Centennial Bread Sampler

Written & compiled in honor of
a century of service
to the homemakers and bakers of America.

Copyright © 1981

 Universal Foods Corporation
Milwaukee, WI 53201

GREETINGS
from RED STAR YEAST – the natural one.

We're celebrating! Yes, our company, Universal Foods Corporation, is 100 years old, and to commemorate this historic and joyous occasion we have published our Centennial Bread Sampler.

We are extremely proud of this yeast breads cookbook, the largest and most complete we have ever published. There are over 300 recipes—some newly created and many historic old favorites. There are recipes for yeast bakers who are beginners and those more experienced. Plus, there are recipes for the occasional baker or the homemaker who bakes several breads every week.

In addition to recipes, we have included many pages of information on yeast baking which will help you bake perfect yeast breads every time.

The eight chapters include recipes you have requested and many you tell us are your all-time favorites. We are in tune with foods being served today, and breads from this cookbook can be the star of a meal or they can complement your meal.

Don't be just a cookbook reader—be a doer and bake a bread today. Yes, we wrote *the* book on bread, and we hope the results of your bread baking will bring joy to family and friends.

Sincerely yours,

Carol Stevens

Carol Stevens
Consumer Services
Universal Foods Corporation

Managing Editor—Neil Reay
Food Editor—Barbara Thornton
Food Consultants—Barbara Thornton Associates®

**CENTENNIAL
UNIVERSAL FOODS
1882-1982**

TABLE OF CONTENTS

KEY TO SYMBOLS, Each recipe in this cookbook may have one or more symbols. These symbols call attention to a special feature of the recipe.

The half moon symbol indicates the recipe can be prepared and refrigerated overnight; then shaped and baked the next day.

The old-fashioned stove indicates the recipe is historic. Most of our historic recipes have new, streamlined methods of preparation, but the baked foods are the same as our grand-mothers and great-grandmothers prepared.

The clock symbol indicates the recipe is faster to prepare and bake than the majority of the recipes.

The Blue Ribbon symbol indicates the recipe was a winner in one of our Recipe Exchange Contests.

The half-filled measuring cup indicates the recipe has a smaller yield— perfect for smaller families.

3

A CENTURY IN PERSPECTIVE

Red Star Yeast traces its roots back to December 4, 1882. On that date the Meadow Springs Distilling Company was incorporated in Milwaukee, Wisconsin. Land for a plant was purchased in the Menomonee River Valley west of the city. Although it was only three miles from the heart of Milwaukee, in 1882 it was the center of a pastoral setting with over 600 head of grazing cattle for neighbors. With many expansions, renovations and modernizations, the original building is still a part of the plant making Red Star Yeast for consumers today.

On July 4, 1883, the Meadow Springs Distilling Company was open for business. Yeast was used to distill the company's principal products: Livingston Whiskey, Mistletoe Gin and Post Hoorn Gin. In May, 1887, the company changed its name to the National Distilling Company.

But yeast had other uses in the young company as well. Under the Red Star name, yeast was also being sold to bakeries and to consumers. In 1887, the Secretary's report recorded the recommendation "that the yeast business be stimulated until full capacity is reached." Early labels carried the direct but ungrammatical claim "Famous because the Best," as well as openly claiming to be "incomparably the best, the purest and strongest yeast in the market." The company's early commitment to selling pure, all-natural yeast was shown in the label statement "contains no chemicals or other injurious substances." In addition to the Red Star® name, yeast was also sold under the Blue Star and White Star names for a time.

In 1890 the company opened its first laboratory to provide scientific control of the yeast manufacturing process. Yeast is a living organism, and because yeast's function in fermentations and in raising dough had not been understood until studied by Louis Pasteur in 1859, there was much to be learned by this pioneering effort. The company has continued to maintain its reputation for the development of ever-improving manufacturing processes and strains of yeast.

In 1891 the company's offices on Water Street next to the Milwaukee River burned to the ground. Undaunted, the company bought land on Buffalo Street and built new offices. The new building was burned to the ground in the great Third Ward Fire in October, 1892. The company rebuilt again and remained on the site until 1962.

In 1917 World War I brought government restrictions that barred the use of grain in distilled spirits for beverages. Existing stocks of liquor could be sold, but none could be manufactured. The National Distilling Company converted to the production of industrial alcohol to support the war effort. When the Eighteenth Amendment to the Constitution, commonly called Prohibition, was enacted in July 1919, the company was at full capacity producing yeast, industrial alcohol, vinegar and dried animal feed (from the grain used to grow the yeast and produce alcohol). In the spirit of the new law prohibiting the sale of liquor, a new sign went up on the company offices in November of 1919 declaring the company to be the Red Star Yeast and Products Company.

In 1920 the company's laboratory made its first major contribution to yeast manufacturing in the United States. Adopting a technique being tried in Europe, they switched from the traditional but short life Vienna yeast to aerated yeast. By continuously bubbling air through the tanks while the yeast is growing, they were able to produce less alcohol and more yeast of a superior quality and with a longer "shelf life" of activity and freshness. The demand for yeast grew at such a fast rate that alcohol and vinegar production were discontinued to devote all efforts to yeast.

The delivery of yeast was also making progress. Originally, the company used two-wheeled, chariot-like carts to deliver yeast. By 1900, four-wheeled enclosed wagons and bicycles were used. In 1919 Model T Ford roadsters with delivery bodies extended the distances over which deliveries could be made. In 1920 Red Star Yeast traveled by rail and truck to 13 regional "cutting" branches, where 75 pound blocks of yeast were cut up and wrapped for delivery to stores and bakeries through 50 sales branches. This marked the first time that many rural midwestern areas had access to fresh, commercially produced yeast. Up until this time, rural homemakers had depended on "wild" yeasts in the air or on the use of a "starter" saved from the last baking for leavening. The company was thus ready for the next major change in distribution when supermarkets developed in the United States starting in 1930.

In 1936 the company's laboratory again initiated a major change in yeast manufacturing techniques. Yeast had always been grown in vats using grains as the food source because baking yeast was originally a by-product of the brewing industry. The laboratory had been studying different food sources since 1920, and now converted to the use of molasses from sugar cane and sugar beets as the food source for the yeast.

The 1940s brought war, and the people at Red Star Yeast and Products Company again pitched in to help. In 1941, under government sponsorship, they developed the first dried yeast for use overseas by United States troops in mobile kitchens. The dried yeast did not need refrigeration like compressed yeast, and had an active life measured in months rather than weeks.

Serving the needs of the home baker has always had high priority for the company. Prior to 1900, yeast wrappers carried recipes developed by the company, as well as careful step-by-step instructions and usage suggestions. By 1917, no doubt influenced by Milwaukee's own diverse ethnic mix, the company had published a series of six booklets entitled "Recipes of all

Nations" containing traditional and modern recipes for American, German, Norwegian, Polish, Jewish and French foods. Each recipe was printed both in English and in the language of the nation in which it originated. The title page of each booklet stated: "In compiling and issuing this series of Recipes for all Nations, it is our desire to perpetuate in the memory of the older folks a record of the dishes they learned to make and enjoy in their 'Fatherland', and give the younger generation an opportunity to revive these memories and learn to prepare for themselves those foods 'that Mother used to make.'" This was one of the earliest efforts to commit to writing recipes that had been passed down only by word of mouth. The full set of six 40-page booklets was available for 10¢, including postage.

The company has continued to provide guidance and new ideas for homemakers. A survey of old files reveals a booklet of "30 minute recipes" from 1949, and a book on "Quick and Easy Batterway Recipes" from 1954 using the no-knead batter breads technique updated for the chapter in this book. For ten years, 1957-1966, the company was a participating sponsor of the Pillsbury Bake-Off contest, and printed the winning yeast recipes each year on Red Star Yeast packages.

In 1967 the company started its own recipe program called "Over the Back Fence." Regular users of Red Star Yeast were asked to submit their favorite recipes to be shared in both booklets and over the radio in many midwestern markets where sales were strongest.

In February 1968 the company introduced its Instant Blend Active Dry Yeast. The smaller particle size allowed the yeast to be blended with part of the flour with an electric mixer, eliminating the need to rehydrate the yeast in water first. The mixer method also allows the use of hotter water (120°-130° F) for a faster start without hurting the yeast. Most of the recipes in this book use the Instant Blend method.

In 1972 the company introduced a new recipe for a yeast-fermented fruit sauce called Vintage® Fruit Sauce. In 1973 a cookbook of uses for this popular fruit sauce was issued, and it remains in demand today. These recipes are included in the last chapter of this book. Starting in 1975, the company ran a series of recipe contests called the Red Star Recipe Exchange. Winning recipes from the first three Recipe Exchanges are included in this book and identified by a blue ribbon symbol.

The Red Star Centennial Bread Sampler is the latest effort in our long tradition of service to the homemaker. Full development of the book took over 18 months. Historical files were reviewed, recipes selected and updated for today's ingredients and put into a standardized format. The oldest of these recipes are designated with a wood-burning stove symbol to indicate their historic background. All recipes in the book have been tested at least twice and by at least two bakers with different brands of ingredients. A panel of trained home economists reviewed and judged the suitability of each recipe and each end product. Consumer letters for several years past were reviewed to determine current baking interests and common baking problems. Special educational chapters on *What's In Bread and Why* and *Yeast Baking Tips* were developed to help all bakers, from the novice to the experienced. Stopwatch and measuring cup symbols indicate recipes suitable when time is short or families are small. A quarter-moon symbol identifies make-ahead recipes. Many new recipes were developed to meet contemporary needs. The chapter on *Main Dishes and Snacks* is especially important in this regard, with many new, innovative and nutritious meal alternatives for your family.

In the 1960s the Red Star Yeast and Products Company began to diversify into other food products. In 1961 they acquired the Universal Foods Company of Chicago, a manufacturer of mixes for the restaurant business. Chili Products Corporation of California was added in 1962. The company then changed its name to Universal Foods Corporation and the yeast business became a division. In 1963 the Stella Cheese Company was acquired. The first of many soft drink bottling operations was added in 1969. The first acquisition in the field of imported gourmet foods took place in 1972.

Today, Universal Foods Corporation is listed on the New York Stock Exchange and is a diversified national manufacturer of specialty foods including yeast (Red Star® brand), cheese and cheese substitutes (Stella® and other brands), soft drinks, dehydrated foods and seasonings, and is a major importer and distributor of gourmet and fancy food items (Ile de France® and other brands). More than 3,000 employees support the company's activities in 30 major facilities throughout the United States. Minority investments are also held in several foreign affiliates.

Universal Foods Corporation is the most diversified yeast manufacturer in the United States, serving consumers, commercial and retail bakeries, the foodservice and restaurant trade, processed food manufacturers and industrial customers, the nutritional and health food industries, and the wine and distilled spirits industries. Innovation, quality and service have been the strength and motivating ideals of the company for the past century. Now they are helping us build the next century.

WHAT'S IN BREAD AND WHY

All yeast breads—from the traditional white loaf to the special holiday coffeecake—use the same basic ingredients: yeast, flour, liquid, sugar, salt and fat. The amounts and form of each ingredient will vary in each type of bread. Additional flavoring ingredients may be added.

The following section will help you to understand the function of each ingredient and the various forms of that ingredient that can be used.

RED STAR® YEAST
FLOUR
LIQUIDS
SUGAR/OTHER SWEETENING INGREDIENTS
SALT
FAT
FLAVORING INGREDIENTS

RED STAR® YEAST

Red Star Yeast is available in two forms: Instant Blend Active Dry Yeast and Compressed Yeast.

Red Star Instant Blend Active Dry Yeast is the all natural one, with no additives or preservatives. It is available in a package or in a jar. Instant Blend Dry Yeast in a strip of three foil lined packages is specially packed to remain fresh for at least twelve months without refrigeration. Store in a cool, dry place. For best results, use before the date shown on the package.

Instant Blend Dry Yeast in the vacuum-packed jar should be stored in the refrigerator after opening and used within two months. Allow the amount of yeast in the recipe to come to room temperature before using. Two and one-fourth teaspoons of yeast equal one package. (Recipes in this book call for a certain number of packages.)

Instant Blend Dry Yeast can be used in two ways. To dissolve separately, use warm water (110-115°F.). For the newer mixer method, blend yeast with part of the flour and the other dry ingredients; use a liquid temperature of 120-130°F. The mixer method eliminates dissolving the yeast in a separate step. By coating the yeast with dry ingredients, warmer temperature liquids can be used without concern that the yeast will be killed.

In order for the yeast to dissolve properly, each package of yeast in a recipe must have ¼ cup water. This water can be deducted from the total liquid amount.

Red Star Compressed Yeast is the traditional form—a moist and creamy white cake, with a firm, fairly brittle texture. Because it is perishable, store in the refrigerator and use within a few days. It can be crumbled into the flour mixture and used in the mixer method. If using conventional dissolve-yeast-first recipes, dissolve in lukewarm water (80-90°F.).

For longer storage, compressed yeast can be frozen. Wrap in foil and freeze at 0°F. for up to six months; defrost overnight in the refrigerator before using. The brittle texture may have disappeared, but this will not affect the quality of the yeast.

Compressed yeast and active dry yeast can be used interchangeably. One ⅝-ounce cake or ⅓ of a 2-ounce cake of Red Star Compressed Yeast equals one ¼-ounce package of Red Star Instant Blend Active Dry Yeast.

Baker's Yeast: Some home bakers may be purchasing yeast in large quantities. You must remember that Baker's Yeast differs from the yeast packaged for consumers. Baker's Compressed Yeast is a different strain and has a much shorter shelf life before it loses its freshness. Yeast should always be purchased in packages with a freshness date and in quantities that can be used in a short time to insure the quality of your baked goods. Baker's Dry Yeast has a different particle size and cannot be used in the mixer method like Instant Blend Yeast.

FLOUR

Choosing the correct flour is important for good bread. Flour isn't just flour. There are several kinds of flour which can be used for bread baking, each with its own properties. The following information will help you understand the basic characteristics of flour and the differences in flour.

FLOUR CHARACTERISTICS

The most common grain used for many different flours is wheat. Wheat flour contains high quality proteins. When flour is mixed with liquid, these proteins form gluten—the rubbery substance which gives structure and elasticity to batters and doughs. The gluten, which is developed by mixing and kneading, stretches like elastic, trapping the bubbles of carbon dioxide gas formed by the yeast and building the framework of the bread.

Wheat flours can be of two types—hard and soft. Hard wheat flours contain more gluten-forming proteins than soft wheat flours. The amount of gluten proteins in the flour will affect the volume and tenderness of breads.

Wheat flour is milled into two categories of flour. They are white flours which include—bread, all-purpose and unbleached flour. The other category, whole grain flours, includes—whole wheat and graham flours and cracked wheat. White flour is milled from the endosperm or inner part of the wheat kernel while the whole grain flours are milled from the entire wheat kernel, which includes the bran and germ.

Most white flours are enriched to replace the nutrients of the bran and germ which are removed during milling; iron and the B vitamins (thiamine, niacin and riboflavin) are added by a process known as enrichment. The whole grain flours are natural flours with no additives.

Breads baked with the whole grain flours are more compact and lower in volume than those made from white flour. The whole grain wheat flours form less gluten than the white flours so they are usually combined with some white flour to insure good volume and appearance in breads. Whole grain wheat flours can be used alone, however, in breads without the addition of white flour; the loaves are heavier and denser, but have an excellent flavor.

Rye flours are also used frequently in breads. Because rye flours form less gluten than wheat flours, they are usually combined with white flour in breads and are not used alone, except in the case of special diets. Rye flours are natural flours with no additives.

The whole grain wheat flours and rye flours add unique flavor, color and texture to breads generally associated with old-fashioned baking.

Flours milled from other grains (corn, rice, barley, soybeans, etc.) are used occasionally in breads. As these flours form no gluten, they are used only as additions with wheat and rye flours.

KINDS OF FLOUR

WHITE FLOURS

Bread Flour—available in some parts of the country, this wheat flour is higher in protein and milled especially for bread baking. It produces breads with higher volume and is ideal to use for loaves.

All-Purpose Flour—a blend of hard and soft wheats which yields a flour that gives good results for many kinds of baked products. Some all-purpose flours are labeled "high protein" and are best to use in loaves. Other all-purpose flours with less protein give better results in the softer, sweeter doughs.

Unbleached Flour—an all-purpose flour with natural whiteness; no bleaching/maturing agent has been used. Like all-purpose flours, unbleached flours can vary in protein level.

Self-Rising Flour—an all-purpose flour to which leavening and salt have been added. The best use for this flour is biscuits and quick breads, not yeast breads.

WHOLE GRAIN WHEAT FLOURS

Whole Wheat and Graham Flours—flour ground from the entire wheat kernel which includes all the natural nutrients. Graham flour may be more coarsely ground than whole wheat flour. Breads baked from these flours have a distinctive flavor derived from the bran and germ of the wheat kernel.

Cracked Wheat—made by "cracking" the entire wheat kernel into small pieces. It is usually combined with white flour for good volume. Cracked wheat adds a crunchiness to breads.

RYE FLOURS

Medium Rye Flour—ground from the endosperm or inner part of the rye kernel. Since it does not include the bran, it is a finer textured flour. "Medium" refers to the color.

Dark Rye, Pumpernickel Rye Flours—coarse-textured flours ground from the entire rye kernel. Because these flours include the bran, they will give bread more texture than medium rye flour. "Pumpernickel" indicates the primary use of the flour is in coarse-textured dark rye breads.

OTHER GRAINS AND CEREALS USED IN BREADS

These are used to add a special flavor or texture to breads.

Wheat Germ—tiny golden flakes which are from the inner part of the wheat kernel. It adds a nutty flavor to breads, as well as extra nutrients.

Cornmeal and Rolled Oats—add a crunchy sweetness to breads.

Rice, Barley, Buckwheat Flours—add the flavor of that particular grain.

Soy Flour—because soy flour is especially high in protein, it is generally added for increased nutrition.

Whole Bran Cereal—adds texture and a characteristic bran flavor.

Natural Cereals/Granola—add crunchiness and sweetness to breads.

Other Cereals—add texture and the flavor of the grain from which the cereal is made.

Seeds/Nuts—products like sesame seeds and salted sunflower nuts are added for crunchiness and a special flavor.

FLOUR TIPS FOR BREAD BAKING

MEASURING FLOUR

Today's flour is sifted during milling so it isn't necessary to sift flour before measuring. All of the recipes in this book have been created and tested with unsifted flour for your convenience. To measure flour—spoon lightly into dry measuring cup, being careful not to pack the flour; level cup with knife or straight edge spatula.

The whole grain wheat and rye flours are never sifted. Since they may settle during storage, stir before measuring to evenly distribute the bran particles.

AMOUNT OF FLOUR TO USE IN RECIPES

Most of the recipes in this book have a ½ cup range of flour due to differences in brands of flour and changing climatic conditions.

Flours absorb liquids differently depending on the protein level of the flour. Flours which are higher in protein absorb more liquid, so less flour will be used. Lower protein flours absorb less liquid, so more flour is needed.

Depending on the weather, the amount of flour used in any given recipe can vary from baking to baking. Moisture levels of flours can vary depending on the temperature and relative humidity; flours can gain or lose moisture to the air. In humid weather, doughs may be more sticky as the flour absorbs moisture from the air; more flour will then be needed. Under dry conditions (or if flour is stored near heat), doughs will lose moisture to the air, so less flour will be used. Some of the batter bread recipes in this book have a given amount of flour. The kind of flour used or the moisture differences in the atmosphere will not affect these batters appreciably.

STORE FLOUR PROPERLY

Always store flour in an airtight container. Empty flour from the bag into an airtight plastic or metal container or place the bag in an airtight container. Store in a cool, dry place away from heat to preserve freshness, moisture and baking quality. To maintain their freshness, store whole grain wheat flours and rye flours in the refrigerator during warm, humid weather if they are not used frequently; since these flours include the oil-rich germ of the kernel, they can become rancid if improperly stored.

For long-term storage, flour can be frozen. Wrap bag in moisture-proof material or empty flour into freezer bags or containers. Because of the low moisture content, flour will not become "solid" when frozen; its appearance will not change. Let flour come to room temperature before using. Freezing is especially helpful for long-term storage of the whole grain wheat and rye flours.

OTHER INGREDIENTS IN BREADS

Besides yeast and flour, most breads include the following basic ingredients.

LIQUIDS

Water and milk are the most commonly used liquids in breads. Breads made with water only will have a more open texture, a more wheaty flavor and

12

a crisper crust. Milk creates breads which are richer and have a more velvety texture; crusts are softer and will brown more quickly due to the sugar and butterfat in milk. Milk also improves the keeping quality of breads and contributes nutrients. Milk is frequently used in the richer, sweeter doughs to give more tenderness.

Eggs may also be used as part of the liquid; they add richness, tenderness and a golden color, as well as nutrients. Occasionally only the egg yolk is added to doughs for more tenderness.

Juices or other liquids may be added for special flavors.

Red Star Instant Blend Dry Yeast must have some water as part of the total liquid in order to dissolve properly — ¼ *cup water for each package of dry yeast.* All the recipes in this book have been created and tested in this way. If you have a special recipe of your own which does not include water, and you are using the mixer method, add ¼ cup water for each package of yeast used and deduct the amount of water from the total liquid in the recipe.

SUGAR/OTHER SWEETENING INGREDIENTS

Sugar provides food for the yeast to grow, adds flavor and helps in browning of the crust. Different sweetening ingredients create different flavors. Brown sugar, honey and molasses are often used in specialty flour breads to bring out the grain flavor. Breads made with honey or molasses brown more quickly. Usually a 25° lower oven temperature is used — or watch carefully and cover with foil the last 5 to 10 minutes of baking.

SALT

Salt controls the speed of rising of the dough for good texture and also adds flavor.

FAT

Butter, margarine, shortening and oil are used in breads to add tenderness, moistness and flavor. Butter or margarine add more flavor than shortening and are often used in the richer, sweeter doughs; butter or margarine can be used interchangeably. The 60-40 combination of margarine and butter, available in sticks, can be substituted for butter or margarine. Whipped butter or margarine or other forms with low fat/high moisture content cannot be substituted satisfactorily.

FLAVORING INGREDIENTS

Herbs, spices, grated rinds, cheese, dried and candied fruits and nuts are frequently added to doughs for special flavors. Fillings and toppings add extra flavor and variety to breads.

YEAST BAKING TIPS

METHODS

Most of the recipes in this book have been developed using the mixer method. Some of the flour is mixed in with the mixer. The mixture will be similar to a thick cake batter. Beating with the mixer at medium speed helps develop the gluten to give bread its structure. Using the mixer for the first part of the mixing also shortens the kneading time.

Recipes have been tested with a counter-top mixer. Either counter-top or portable mixers can be used. If a portable mixer is used, beat about one minute longer as portable mixers have less power.

Many brands of mixers now provide a dough hook, and there are several brands offering "extra power" mixers. We recommend following the manufacturer's directions for using the dough hook. In our testing with the dough hook we have found that breads may be slightly drier because more flour can be worked in with the dough hook during the kneading stage.

We have not tested any of our recipes using a food processor for the mixing or kneading. There are some publications which feature the use of the equipment for bread making.

The recipes can also be mixed by hand with a spoon. Knead the dough longer when mixing by hand to develop the gluten.

LIQUID TEMPERATURE

The mixer method allows for higher temperature liquid to dissolve the yeast. Because the yeast is combined with other dry ingredients, liquid temperature can be 120-130°F. When dissolving the yeast in the liquid, a temperature of 110-115°F. should be used. All of the recipes in this book follow one of these two methods. Use a yeast or candy thermometer for greatest accuracy. If too warm a liquid temperature is used it will kill the yeast. If too cool a liquid temperature is used the yeast will not be activated.

KNEADING

Basically, breads are of two types—kneaded and batter. For kneaded breads, after the mixing, flour is stirred in to make a firm or soft dough; additional flour is kneaded into the dough. The range of flour given in a recipe includes the flour used for kneading.

Firm doughs are needed for loaves and some dinner rolls. Doughs which are baked on cookie sheets need to be firm to hold their shape. Soft doughs are needed for richer coffeecakes and sweet rolls where tenderness is important. The less flour that is added, the more tender the coffeecake or rolls will be. The dough should be soft but not so sticky that it can't be handled easily.

Batter breads are not kneaded. The first addition of flour is beaten in with the mixer; less flour is stirred in so the dough is stickier. The dough is allowed to rise, then baked. For more information on batter breads, see the Batter Bread Chapter.

Kneading is the process of developing dough into a smooth, elastic ball. Kneading develops the gluten by making it stronger and more elastic for better volume. Kneading also produces a finer grain or texture in breads.

To knead dough: Place on lightly floured surface, turning dough over several times to make it easier to handle. With curved fingers, fold dough in half towards you. Then push down and away, firmly but lightly, with heel of hand in a rolling motion. Give dough a quarter turn. Repeat folding, pushing and turning until dough is smooth and velvety on the outside, springy when pressed with the fingers and little blisters can be seen under the surface.

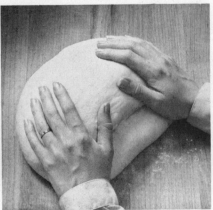

Specialty flour doughs require less kneading—5 minutes is usually sufficient. Because there is less gluten, overkneading increases stickiness and makes doughs more difficult to handle.

RISING

Rising improves the flavor and texture of breads. Place kneaded dough in a lightly greased bowl, turning dough to grease top to prevent the dough from drying out. Cover bowl with plastic wrap, foil, or towel. A warm place with an even temperature of 80-85°F. is best for rising; higher temperatures may kill the yeast and keep the dough from rising.

The oven is ideal. Most of the breads in this book have been tested with oven rising of the dough. If your dough rises at room temperature, it may take longer to rise than the times indicated in the recipes. In some of the recipes in this book, room temperature rising is recommended.

In a gas oven, the pilot light will provide enough warmth. For a gas oven with electronic ignition or an electric oven, turn oven to lowest setting for one minute; turn off oven. Place bowl on center rack and close door. Another method for rising is to place bowl of dough on a rack over a pan or bowl of hot water; cover with towel.

To test for double in size: press two fingers lightly and quickly into dough. If the indentation remains, the dough is double.

For doughs which are refrigerated instead of the first rising, cover bowl with plastic wrap and foil to prevent the dough from drying out. A refrigerator temperature of 38-41°F. will give best results.

The microwave oven can also be used for the first rising of doughs. Follow the manufacturer's instructions for the method to use. If your instruction manual does not recommend using the microwave for dough rising, use a conventional oven instead. Some of the older models do not have a low enough power setting to use for dough rising, and the dough will cook. Remember not to use metal bowls or pans.

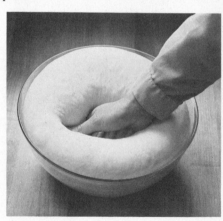

PUNCHING DOWN DOUGH
Punching down the dough releases the large air bubbles formed by the yeast during rising; this produces a finer texture. When the dough has doubled in size, push your fist quickly into the center of the dough. Then pull edges of the dough to the center. Turn over and shape dough into a ball. Kneading the dough two or three times will help release additional air bubbles.

LET DOUGH REST
If you have the time, let the dough rest 10 to 15 minutes after punching down and before shaping. Cover with an inverted bowl. This relaxes the gluten in the dough and makes the dough easier to roll out and shape. Some doughs are quite elastic and will "pull back" at first when rolling out.

SHAPING

Follow recipe for shaping. Following are a few hints:

To divide dough: weigh the dough on a kitchen scale to obtain loaves and rolls which are of uniform size.

Rolling out dough: using a rolling pin will help eliminate air bubbles in the dough and prevent "holes" in the bread.

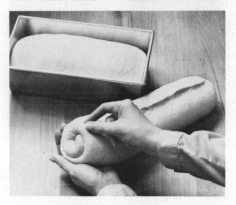

Sealing edges and ends: moisten the edges of dough with cold water before pinching to help seal them. This is especially helpful for doughs which have a moist filling.

Shaping and sealing ends of loaves: pinch ends together and smooth out or tuck sealed ends under loaf.

SECOND RISING

Many doughs will have a second rising which is in the pan. The second rising gives better volume, a more mellow yeast flavor and a finer texture to breads.

Depending on the bread, some doughs will rise until almost doubled while others will rise until double. Follow specific instructions in the recipe.

Some doughs with less gluten, such as specialty flour doughs, could fall during baking if they rise until double.

To test for double in size: press finger lightly into dough near the edge; if the indentation remains, the dough is double.

PANS

All names used for pans in this book are the latest terms used by the bakeware industry. Use the pan size recommended in the recipe for best results.

For some loaves, either a 9x5 or an 8x4-inch bread pan is satisfactory so

17

both sizes have been given. If an alternative pan is satisfactory, it will usually be listed in the recipe. For example, some coffeecakes can be baked in either a 12-cup Bundt® pan or a 10-inch tubed cake pan. However, for coffeecakes where melted butter or a filling may run out of a loose bottom tubed cake pan, only the Bundt® pan is given. In some cases, if you don't have the pan which is listed in the recipe, you could substitute a similar pan; for example, a jelly roll pan could be used for large braids if a large cookie sheet is not available.

PAN TYPES

Uncoated aluminum pans give the most even browning and uniform baking results. Aluminum pans come in three different weights. The lighter weight aluminum pans are less satisfactory for baking; they absorb heat more quickly and less uniformly so can cause over-browning and uneven browning.

While glass pans, pans with a non-stick coating or pans with a colored exterior can be used, they do absorb more heat and will produce a harder crust than an uncoated aluminum pan will. Dull or darkened pans absorb more heat than light-colored metal pans so crusts may turn out too dark or too crisp. Check for doneness before the recommended baking time when using darker pans.

Although stainless steel pans are easy to keep clean and do not discolor, they do not absorb heat as evenly as aluminum and are less satisfactory for baking. Very shiny metal pans, such as tin, reflect heat away from the bread; the breads will not brown as well or develop a crust.

We have tested the breads in this book with heavier, light-colored aluminum pans. We have not done any testing with clay pans or the pyroceram microwave pans. If using these pans for baking, follow the manufacturer's recommendations.

CRUST TREATMENTS

Do you like crisp, chewy crusts or soft, tender crusts on breads? Here are some techniques to help you achieve the type of bread you would like.

For a chewy or crisp crust on breads and rolls:

- Use a recipe which calls for water as the liquid in the dough.
- Brush or spray loaves or rolls with cold water before baking and again several times during baking. This is ideal for getting a crispy, crackly crust on French or sourdough breads.
- Brush dough with an Egg White Glaze before baking, as in the *Chicken Dressing Braid* recipe. Combine 1 slightly beaten egg white with 1 tablespoon water.
- Brush dark rye breads and rolls with Delicatessen Glaze towards the end of baking, as in the *Delicatessen Black Bread* recipe. In small sauce-

pan, combine ¼ cup cold water and ½ teaspoon cornstarch; bring to a boil; cool slightly. Remove loaves or rolls from oven 5 minutes before end of baking; brush with Glaze. Return breads to oven to finish baking. This Glaze also gives a glossy appearance.

For a softer, tender crust on breads and rolls:

- Use a recipe which calls for milk and water as the liquid in the dough. Milk adds tenderness.

- Brush crusts with butter or margarine immediately after baking.

For a shiny, golden crust, brush with an Egg Glaze, Egg Yolk Glaze or slightly beaten egg before baking.

- Egg Glaze, as in the *Easy Croissants* recipe. Combine 1 slightly beaten egg with 1 tablespoon water or milk.

- Egg Yolk Glaze, as in the *Brioche* recipe. Combine 1 slightly beaten egg yolk with 1 tablespoon water or milk.

- Beat 1 whole egg slightly and brush on bread, as in the *Finnish Pulla* recipe.

The Egg White Glaze can also be used for a shiny crust. Because the yolk is not used, the crust will not be as golden in color.

Brushing the dough with milk before baking will also give a shiny crust, but not as shiny as when using one of the egg glazes.

Doughs are usually brushed with an egg glaze after rising in the pan and before baking to allow for optimum rising of the dough. Brush doughs gently with a soft pastry brush or a feather brush so as not to puncture the dough.

ADDING TOPPINGS TO BREADS

Egg glazes are usually used when seeds or other toppings are desired on breads. Because the glaze is sticky, it will hold the seeds or other ingredients, such as cereals or nuts, in place.

Brush dough before baking with any of the egg glazes. Sprinkle with sesame seeds or poppy seeds. For breads using cereals, sprinkling some of the cereal on top gives an attractive appearance. If the cereal is in larger pieces, such as granola, crush the cereal first. The *Molasses Oatmeal Bread* has rolled oats sprinkled on the crust. If desired, the oats could be chopped in a blender or food processor. For breads using wheat germ, sprinkle additional wheat germ on top.

Use chopped nuts to add crunchiness. The *Seed And Wheat Bread* has chopped salted sunflower nuts sprinkled on top.

Brushing the dough with milk before baking will also hold seeds in place.

Pearl sugar is used occasionally to sprinkle on the top of coffeecakes for a decorative appearance. Pearl sugar is a decorating sugar in large white crystals, which do not dissolve during baking. It can be found in larger supermarkets or in specialty food shops. The *Fruit Filled Lattice Coffeecake* is brushed with an Egg White Glaze and sprinkled with pearl sugar.

Coarse salt may be used to sprinkle on the tops of rolls and is frequently used to sprinkle on specialty breads like bread sticks and pretzels. Coarse salt, sometimes called coarse kosher salt, is in large sparkling crystals. It is not the same as coarse salt made to use in freezing ice cream. Except for bread sticks, baked products sprinkled with coarse salt are best eaten the day they are made; when stored, the salt will absorb moisture and dissolve, causing the tops of soft baked products to become moist and wrinkled in appearance. The *Soft Pretzels* are brushed with an Egg White Glaze and sprinkled with coarse salt.

OTHER CRUST TREATMENTS

You will find recipes in this book with other crust treatments.

The top of the *90-Minute Buttercrust Bread* is slashed lengthwise down the center of the loaf before baking. Melted butter, which is poured into the slash, soaks into the dough. The *Orange Raisin Butter Bread* also uses this technique.

Many of the breads, such as the *French Bread* and some of the rye and whole wheat breads, have a decorative crust design achieved by slashing the top of the loaves. With a very sharp knife, cut slashes about ¼-inch deep in the top of the loaf; slash carefully so as not to flatten the loaf. Slashing loaves after rising will produce a more prominent design than when the loaves are slashed before rising. Diagonal slashes are attractive on long loaves. For round loaves, cut diagonal slashes or make an "X" or a criss-cross design.

The *Grecian Sweet Braid* is brushed with an egg-milk glaze and sprinkled with sugar, almonds and sesame seed before baking for a "frosty" appearance.

BAKING

For best volume and texture, preheat oven before baking yeast breads. The final expansion of the dough, called "oven spring," takes place in the first 10 to 15 minutes of baking in a hot oven. If the oven has been used for the rising of the dough, remove dough before preheating the oven.

PLACEMENT POINTERS

Air must circulate freely in the oven for even baking. When using one rack, position it in the center of the oven for cookie sheets or flatter pans. For bread pans, Bundt® pans and tubed cake pans, use a lower oven rack for best results; then as heat rises in the oven the tops of loaves and coffee-cakes will not become too brown before they are completely baked.

When using two racks, place them so they divide the oven in thirds. Stagger pans so that one is not directly above another. Arrange the pans so there is about two inches for air to circulate on all sides. Switch pans halfway through baking for more even browning.

Although breads can be baked in a microwave oven, the results are not the same as in a conventional oven. Breads baked in a microwave oven do not brown or develop a crust as there is no hot air to dry out the surfaces. All breads in this book have been developed for baking in conventional ovens.

TESTS FOR DONENESS

The most common tests for doneness of breads are golden brown color and a hollow sound. The "hollow sound" test is best for loaves. Tap the crust lightly with finger; if done, it will have a hollow sound.

COOLING

For most breads, remove from pan immediately after baking and cool on racks to prevent the bottom crust from becoming moist and soggy. For some richer coffeecakes baked in tubed cake pans, cool in pan for 10 minutes to prevent coffeecake from breaking apart.

Unless the bread is to be served warm, cool before slicing. Use a serrated knife with a gentle "sawing" motion for cutting. An electric knife is particularly good for slicing warm breads.

STORAGE OF BREADS

Cool breads completely before storing. To maintain freshness, place breads in airtight plastic bags or wrap tightly in plastic wrap or foil and store at room temperature. Placing breads in the refrigerator is helpful in warm, humid weather to prevent molding, but it does cause the breads to dry out more quickly. If the bread contains meat, however, it should be refrigerated.

A good rule to follow is "Bake first, then freeze." Unless doughs have been specifically created for freezing, they may not freeze well.

For freezing baked breads, wrap in heavy foil, freezer wrap or place in heavy plastic bags; seal tightly. For best results, breads should not be frosted or glazed before freezing. For best quality, use breads within 3 months; longer storage means some loss of flavor and moistness.

Basic loaves and rolls will maintain their quality better when frozen than the richer, sweeter coffeecakes and rolls. Some richer doughs will dry slightly.

Thaw breads in their original freezer wrapping at room temperature. Breads will thaw in 2 to 3 hours, depending on the room temperature and the size of the bread. Rolls will thaw more quickly.

To reheat coffeecakes and rolls, wrap in foil and heat in a 300° oven for 15 to 20 minutes, depending on the size of the bread. Glaze or decorate after reheating. A microwave oven may be used for reheating breads; follow the manufacturer's recommendations for the setting and time.

Basic breads & rolls

Honey Of A Whole Wheat Bread

"Wild Fire" Rye Bread

Onion Mustard Buns

Old Milwaukee Rye Bread

Refrigerator Rolls — Knot shape

23

BASIC BREADS AND ROLLS

This chapter is for all bakers, from the beginner to the experienced! If you're just discovering the joys of baking yeast breads, these breads and rolls are easy to mix and shape and will give you a satisfying experience from your very first baking. If you're an experienced baker, you'll find breads with intriguing flavors, textures and shapes to add to your yeast baking repertoire.

In this chapter you'll find all the traditional white breads, the deliciously hearty whole grain breads and the classic sourdough breads, plus an array of dinner and sandwich rolls and "little" breads such as pretzels, bagels, English muffins, pancakes and waffles. For white breads, you can choose from the traditional loaves, variations such as *90-Minute Buttercrust Bread* and *Rich Raisin Bread*, and the familiar crusty *French Bread*. A more glamorous white bread is the *Easy Egg Braid*. Whole grain breads include many varieties of whole wheat and rye loaves and rolls. Although sourdough may seem mysterious, following the suggestions and recipes in that section will make this an exciting adventure for you.

Yeast bread bakers want the old-fashioned goodness of home-baked breads, yet want bread baking to fit into their busy schedule. To help accomplish these goals, most of our recipes use the easy mixer method. You don't have to dissolve the yeast separately; just mix with part of the flour and other dry ingredients. Then add the liquid ingredients and use the mixer for mixing. Using the mixer helps develop the gluten in the bread so it shortens the kneading time. Letting the dough rise in the oven shortens the total rising time. If you find yourself with a limited time schedule, there are breads which require less time—choose *Refrigerator White Bread* or *Sauerkraut Rye Bread* with only one rise.

Using a higher protein all-purpose flour or bread flour for these breads will give you better results. You'll get breads with higher volume, tender eating texture and finer grain. These breads all freeze well, so enjoy a loaf of bread or pan of rolls now and freeze one for later.

Read the information section in the front part of this book for more detailed information on bread ingredients and tips on yeast baking.

Swedish Chocolate Bread

*This delectable bread makes a beautiful presentation and
a tasty remembrance.*
To be made in a Bread Machine

DOUGH:
1 cup warm milk
1/2 cup butter or margarine
1/4 cup sugar
1/2 tsp. salt
3 cups flour
1 1/2 tsp. rapid or quick yeast

FILLING: 1/3 - 1/2 cup Roasted Nut Crunch or Milk Chocolate
Almond Crunch from Moon Shine Trading Co.

WASH: 1 egg beaten with 1-2 T. milk

PROCEDURE: Remove dough from the machine upon completion
of the dough cycle. Roll on a lightly floured surface into a large
rectangle. Spread the Chocolate Nut Creme filling on the middle
third of the dough. With a knife or pastry scissors, cut 1-inch strips
down both sides of the dough from filling to edge. Fold the top of
filled end over dough and then alternate fold side strips over filling,
angling each folded strip down to form a braided appearance.

Place on a greased baking sheet, cover and let rise for about 1
hour. Brush with egg wash and bake in a preheated 350° oven for
20 to 25 minutes.

This versatile bread can be served immediately or frozen for
future use. Its taste and texture is so wonderful, you will make it
again and again!

Moon Shine Trading Co. • Woodland, CA • 800-678-1226
Honeys • Nut Butters • Fruit Spreads
Chocolate & Vanilla Nut Spread Cremes

Swedish Chocolate Bread

*This delectable bread makes a beautiful presentation and
a tasty remembrance.*
To be made in a Bread Machine

DOUGH:
1 cup warm milk
1/2 cup butter or margarine
1/4 cup sugar
1/2 tsp. salt
3 cups flour
1 1/2 tsp. rapid or quick yeast

FILLING:
1/3 - 1/2 cup Roasted Nut Crunch or Milk Chocolate
Almond Crunch from Moon Shine Trading Co.

WASH:
1 egg beaten with 1-2 T. milk

PROCEDURE: Remove dough from the machine upon completion
of the dough cycle. Roll on a lightly floured surface into a large
rectangle. Spread the Chocolate Nut Creme filling on the middle
third of the dough. With a knife or pastry scissors, cut 1-inch strips
down both sides of the dough from filling to edge. Fold the top of
filled end over dough and then alternate fold side strips over filling,
angling each folded strip down to form a braided appearance.

Place on a greased baking sheet, cover and let rise for about 1
hour. Brush with egg wash and bake in a preheated 350° oven for
20 to 25 minutes.

This versatile bread can be served immediately or frozen for
future use. Its taste and texture is so wonderful, you will make it
again and again!

Moon Shine Trading Co. • Woodland, CA • 800-678-1226
Honeys • Nut Butters • Fruit Spreads
Chocolate & Vanilla Nut Spread Cremes

Swedish Chocolate Bread

*This delectable bread makes a beautiful presentation and
a tasty remembrance.*
To be made in a Bread Machine

DOUGH:
1 cup warm milk
1/2 cup butter or margarine
1/4 cup sugar
1/2 tsp. salt
3 cups flour
1 1/2 tsp. rapid or quick yeast

FILLING:
1/3 - 1/2 cup Roasted Nut Crunch or Milk Chocolate
Almond Crunch from Moon Shine Trading Co.

WASH:
1 egg beaten with 1-2 T. milk

PROCEDURE: Remove dough from the machine upon completion
of the dough cycle. Roll on a lightly floured surface into a large
rectangle. Spread the Chocolate Nut Creme filling on the middle
third of the dough. With a knife or pastry scissors, cut 1-inch strips
down both sides of the dough from filling to edge. Fold the top of
filled end over dough and then alternate fold side strips over filling,
angling each folded strip down to form a braided appearance.

Place on a greased baking sheet, cover and let rise for about 1
hour. Brush with egg wash and bake in a preheated 350° oven for
20 to 25 minutes.

This versatile bread can be served immediately or frozen for
future use. Its taste and texture is so wonderful, you will make it
again and again!

Moon Shine Trading Co. • Woodland, CA • 800-678-1226
Honeys • Nut Butters • Fruit Spreads
Chocolate & Vanilla Nut Spread Cremes

Swedish Chocolate Bread

This delectable bread makes a beautiful presentation and
a tasty remembrance.
To be made in a Bread Machine

DOUGH:
1 cup warm milk
1/2 cup butter or margarine
1/4 cup sugar
1/2 tsp. salt
3 cups flour
1 1/2 tsp. rapid or quick yeast

FILLING:
1/3 - 1/2 cup Roasted Nut Crunch or Milk Chocolate Almond Crunch from Moon Shine Trading Co.

WASH:
1 egg beaten with 1-2 T. milk

PROCEDURE: Remove dough from the machine upon completion of the dough cycle. Roll on a lightly floured surface into a large rectangle. Spread the Chocolate Nut Creme filling on the middle third of the dough. With a knife or pastry scissors, cut 1-inch strips down both sides of the dough from filling to edge. Fold the top of filled end over dough and then alternate fold side strips over filling, angling each folded strip down to form a braided appearance.

Place on a greased baking sheet, cover and let rise for about 1 hour. Brush with egg wash and bake in a preheated 350° oven for 20 to 25 minutes.

This versatile bread can be served immediately or frozen for future use. Its taste and texture is so wonderful, you will make it again and again!

Moon Shine Trading Co. • Woodland, CA • 800-678-1226
Honeys • Nut Butters • Fruit Spreads
Chocolate & Vanilla Nut Spread Cremes

Swedish Chocolate Bread

*This delectable bread makes a beautiful presentation and
a tasty remembrance.*
To be made in a Bread Machine

DOUGH:　　1 cup warm milk
　　　　　　　1/2 cup butter or margarine
　　　　　　　1/4 cup sugar
　　　　　　　1/2 tsp. salt
　　　　　　　3 cups flour
　　　　　　　1 1/2 tsp. rapid or quick yeast

FILLING:　　1/3 - 1/2 cup Roasted Nut Crunch or Milk Chocolate
　　　　　　　Almond Crunch from Moon Shine Trading Co.

WASH:　　1 egg beaten with 1-2 T. milk

PROCEDURE: Remove dough from the machine upon completion
of the dough cycle. Roll on a lightly floured surface into a large
rectangle. Spread the Chocolate Nut Creme filling on the middle
third of the dough. With a knife or pastry scissors, cut 1-inch strips
down both sides of the dough from filling to edge. Fold the top of
filled end over dough and then alternate fold side strips over filling,
angling each folded strip down to form a braided appearance.

　　　Place on a greased baking sheet, cover and let rise for about 1
hour. Brush with egg wash and bake in a preheated 350° oven for
20 to 25 minutes.
　　　This versatile bread can be served immediately or frozen for
future use. Its taste and texture is so wonderful, you will make it
again and again!

Moon Shine Trading Co. • Woodland, CA • 800-678-1226
Honeys • Nut Butters • Fruit Spreads
Chocolate & Vanilla Nut Spread Cremes

White Bread

A white bread recipe that will always win you a blue ribbon.

6½ to 7 cups all-purpose flour
2 packages Red Star Instant Blend Dry Yeast
3 tablespoons sugar
1 tablespoon salt
1¼ cups water
1 cup milk
2 tablespoons shortening

Oven 400°   **2 Loaves**

In large mixer bowl, combine 3 cups flour, yeast, sugar and salt; mix well. In saucepan, heat water, milk and shortening until warm (120-130°; shortening does not need to melt). Add to flour mixture. Blend at low speed until moistened; beat 3 minutes at medium speed. By hand, gradually stir in enough remaining flour to make a firm dough. Knead on floured surface until smooth and elastic, 5 to 8 minutes. Place in greased bowl, turning to grease top. Cover; let rise in warm place until light and doubled, about 1 hour.

Punch down dough. Divide into 2 parts. On lightly floured surface, roll or pat each half to a 14x7-inch rectangle. Starting with shorter side, roll up tightly, pressing dough into roll with each turn. Pinch edges and ends to seal. Place in greased 9x5 or 8x4-inch bread pans. Cover; let rise in warm place until double, about 30 minutes. Bake at 400° for 35 to 40 minutes until golden brown. Remove from pans; cool.

White Bread – Compressed Yeast

 Our blue ribbon white bread recipe that uses Red Star Compressed Yeast in the mixer method.

6½ to 7 cups all-purpose flour
2 cakes (⅝ oz. each) Red Star Compressed Yeast
3 tablespoons sugar
1 tablespoon salt
1¼ cups water
1 cup milk
2 tablespoons shortening

Oven 400°   **2 Loaves**

In large mixer bowl, combine 3 cups flour and compressed yeast; blend at low speed until thoroughly combined and crumbly. Add sugar and salt; mix well. In saucepan, heat water, milk and shortening until warm (120-130°; shortening does not need to melt). Add to flour mixture. Blend at low speed until moistened; beat 3 minutes at medium speed. By hand, gradually stir in enough remaining flour to make a firm dough. Knead on floured surface until smooth and elastic, 5 to 8 minutes. Place in greased bowl, turning to grease top. Cover; let rise in warm place until light and doubled, about 1 hour.

Punch down dough. Divide into 2 parts. On lightly floured surface, roll or pat each half to a 14x7-inch rectangle. Starting with shorter side, roll up tightly, pressing dough into roll with each turn. Pinch edges and ends to seal. Place in greased 8x4 or 9x5-inch bread pans. Cover; let rise in warm place until double, about 30 minutes. Bake at 400° for 35 to 40 minutes until golden brown. Remove from pans; cool.

White Bread – Four Loaves

Here's the perfect white bread recipe for the ambitious homemaker who always serves her family homemade bread.

11 to 11½ cups unbleached flour
3 packages Red Star Instant
Blend Dry Yeast
⅓ cup sugar
2 tablespoons salt
2½ cups water
1½ cups milk
⅓ cup shortening

Oven 400°   **4 Loaves**

In large mixer bowl, combine 5 cups flour, yeast, sugar and salt; mix well. In saucepan, heat water, milk and shortening until warm (120-130°; shortening does not need to melt). Add to flour mixture. Blend at low speed until moistened; beat 3 minutes at medium speed. By hand, gradually stir in enough remaining flour to make a firm dough. Knead on floured surface until smooth and elastic, about 10 minutes. Place in greased bowl, turning to grease top. Cover; let rise in warm place until light and double, about 1 hour.

Punch down dough. Divide into 4 parts. On lightly floured surface, roll or pat each fourth to a 14x7-inch rectangle. Starting with shorter side, roll up tightly, pressing dough into roll with each turn. Pinch edges and ends to seal. Place in greased 8x4 or 9x5-inch bread pans. Cover; let rise in warm place until double, about 30 minutes. Bake at 400° for 35 to 40 minutes until golden brown. Remove from pans; cool.

Refrigerator White Bread

☽ An excellent bread for busy homemakers. The refrigerator rising allows you to prepare the bread one day and bake it the next.

6½ to 7 cups all-purpose flour
2 packages Red Star Instant
Blend Dry Yeast
3 tablespoons sugar
1 tablespoon salt
2⅓ cups water
⅓ cup butter or margarine
Oil

Oven 400°   **2 Loaves**

In large mixer bowl, combine 3 cups flour, yeast, sugar and salt; mix well. In saucepan, heat water and butter until warm (120-130°; butter does not need to melt). Add to flour mixture. Blend at low speed until moistened; beat 3 minutes at medium speed. By hand, gradually stir in enough remaining flour to make a firm dough. Knead on floured surface until smooth and elastic, 5 to 8 minutes. Cover; let rest 20 minutes.

Punch down dough. Divide into 2 parts. On lightly floured surface, roll or pat each half to a 14x7-inch rectangle. Starting with shorter side, roll up tightly, pressing dough into roll with each turn. Pinch edges and ends to seal. Place in greased 8x4 or 9x5-inch bread pans. Gently brush loaves with oil. Cover pans loosely with plastic wrap. Refrigerate 2 to 24 hours. When ready to bake, remove from refrigerator. Uncover; let stand 10 minutes while preheating oven. Bake at 400° for 35 to 40 minutes until golden brown. If too dark, cover loosely with foil last 5 to 10 minutes of baking. Remove from pans; cool.

Modern Sponge White

With this recipe you can make bread the way your grandmother did. It takes more time, but you'll love the flavor and texture of these loaves. It is similar to English Muffin bread.

1 cup warm water
1 package Red Star Instant Blend Dry Yeast
6½ to 7 cups all-purpose flour
1½ cups milk
3 tablespoons sugar
1 tablespoon salt
2 tablespoons shortening

Oven 400°   **2 Loaves**

In large mixer bowl, combine warm water (110-115°) and yeast; let stand 5 minutes. Add 3 cups flour. In saucepan, heat milk until warm (110-115°). Add to flour mixture. Beat until smooth, about 100 strokes. Cover bowl with plastic wrap and foil. Let stand at room temperature for 6 to 24 hours. Add sugar, salt and shortening. By hand, gradually stir in enough remaining flour to make a firm dough. Knead on floured surface until smooth and elastic, 5 to 8 minutes. Place in greased bowl, turning to grease top. Cover; let rise in warm place until light and doubled, about 1 hour.

Punch down dough. Divide into 2 parts. On lightly floured surface, roll or pat each half to a 14x7-inch rectangle. Starting with shorter side, roll up tightly, pressing dough into roll with each turn. Pinch edges and ends to seal. Place in greased 8x4 or 9x5-inch bread pans. Cover; let rise until double, about 1 hour. Bake at 400° for 35 to 40 minutes until golden brown. Remove from pans; cool.

90-Minute Buttercrust Bread

A traditional, basic white bread made easy by a streamlined method. It's special with butter in the bread and on top too.

5½ to 6 cups all-purpose flour
2 packages Red Star Instant Blend Dry Yeast
2 tablespoons sugar
1 tablespoon salt
1 cup milk
1¼ cups water
3 tablespoons butter or margarine
1 tablespoon butter or margarine, melted

Oven 400°   **2 Loaves**

In large mixer bowl, combine 2½ cups flour, yeast, sugar and salt; mix well. In saucepan, heat milk, water, and 3 tablespoons butter until warm (120-130°; butter does not need to melt). Add to flour mixture. Beat at low speed until moistened; beat 3 minutes at medium speed. By hand, gradually stir in enough remaining flour to make a firm dough. Knead on floured surface until smooth and elastic, 5 to 8 minutes. Place in greased bowl, turning to grease top. Cover; let rise in warm oven (Turn oven to lowest setting for 1 minute, turn off.) for 20 minutes.

Punch down dough. Divide into 2 parts. On lightly floured surface, roll or pat each half to a 14x7-inch rectangle. Starting with shorter side, roll up tightly, pressing dough into roll with each turn. Pinch edges and ends to seal. Place in greased 8x4 inch bread pans. Cover; let rise in warm oven until almost doubled, about 30 minutes. With very sharp knife, make a slash across the top of each loaf and pour melted butter into each slash. Bake at 400° for 20 to 25 minutes until golden brown. Remove from pans; cool.

27

French Bread

An American version of the classic French bread. Spray or brush with cold water during baking for a crispy crust. The bread is best eaten the day it is made. If stored before slicing, leave uncovered at room temperature to keep the crust crisp.

1 package Red Star Instant Blend Dry Yeast
1¼ cups warm water
2¾ to 3 cups all-purpose flour
1 teaspoon salt
Cornmeal

Oven 425°   **1 Loaf**

Dissolve yeast in warm water (110-115°); let stand 5 minutes. By hand, stir in 1½ cups flour and salt. Gradually stir in just enough remaining flour to make a soft dough. Knead on floured surface until smooth and elastic, about 10 minutes. Place in greased bowl, turning to grease top. Cover; let rise at room temperature until double, 2½ to 3 hours.

Punch down dough. On lightly floured surface, roll or pat dough to a 12x6-inch rectangle. Starting with longer side, roll up tightly, pressing dough into roll with each turn. Pinch edges and ends to seal. Place on greased cookie sheet sprinkled with cornmeal. Cover; let rise at room temperature until more than doubled, 1 to 1½ hours. With very sharp knife, make 2 or 3 diagonal slashes across top of loaf. Spray or brush loaf with cold water. Bake at 425° for 25 to 30 minutes until golden brown. Spray or brush loaf with water several times during baking for a crispier crust. Remove from cookie sheet; cool.

Rich Raisin Bread

An old favorite that's delicious toasted!

5 to 5½ cups all-purpose flour
2 packages Red Star Instant Blend Dry Yeast
½ cup sugar
1 teaspoon salt
¾ cup milk
½ cup water
½ cup butter or margarine
2 eggs
1 cup raisins

Oven 350°   **2 Loaves**

In large mixer bowl, combine 2½ cups flour, yeast, sugar and salt; mix well. In saucepan, heat milk, water, and butter until warm (120-130°; butter does not need to melt). Add to flour mixture. Add eggs. Blend at low speed until moistened; beat 3 minutes at medium speed. By hand, gradually stir in raisins and enough remaining flour to make a firm dough. Knead on floured surface 5 to 8 minutes. Place in greased bowl, turning to grease top. Cover; let rise in warm place until double, about 1 hour.

Punch down dough. Divide into 2 parts. On lightly floured surface, roll or pat each half to a 14x7-inch rectangle. Starting with shorter side, roll up tightly, pressing dough into roll with each turn. Pinch edges and ends to seal. Place in greased 8x4 or 9x5-inch bread pans. Cover; let rise in warm place until double, 45 to 60 minutes. Bake at 350° for 40 to 45 minutes until golden brown. If too dark, cover loosely with foil last 5 to 10 minutes of baking. Remove from pans; cool.

Classic Rich Bread

🎗 A rich white bread—perfect to accompany a meal, to serve toasted for breakfast or to use for French toast.

8 to 8½ cups all-purpose flour
2 packages Red Star Instant
Blend Dry Yeast
¾ cup sugar
1 tablespoon salt
1½ cups milk
½ cup water
¾ cup butter or margarine
4 eggs

Oven 375°   **3 Loaves**

In large mixer bowl, combine 3 cups flour, yeast, sugar, and salt; mix well. In saucepan, heat milk, water, and butter until warm (120-130°; butter does not need to melt). Add to flour mixture. Add eggs. Blend at low speed until moistened; beat 3 minutes at medium speed. By hand, gradually stir in enough remaining flour to make a firm dough. Knead on floured surface until smooth and elastic, 5 to 8 minutes. Place in greased bowl, turning to grease top. Cover; let rise in warm place until light and doubled, about 1½ hours.

Punch down dough. Divide into 3 parts. On lightly floured surface, roll or pat each third to a 14x7-inch rectangle. Starting with shorter side, roll up tightly, pressing dough into roll with each turn. Pinch edges and ends to seal. Place in greased 8x4-inch bread pans. Cover; let rise in warm place until double, about 45 minutes. Bake at 375° for 25 to 30 minutes until golden brown. Remove from pans; cool.

Hearty White Bread

🎗 A white bread baked with three hearty ingredients.

6 to 6½ cups all-purpose flour
2 packages Red Star Instant
Blend Dry Yeast
½ cup wheat germ
¼ cup potato flakes
¼ cup nonfat dry milk solids
2 tablespoons sugar
1 tablespoon salt
2 cups water
2 tablespoons oil
3 eggs

Oven 400°   **2 Loaves**

In large mixer bowl, combine 3 cups flour, yeast, wheat germ, potato flakes, dry milk solids, sugar, and salt; mix well. In saucepan, heat water and oil until warm (120-130°). Add to flour mixture. Add eggs. Blend at low speed until moistened; beat 3 minutes at medium speed. By hand, gradually stir in enough remaining flour to make a firm dough. Knead on floured surface until smooth and elastic, 5 to 8 minutes. Place in greased bowl, turning to grease top. Cover; let rise in warm place until light and doubled, about 1 hour.

Punch down dough. Divide into 2 parts. On lightly floured surface, roll or pat each half to a 14x7-inch rectangle. Starting with shorter side, roll up tightly, pressing dough into roll with each turn. Pinch edges and ends to seal. Place in greased 9x5 or 8x4-inch bread pans. Cover; let rise in warm place until double, about 45 minutes. Bake at 400° for 35 to 40 minutes until golden brown. Remove from pans; cool.

Grated Potato Bread

🏵 Grated potatoes and wheat germ add two nutritious ingredients to these delicious loaves.

2 medium potatoes, peeled
1 cup water
6 to 6½ cups unbleached flour
2 packages Red Star Instant Blend Dry Yeast
⅓ cup nonfat dry milk solids
¼ cup wheat germ
2 tablespoons sugar
1 tablespoon salt
¼ teaspoon ginger
1 cup water
¼ cup oil
Butter, melted

Oven 375°　　　　**2 Loaves**

Grate potatoes into 1 cup water. In large mixer bowl, combine 2½ cups flour, yeast, dry milk, wheat germ, sugar, salt, and ginger; mix well. In saucepan, heat 1 cup water and oil until warm (120-130°). Add water, oil and potatoes to flour mixture. Blend at low speed until moistened; beat 3 minutes at medium speed. By hand, gradually stir in enough remaining flour to make a firm dough. Knead on floured surface until smooth and elastic, 5 to 8 minutes. Place in greased bowl, turning to grease top. Cover; let rise in warm place until light and doubled, about 1 hour.

Punch down dough. Divide into 2 parts. On lightly floured surface, roll or pat each half to a 14x7-inch rectangle. Starting with shorter side, roll up tightly, pressing dough into roll with each turn. Pinch edges and ends to seal. Place in greased 8x4-inch bread pans. Cover; let rise in warm place until double, about 45 minutes. Bake at 375° for 30 to 35 minutes until golden brown. Brush with melted butter. Remove from pans; cool.

Easy Egg Braid

 An attractive egg braid—extra rich and good!

4 to 4½ cups all-purpose flour
2 packages Red Star Instant Blend Dry Yeast
2 tablespoons sugar
2 teaspoons salt
½ cup water
½ cup milk
2 tablespoons shortening
3 eggs, slightly beaten (reserve 1 tablespoon)

Oven 400°　　　　**1 Large Braid**

In large mixer bowl, combine 2 cups flour, yeast, sugar and salt; mix well. In saucepan, heat water, milk and shortening until warm (120-130°; shortening does not need to melt). Add to flour mixture. Add eggs. Blend at low speed until moistened; beat 3 minutes at medium speed. By hand, gradually stir in enough remaining flour to make a firm dough. Knead on floured surface until smooth and elastic, 5 to 8 minutes. Place in greased bowl, turning to grease top. Cover; let rise in warm place until light and doubled, about 1 hour.

Punch down dough. Divide into 3 parts. On lightly floured surface, roll each third to a 15-inch rope. On greased cookie sheet loosely braid from center to ends. Pinch ends and tuck under to seal. Cover; let rise in warm place until almost doubled, about 30 minutes. Brush with reserved 1 tablespoon egg. Bake at 400° for 25 to 30 minutes until golden brown. Remove from cookie sheet; cool.

Sugar Free Bread

If you're on a special diet, you don't have to give up basic foods. Our sugar free bread recipe makes a very good loaf.

6½ to 7 cups all-purpose flour
2 packages Red Star Instant Blend Dry Yeast
Artificial sweetener to equal 2 tablespoons sugar
1 tablespoon salt
2½ cups water
2 tablespoons shortening
Butter

Oven 400°   **2 Loaves**

In large mixer bowl, combine 2½ cups flour, yeast, artificial sweetener and salt; mix well. In saucepan, heat water and shortening until warm (120-130°; shortening does not need to melt). Add to flour mixture. Blend at low speed until moistened; beat 3 minutes at medium speed. By hand, gradually stir in enough remaining flour to make a firm dough. Knead on floured surface until smooth and elastic, 5 to 8 minutes. Place in greased bowl, turning to grease top. Cover; let rise in warm place until light and doubled, about 1 hour.

Punch down dough. Divide into 2 parts. On lightly floured surface, roll or pat each half to a 14x7-inch rectangle. Starting with shorter side, roll up tightly, pressing dough into roll with each turn. Pinch edges and ends to seal. Place in greased 8x4 or 9x5-inch bread pans. Cover; let rise in warm place until double, about 1 hour. Bake at 400° for 35 to 40 minutes until golden brown. Remove from pans; brush with butter. Cool.

PAN ROLL VARIATION: Divide dough into 2 parts. Divide each half into 12 pieces. Shape each piece into a smooth ball. Place 12 balls in greased 8-inch square cake pan. Cover; let rise until double, about 30 minutes. Bake at 400° for 25 to 30 minutes until golden brown. Remove from pans; brush with butter. Cool. Makes 24 Rolls.

My Notes: _____

_____

_____

_____

_____

_____

_____

_____

_____

_____

_____

_____

_____

_____

Rich Refrigerator Rolls

☽ A rich, golden, tender roll that's easy to make—no kneading required. From this one dough you can make four different kinds of rolls: the traditional Cloverleaf, the fun-to-serve Miniature roll, the Parker House which is square instead of the usual round shape, and the Crescent. The number of rolls from this recipe will depend on the kind you make.

5 to 5½ cups all-purpose flour
2 packages Red Star Instant Blend Dry Yeast
½ cup sugar
1 teaspoon salt
1 cup water
½ cup butter or margarine
3 eggs

Oven 400°　　　24 to 48 Rolls

In large mixer bowl, combine 2 cups flour, yeast, sugar and salt; mix well. In saucepan, heat water and butter until warm (120-130°; butter does not need to melt). Add to flour mixture. Add eggs. Blend at low speed until moistened; beat 3 minutes at medium speed. By hand, gradually stir in enough remaining flour to make a soft dough. Cover with plastic wrap and foil. Refrigerate 6 to 12 hours.

While dough is chilling, punch down several times. Shape into rolls as follows: Divide into 4 parts. Shape each fourth into Cloverleaf, Miniature, Parker House or Crescent rolls. Refrigerate remaining dough until ready to use. Place rolls in greased muffin pan cups or on greased cookie sheets, depending on the roll. Cover; let rise at room temperature until almost doubled, 10 to 15 minutes. Bake at 400° for the time specified until golden brown. Remove from pans or cookie sheets. Serve warm or cold.

Cloverleaf Rolls

¼ Recipe Rich Refrigerator Rolls dough

6 Rolls

Divide dough into 3 parts. Divide each third into 6 pieces. Shape each piece into a smooth ball. Place 3 balls in each greased muffin pan cup. Cover, let rise. Bake 8 to 10 minutes.

Miniature Rolls

¼ Recipe Rich Refrigerator Rolls dough

12 Rolls

Divide dough into 3 parts. Divide each third into 4 pieces. Shape each piece into a smooth ball. Place one ball in each greased miniature muffin pan cup. Cover; let rise. Bake 8 to 10 minutes.

Parker House Rolls

¼ Recipe Rich Refrigerator Rolls dough
1 tablespoon butter, melted

12 Rolls

On lightly floured surface, roll dough to a 12x9-inch rectangle. Cut into 12 squares. Brush with butter. Make an off-center crease in each square. Fold so top half overlaps slightly. Press edges together. Place 2 to 3 inches apart on greased cookie·sheets. Cover; let rise. Bake 6 to 8 minutes.

Crescent Rolls

¼ Recipe Rich Refrigerator Rolls dough
1 tablespoon butter, melted

10 Rolls

On lightly floured surface, roll dough to a 12-inch circle. Brush with butter. Cut into 10 wedges. Starting with wide end of wedge, roll toward point. Place point down, 2 to 3 inches apart, on greased cookie sheets; curve to form a crescent shape. Cover; let rise. Bake 6 to 8 minutes.

Refrigerator Rolls

A convenient roll that can be made the night before and re-frigerated, then shaped and baked the next morning. Or make in the morning to have fresh-from-the-oven rolls for dinner. The rolls are easy to shape—they are all made by roll-ing the dough into ropes. They rise quickly— 10 to 15 minutes at room temperature. The egg glaze gives the rolls a shiny, golden top. The glaze, as well as the seeds, may be omitted, if desired.

6½ to 7 cups all-purpose flour
2 packages Red Star Instant Blend Dry Yeast
½ cup sugar
2 teaspoons salt
2 cups water
⅓ cup butter or margarine
2 eggs
1 egg, slightly beaten
1 tablespoon water
Sesame seeds or poppy seeds

Oven 400°　　　　　**36 Rolls**

In large mixer bowl, combine 2½ cups flour, yeast, sugar and salt; mix well. In saucepan, heat 2 cups water and butter until warm (120-130°; butter does not need to melt). Add to flour mixture. Add 2 eggs. Blend at low speed until moistened; beat 3 minutes at medi-um speed. By hand, gradually stir in enough remaining flour to make a soft dough. Knead on floured surface until smooth and elastic, about 5 minutes. Place in greased bowl, turning to grease top. Cover with plastic wrap and foil. Refrig-erate 6 to 12 hours.

While dough is chilling, punch down several times. Shape into rolls as follows: Divide into 4 parts. Shape each fourth into Knots, Swirls, Rosettes or S's. Refrigerate remain-ing dough until ready to use. Place rolls 2 to 3 inches apart on greased cookie sheets. Cover; let rise at room temperature until almost doubled, 10 to 15 minutes. Combine egg and water; gently brush rolls. Sprinkle with sesame or poppy seed. Bake at 400° for 8 to 10 minutes until golden brown. Remove from cookie sheets. Serve warm or cold.

Knots

¼ Recipe Refrigerator Rolls dough
　　　　　　　　9 Rolls

Divide dough into 9 pieces. On light-ly floured surface, roll each piece to a 10-inch rope. Tie a loose knot, stretching rope gently if needed.

Swirls

¼ Recipe Refrigerator Rolls dough
　　　　　　　　9 Rolls

Divide dough into 9 pieces. On light-ly floured surface, roll each piece to a 10-inch rope. Loosely coil each rope.

Rosettes

¼ Recipe Refrigerator Rolls dough
　　　　　　　　9 Rolls

Divide dough into 9 pieces. On lightly floured surface, roll each piece to a 12-inch rope. Tie a loose knot, stretching rope gently if needed to leave two long ends. Tuck top end under roll. Bring bottom end up and tuck into center of roll.

S's

¼ Recipe Refrigerator Rolls dough
　　　　　　　　9 Rolls

Divide dough into 9 pieces. On lightly floured surface, roll each piece to a 10-inch rope. Form a figure "S".

Vienna Hoagie Buns

Chewy buns just right for Hoagie sandwiches. Bake the dough in two loaves for Vienna Bread.

5¾ to 6¼ cups all-purpose flour
2 packages Red Star Instant
 Blend Dry Yeast
1 tablespoon sugar
1 tablespoon salt
1¼ cups water
1 cup milk
1 tablespoon shortening
 Cornmeal
1 egg white, slightly beaten
1 tablespoon water

Oven 425° **8 Buns**

In large mixer bowl, combine 2½ cups flour, yeast, sugar and salt; mix well. In saucepan, heat 1¼ cups water, milk and shortening until warm (120-130°; shortening does not need to melt). Add to flour mixture. Blend at low speed until moistened; beat 3 minutes at medium speed. By hand, gradually stir in enough remaining flour to make a firm dough. Knead on floured surface until smooth and elastic, 5 to 8 minutes. Place in greased bowl, turning to grease top. Cover; let rise in warm place until light and doubled, about 1 hour.

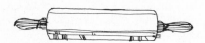

Punch down dough. Divide into 4 parts. Divide each fourth into 2 pieces. On lightly floured surface, roll or pat each piece to an 8x4-inch rectangle. Starting with longer side, roll up tightly, pressing dough into roll with each turn. Pinch edges and ends to seal. Place on greased cookie sheets sprinkled with cornmeal. With very sharp knife, make 2 or 3 diagonal slashes across the top of each bun. Cover; let rise in warm place until double, about 20 minutes. Combine slightly beaten egg white and 1 tablespoon water; brush on buns. Bake at 425° for 15 to 20 minutes until golden brown. Remove from cookie sheets; cool.

Vienna Bread

Oven 400° **2 Loaves**

Prepare dough for Vienna Hoagie Buns as directed *except* divide dough into 2 parts. On lightly floured surface, roll or pat each half to a 12x6-inch rectangle. Starting with longer side, roll up tightly, pressing dough into roll with each turn. Pinch edges and ends to seal. Place on greased cookie sheets sprinkled with cornmeal. With very sharp knife, make 2 or 3 diagonal slashes across the top of each loaf. Cover; let rise in warm place until double, about 30 minutes. Combine slightly beaten egg white and 1 tablespoon water; brush on loaves. Bake at 400° for 30 to 35 minutes until golden brown. Remove from cookie sheets; cool.

Easy Croissants

🎖 A quick version of the delicate French rolls called croissants.

5 cups all-purpose flour
2 packages Red Star Instant Blend Dry Yeast
¼ cup sugar
2 teaspoons salt
1 cup water
¾ cup evaporated milk
¼ cup butter or margarine
1 egg
1 cup butter or margarine, refrigerator temperature, cut into pieces
1 egg
1 tablespoon water

Oven 350°　　　　　　**40 Rolls**

In large mixer bowl, combine 1 cup flour, yeast, sugar and salt; mix well. In saucepan, heat 1 cup water, milk and ¼ cup butter until warm (120-130°; butter does not need to melt). Add to flour mixture. Add 1 egg. Blend at low speed until moistened; beat 3 minutes at medium speed. Set aside. In large bowl, cut 1 cup firm butter into remaining 4 cups flour until butter particles are the size of large peas. Pour yeast mixture over flour-butter mixture and fold in until all flour is moistened. Cover; refrigerate 2 hours.

Place dough on floured surface; knead about 6 times to release air bubbles. Divide into 4 parts. Roll each fourth to a 14-inch circle. With a sharp knife, cut into 10 pie-shape wedges. Starting with wide edge, roll each wedge toward the point. Place on ungreased cookie sheets, point side down, and curve into croissants. Cover; let rise in warm place until almost doubled, 1 to 1½ hours. Combine 1 slightly beaten egg and 1 tablespoon water; brush rolls with egg mixture. Bake at 350° for 15 to 18 minutes until golden brown. Remove from cookie sheets; cool.

Quick Buttermilk Rolls

⏱ 🎖 What could be easier than preparing and baking a pan of buttermilk yeast rolls in about and hour and a half? They're light and tender—simply delicious!

4 to 4½ cups all-purpose flour
2 packages Red Star Instant Blend Dry Yeast
3 tablespoons sugar
1 teaspoon salt
½ teaspoon soda
1¼ cups buttermilk
½ cup water
½ cup shortening

Oven 400°　　　　　　**24 Rolls**

In large mixer bowl, combine 1½ cups flour, yeast, sugar, salt and soda; mix well. In saucepan, heat buttermilk, water and shortening until warm (120-130°; shortening does not need to melt). Add to flour mixture. Blend at low speed until moistened; beat 3 minutes at medium speed. By hand, gradually stir in enough remaining flour to make a firm dough. Knead on floured surface until smooth and elastic, 5 to 8 minutes. Place in greased bowl, turning to grease top. Cover; let rise in warm place until light and doubled, about 20 minutes.

Punch down dough. Divide into 4 parts. Divide each fourth into 6 pieces. Shape each piece into a smooth ball. Place in greased 15x10-inch jelly roll pan. Cover; let rise in warm place until almost doubled, about 20 minutes. Bake at 400° for 15 to 20 minutes until golden brown. Remove from pan; cool.

Bread Sticks

Bread sticks keep several days in a loosely covered container and are fun to serve with salads, as a snack with beverages, or with first courses.

2¼ to 2¾ cups all-purpose flour
1 package Red Star Instant Blend Dry Yeast
1 tablespoon sugar
2 teaspoons salt
1 cup water
2 tablespoons shortening
1 egg white, slightly beaten
1 tablespoon water
3 to 4 tablespoons poppy or sesame seeds

Oven 400°   24 Bread Sticks

In large mixer bowl, combine 1 cup flour, yeast, sugar and salt; mix well. In saucepan, heat water and shortening until warm (120-130°; shortening does not need to melt). Add to flour mixture. Blend at low speed until moistened; beat 3 minutes at medium speed. By hand, gradually stir in enough remaining flour to make a soft dough. Knead on floured surface until smooth and elastic, 5 to 8 minutes. Place in greased bowl, turning to grease top. Cover; let rise in warm place until double, about 45 minutes.

Punch down dough. Divide into 4 parts. Divide each fourth into 6 pieces. On lightly floured surface, roll each piece to an 8-inch rope. Place on greased cookie sheets. Combine egg white and water; brush tops of bread sticks. Sprinkle with poppy or sesame seed. Cover; let rise in warm place about 15 minutes. Bake at 400° for 15 to 20 minutes until deep golden brown. Remove from cookie sheets; cool.

Pepper Bread Sticks

These "specially" flavored bread sticks are perfect with soup.

3½ to 4 cups all-purpose flour
1 package Red Star Instant Blend Dry Yeast
2 teaspoons salt
1 teaspoon sugar
1 teaspoon dried rosemary, crushed
1 tablespoon grated Stella Parmesan Cheese
⅛ teaspoon white pepper
1¼ cups water
3 tablespoons oil
1 egg white, slightly beaten
1 tablespoon water
3 to 4 tablespoons sesame seeds

Oven 400°   24 Bread Sticks

In large mixer bowl, combine 1½ cups flour, yeast, salt, sugar, rosemary, Parmesan cheese and pepper; mix well. In saucepan, heat water and oil until warm (120-130°). Add to flour mixture. Blend at low speed until moistened; beat 3 minutes at medium speed. By hand, gradually stir in enough remaining flour to make a firm dough. Knead on floured surface, 5 to 8 minutes. Place in greased bowl, turning to grease top. Cover; let rise in warm place until double, about 45 minutes.

Punch down dough. Divide into 4 parts. Divide each fourth into 6 pieces. Roll each piece into a 12-inch rope. Place 1 inch apart on greased cookie sheets. Combine egg white and water; brush tops of bread sticks. Sprinkle with sesame seed. Bake at 400° for 25 to 30 minutes until deep golden brown. Remove from cookie sheets; cool.

Burger Buns

Wheat Germ Snack Buns

Make your hamburgers "special" with these easy-to-make buns.

4½ to 5 cups all-purpose flour
2 packages Red Star Instant Blend Dry Yeast
2 tablespoons sugar
1½ teaspoons salt
1 cup milk
½ cup water
¼ cup margarine
1 egg

Oven 400°   **12 Burger Buns or Hot Dog Buns**

In large mixer bowl, combine 1¾ cups flour, yeast, sugar and salt; mix well. In saucepan, heat milk, water and margarine until warm (120-130°; margarine does not need to melt). Add to flour mixture. Add egg. Blend at low speed until moistened; beat 3 minutes at medium speed. By hand, gradually stir in enough remaining flour to make a firm dough. Knead on floured surface until smooth and elastic, 5 to 8 minutes. Cover with plastic wrap, then a towel; let rest 20 minutes.

Divide dough into 2 parts. Divide each half into 6 pieces. Shape each piece into a smooth ball. Place on greased cookie sheet. Flatten to 4-inch diameter. Cover; let rise in warm place until double, about 20 minutes. Bake at 400° for 10 to 12 minutes until golden brown. Remove from cookie sheets; cool.

HOT DOG BUN VARIATION: Shape each piece into a 6x4-inch rectangle. Starting with longer side, roll up tightly, pressing dough into roll with each turn. Pinch edges and ends to seal. Place on greased cookie sheet. Let rise and bake as directed above.

Surprise your family or friends with these delicious small buns. The flavor of the bread complements any filling.

3¾ cups all-purpose flour
¾ cup wheat germ
2 packages Red Star Instant Blend Dry Yeast
2 tablespoons sugar
1¾ teaspoons salt
1 cup milk
½ cup water
¼ cup butter or margarine
1 egg

Oven 400°   **36 Small Buns**

In large mixer bowl, combine 1¾ cups flour, wheat germ, yeast, sugar and salt; mix well. In saucepan, heat milk, water and butter until warm (120-130°; butter does not need to melt). Add to flour mixture. Add egg. Blend at low speed until moistened; beat 3 minutes at medium speed. By hand, gradually stir in enough remaining flour to make a firm dough. Knead on floured surface until smooth and elastic, about 5 minutes. Cover with plastic wrap, then a towel. Let rest 20 minutes.

Divide dough into 4 parts. Divide each fourth into 9 pieces. Shape each piece into a smooth ball. Place on greased cookie sheets. Cover; let rise in warm place until double, about 20 minutes. Bake at 400° for 8 to 10 minutes until golden brown. Remove from cookie sheets; cool.

Beer Rye Dinner Rolls

Light rye rolls, flavored with beer and molasses, are ideal to serve with barbecued meats. Bake as round rolls or as pan rolls.

**3 to 3½ cups all-purpose flour
2 packages Red Star Instant
Blend Dry Yeast
¼ cup sugar
1 tablespoon salt
1½ cups beer
½ cup water
¼ cup dark molasses
3 tablespoons shortening
3 cups medium rye flour
Butter**

Oven 375°   **24 Rolls**

In large mixer bowl, combine 2½ cups all-purpose flour, yeast, sugar and salt; mix well. In saucepan, heat beer, water, molasses and shortening until warm (120-130°; shortening does not need to melt). Add to flour mixture. Blend at low speed until moistened; beat 3 minutes at medium speed. By hand, gradually stir in rye flour and enough remaining all-purpose flour to make a firm dough. Knead on floured surface until smooth and elastic, about 5 minutes. (Dough will be slightly sticky.) Place in greased bowl, turning to grease top. Cover; let rise in warm place until double, about 1 hour.

Punch down dough. Divide into 4 parts. Divide each fourth into 6 pieces. Shape each piece into a smooth ball. Place on greased cookie sheet. Cover; let rise in warm place until almost doubled, about 15 minutes. Bake at 375° for 15 to 20 minutes until rolls sound hollow when tapped. Remove from cookie sheets; brush with butter. Serve warm or cold.

PAN ROLL VARIATION: Place 12 balls in greased 9-inch square cake pan. Cover; let rise until almost doubled, about 30 minutes. Bake at 375° for 20 to 25 minutes. Remove from pans; brush with butter. Serve warm or cold.

Onion Mustard Buns

Onion and mustard, favorite additions to a hamburger, are included in these unusual buns.

**5½ to 6 cups all-purpose flour
2 packages Red Star Instant
Blend Dry Yeast
2 tablespoons sugar
1 tablespoon salt
¼ teaspoon white pepper
1 cup milk
1 cup water
2 tablespoons oil
1 tablespoon prepared mustard
2 tablespoons instant minced onion
1 egg
¼ cup water
2 tablespoons instant minced onion
1 egg, slightly beaten**

Oven 375°   **18 Buns**

In large mixer bowl, combine 3 cups flour, yeast, sugar, salt and pepper; mix well. In saucepan, heat milk, 1 cup water and oil until warm (120-130°). Add to flour mixture. Add mustard, 2 tablespoons instant minced onion and egg. Blend at low speed until moistened; beat 3 minutes at medium speed. By hand, gradually stir in enough remaining flour to make a firm dough. Knead on floured surface until smooth and elastic, 5 to 8 minutes. Place in greased bowl, turning to grease top. Cover; let rise in warm place until double, about 1 hour.

Punch down dough. Divide into 3 parts. Divide each third into 6 pieces. Shape each piece into a smooth ball. Place on greased cookie sheets; flatten to a 3-inch diameter. Cover; let rise in warm place until double, about 30 minutes. Combine ¼ cup water and 2 tablespoons instant minced onion; let stand while rolls are rising. Combine slightly beaten egg and onion mixture and brush tops of rolls. Bake at 375° for 15 to 20 minutes until golden brown. Remove from cookie sheets; cool.

Dark Pumpernickel Rye Rolls

Dinner rolls supreme! Dark and flavor filled. Made with pumpernickel rye flour. Break one open to capture the wonderful aroma of onion, coffee and molasses.

4 to 4½ cups all-purpose flour
2 packages Red Star Instant Blend Dry Yeast
2 tablespoons sugar
1 tablespoon instant coffee
1 tablespoon salt
2 teaspoons onion powder
1 cup milk
1 cup water
½ cup dark molasses
¼ cup shortening
1 square (1 oz.) unsweetened chocolate
2 cups pumpernickel rye flour

Oven 375°   **24 Rolls or 18 Sandwich Buns**

In large mixer bowl, combine 3 cups all-purpose flour, yeast, sugar, instant coffee, salt and onion powder; mix well. In saucepan, heat milk, water, molasses, shortening and chocolate until warm (120-130°; shortening and chocolate do not need to melt). Add to flour mixture. Blend at low speed until moistened; beat 3 minutes at medium speed. By hand, gradually stir in rye flour and enough remaining all-purpose flour to make a firm dough. Knead on floured surface until smooth and elastic, 5 to 8 minutes. Place in greased bowl, turning to grease top. Cover; let rise in warm place until double, about 1 hour.

Punch down dough. Divide into 4 parts. Divide each fourth into 6 pieces. Shape each piece into a smooth ball. Place on greased cookie sheets. Cover; let rise in warm place until double, about 15 minutes. Bake at 375° for 15 to 18 minutes. Remove from cookie sheets; cool.

VARIATION: For Sandwich Buns, divide dough into 3 parts. Divide each third into 6 pieces. Shape each piece into a smooth ball. Place on greased cookie sheet. Flatten to a 3½-inch circle. Let rise and bake as directed above.

Easy Savory Pan Rolls

Simple-to-make pan rolls, flavored with onion and poultry seasoning, are the perfect accompaniment for any holiday menu.

3¼ to 3¾ cups all-purpose flour
½ cup wheat germ
2 packages Red Star Instant Blend Dry Yeast
2 tablespoons sugar
2 teaspoons salt
1 tablespoon instant minced onion
½ teaspoon poultry seasoning
½ cup water
½ cup milk
2 tablespoons butter or margarine
1 egg
2 tablespoons melted butter or margarine
2 tablespoons sesame seeds

Oven 375°   **15 Rolls**

In large mixer bowl, combine 1½ cups flour, wheat germ, yeast, sugar, salt, onion and poultry seasoning. In saucepan, heat water, milk and butter until warm (120-130°; butter does not need to melt). Add to flour mixture. Add egg. Blend at low speed until moistened; beat 3 minutes at medium speed. By hand, gradually stir in enough remaining flour to make a firm dough. Knead on floured surface, 5 to 8 minutes. Place in greased bowl, turning to grease top. Cover; let rise in warm place until light and double, about 1 hour.

Punch down dough. Divide into 3 parts. Divide each third into 5 pieces. Shape each piece into a smooth ball. Dip tops into melted butter. Place in greased 13x9-inch cake pan. Sprinkle with sesame seed. Cover; let rise in warm place until double, about 30 minutes. Bake at 375° for 20 to 25 minutes until golden brown. Remove from pan; cool.

Whole Wheat Cottage Cheese Rolls

A nutritious and light whole wheat roll.

1½ to 2 cups all-purpose flour
2 cups whole wheat flour
2 packages Red Star Instant Blend Dry Yeast
¼ cup packed brown sugar
2 teaspoons salt
½ teaspoon baking soda
½ cup water
1½ cups (12 oz. carton) small curd creamed cottage cheese
2 tablespoons butter or margarine
2 eggs
Butter or margarine

Oven 375°   **24 Rolls**

In large mixer bowl, combine ¾ cup all-purpose flour, ¾ cup whole wheat flour, yeast, brown sugar, salt and baking soda; mix well. In saucepan, heat water, cottage cheese and butter until warm (120-130°; butter does not need to melt). Add to flour mixture. Add eggs. Blend at low speed until moistened; beat 3 minutes at medium speed. By hand, gradually stir in remaining whole wheat flour and enough all-purpose flour to make a firm dough. Knead on floured surface until smooth and elastic, 5 to 8 minutes. Place in greased bowl, turning to grease top. Cover; let rise in warm place until double, about 1 hour.

Punch down dough. Divide into 6 parts. Divide each part into 6 pieces. Shape each piece into a smooth ball. Place in greased muffin pan cups. Cover and let rise in warm place until double, about 45 minutes. Bake at 375° for 12 to 15 minutes. Brush with butter. Remove from pans; cool.

Graham Bread

An old-fashioned bread with a delicious "nutty" flavor! For a darker color, use molasses.

**4½ cups all-purpose flour
2 packages Red Star Instant
   Blend Dry Yeast
½ cup packed brown sugar
2 tablespoons salt
2 cups milk
1½ cups water
⅓ cup shortening
5 to 5½ cups graham flour**

Oven 375°   3 Round Loaves

In large mixer bowl, combine 4 cups all-purpose flour, yeast, sugar, and salt; mix well. In saucepan, heat milk, water and shortening until warm (120-130°; shortening does not need to melt). Add to flour mixture. Blend at low speed until moistened; beat 3 minutes at medium speed. By hand, gradually stir in remaining all-purpose flour and enough remaining graham flour to make a firm dough. Knead on floured surface 5 to 8 minutes. Place in greased bowl, turning to grease top. Cover; let rise in warm place until double, about 1 hour.

Punch down dough. Divide into 3 parts. On lightly floured surface, shape each third into a round loaf. Place on greased cookie sheets. Cover; let rise in warm place until almost doubled, 30 to 45 minutes. Bake at 375° for 25 to 30 minutes until loaves sound hollow when tapped. Remove from cookie sheets; cool.

VARIATION: ½ cup light molasses may be substituted for the brown sugar. Heat molasses with the milk, water and shortening.

Honey of a Whole Wheat Bread

The sweet, nutty flavor of honey and whole wheat make these tasty loaves special.

**3½ to 4 cups all-purpose flour
2½ cups whole wheat flour
2 packages Red Star Instant
   Blend Dry Yeast
1 tablespoon salt
1 cup milk
1 cup water
½ cup honey
3 tablespoons shortening
1 egg**

Oven 375°   2 Loaves

In large mixer bowl, combine 2 cups all-purpose flour, 1 cup whole wheat flour, yeast and salt; mix well. In saucepan, heat milk, water, honey and shortening until warm (120-130°; shortening does not need to melt). Add to flour mixture. Add egg. Blend at low speed until moistened; beat 3 minutes at medium speed. By hand, gradually stir in remaining whole wheat flour and enough remaining all-purpose flour to make a firm dough. Knead on floured surface 5 to 8 minutes. Place in greased bowl, turning to grease top. Cover; let rise in warm place until double, about 1 hour.

Punch down dough. Divide into 2 parts. On lightly floured surface, roll or pat each half to a 14x7-inch rectangle. Starting with shorter side, roll up tightly, pressing dough into roll with each turn. Pinch edges and ends to seal. Place in greased 9x5 or 8x4-inch bread pans. Cover; let rise in warm place until double, 30 to 40 minutes. Bake at 375° for 35 to 40 minutes until golden brown. Remove from pans; cool.

41

100% Whole Wheat Bread

This is a classic whole wheat bread. You'll enjoy thick slices with soup or for sandwiches.

8 to 8½ cups whole wheat flour
2 packages Red Star Instant Blend Dry Yeast
4 teaspoons salt
3 cups water
½ cup dark molasses
¼ cup oil

Oven 375°   2 Round Loaves

In large mixer bowl, combine 3½ cups flour, yeast, and salt; mix well. In saucepan, heat water, molasses, and oil until warm (120-130°). Add to flour mixture. Blend at low speed until moistened; beat 3 minutes at medium speed. By hand, gradually stir in enough remaining flour to make a firm dough. Knead on floured surface 5 to 8 minutes. Place in greased bowl, turning to grease top. Cover; let rise in warm place until double, 1 to 1½ hours.

Punch down dough. Divide into 2 parts. On lightly floured surface, shape each half into a round loaf. Place in greased 9-inch layer cake pans. With very sharp knife, make 6 slashes, ¼-inch deep, across the top of each loaf (spoke fashion). Cover; let rise in warm place until almost doubled, about 30 minutes. Bake at 375° for 40 to 45 minutes, until loaves sound hollow when tapped. Remove from pans; cool.

Special Whole Wheat Bread

An excellent whole wheat bread made special with cottage cheese and honey.

4 to 4½ cups all-purpose flour
2 cups whole wheat flour
2 packages Red Star Instant Blend Dry Yeast
1 tablespoon salt
1½ cups milk
½ cup water
½ cup small curd cottage cheese
¼ cup honey
¼ cup butter or margarine

Oven 375°   2 Loaves

In large mixer bowl, combine 1 cup all-purpose flour, whole wheat flour, yeast, and salt; mix well. In saucepan, heat milk, water, cottage cheese, honey and butter until warm (120-130°; butter does not need to melt). Add to flour mixture. Blend at low speed until moistened; beat 3 minutes at medium speed. By hand, gradually stir in enough remaining all-purpose flour to make a firm dough. Knead on floured surface until smooth and elastic, 5 to 8 minutes. Place in greased bowl, turning to grease top. Cover; let rise in warm place until double, about 1 hour.

Punch down dough. Divide into 2 parts. On lightly floured surface, roll or pat each half to a 14x7-inch rectangle. Starting with shorter side, roll up tightly, pressing dough into roll with each turn. Pinch edges and ends to seal. Place in greased 9x5-inch bread pans. Cover; let rise in warm place until double, about 1 hour. Bake at 375° for 35 to 40 minutes until loaves sound hollow when tapped. Remove from pans; cool.

Whole Wheat Bran Sandwich Buns

A delicious bun to serve with hamburgers or cheeses and luncheon meats. Make larger to serve as snack buns.

2½ to 3 cups all-purpose flour
  2 packages Red Star Instant Blend Dry Yeast
  1 cup whole bran cereal
  ¼ cup packed brown sugar
  1 teaspoon salt
  1¼ cups milk
  ½ cup water
  2 tablespoons shortening
  1 egg
  1½ cups whole wheat flour
  1 egg white, slightly beaten
  1 tablespoon water
  1 to 1½ tablespoons sesame seeds

Oven 375°   12 Sandwich Buns

In large mixer bowl, combine 1½ cups all-purpose flour, yeast, cereal, sugar and salt; mix well. In saucepan, heat milk, ½ cup water and shortening until warm (120-130°; shortening does not need to melt). Add to flour mixture. Add egg. Blend at low speed until moistened; beat 3 minutes at medium speed. By hand, gradually stir in whole wheat flour and enough remaining all-purpose flour to make a firm dough. Knead on floured surface about 5 minutes. Place in greased bowl, turning to grease top. Cover; let rise in warm place until doubled, 1 to 1½ hours.

Punch down dough. Divide into 4 parts. Divide each fourth into 3 pieces. Shape each piece into a smooth ball. Place on greased cookie sheets. Flatten to a 4-inch diameter. Cover; let rise in warm place until almost doubled, about 20 minutes. Combine egg white and 1 tablespoon water. Brush tops of buns. Sprinkle with sesame seeds. Bake at 375° for 15 to 18 minutes until golden brown. Remove from cookie sheets; cool.

For Steak Buns: Divide dough into 2 parts. Divide each half into 5 pieces. Shape each piece into a smooth ball. Place on greased cookie sheets. Flatten to a 5-inch diameter. Let rise about 25 minutes. Bake for 15 to 20 minutes. Makes 10 steak buns.

Cracked Wheat Bread

Slice these crunchy textured round loaves on a decorative bread board at the table.

5½ to 6 cups all-purpose flour
  2 packages Red Star Instant Blend Dry Yeast
  ¼ cup packed brown sugar
  4 teaspoons salt
  2½ cups warm water
  2 tablespoons oil
  1 cup graham flour
  ¾ cup cracked wheat

Oven 375°   2 Round Loaves

In large mixer bowl, combine 2¼ cups all-purpose flour, yeast, brown sugar and salt; mix well. Add warm water (120-130°) and oil to flour mixture. Blend at low speed until moistened; beat 3 minutes at medium speed. By hand, gradually stir in graham flour, cracked wheat and enough remaining all-purpose flour to make a firm dough. Knead on floured surface until smooth and elastic, 5 to 8 minutes. Place in greased bowl, turning to grease top. Cover; let rise in warm place until double, about 1 hour.

Punch down dough. Divide into 2 parts. On lightly floured surface, shape each half to a round loaf. Place on greased cookie sheet. Cover; let rise in warm place until double, about 30 minutes. Bake at 375° for 25 to 30 minutes until golden brown. Remove from cookie sheets; cool.

43

Molasses Oatmeal Bread

This bread uses the "old world" technique of soaking grains in boiling water to soften them. Molasses adds a delicious flavor to the moist, old-fashioned loaves. Sprinkle oats on top for an attractive appearance.

2 packages Red Star Instant Blend Dry Yeast
½ cup warm water
2 cups quick rolled oats
2 tablespoons shortening
2 cups boiling water
½ cup molasses
4 teaspoons salt
5½ to 6 cups all-purpose flour
1 egg white, slightly beaten
1 tablespoon water
2 tablespoons quick rolled oats

Oven 400° **2 Loaves**

Dissolve yeast in ½ cup warm water (110-115°); set aside. In large bowl, place 2 cups rolled oats and shortening; pour in boiling water; stir. Cool to lukewarm, about 10 minutes. Stir in dissolved yeast, molasses and salt. By hand, stir in half the flour; then gradually stir in enough remaining flour to make a firm dough. Knead on floured surface 5 to 8 minutes. Place in greased bowl, turning to grease top. Cover; let rise in warm place until double, about 1 hour.

Punch down dough. Divide into 2 parts. On lightly floured surface, roll or pat each half to a 14x7-inch rectangle. Starting with shorter side, roll up tightly, pressing dough into roll with each turn. Pinch edges and ends to seal. Place in greased 9x5-inch bread pans. Cover; let rise in warm place until double, about 1 hour. Combine egg white and 1 tablespoon water; brush tops of loaves. Sprinkle with 2 tablespoons rolled oats. Bake at 400° for 35 to 40 minutes until golden brown. Remove from pans; cool.

Mom's Nut Bread

A yeast version of the popular nut bread! This recipe was updated from a recipe brought from Europe in 1882. Nut bread was a favorite tea time snack served with "Bar-le-duc"—cream cheese and currant jelly.

3 to 3½ cups all-purpose flour
2 cups whole wheat flour
2 packages Red Star Instant Blend Dry Yeast
½ cup packed brown sugar
1 tablespoon salt
2 cups water
2 tablespoons shortening
1 cup chopped walnuts

Oven 375° **2 Loaves**

In large mixer bowl, combine 1 cup all-purpose flour, whole wheat flour, yeast, sugar and salt; mix well. In saucepan, heat water and shortening until warm (120-130°; shortening does not need to melt). Add to flour mixture. Blend at low speed until moistened; beat 3 minutes at medium speed. By hand, gradually stir in nuts and enough remaining flour to make a firm dough. Knead on floured surface 5 to 8 minutes. Place in greased bowl, turning to grease top. Cover; let rise in warm place until double, about 1 hour.

Punch down dough. Divide into 2 parts. On lightly floured surface, roll or pat each half to a 14x7-inch rectangle. Starting with shorter side, roll up tightly, pressing dough into roll with each turn. Pinch edges and ends to seal. Place in greased 8x4-inch bread pans. Cover; let rise in warm place until double, about 1 hour. Bake at 375° for 35 to 40 minutes until loaves sound hollow when tapped. Remove from pans; cool.

Pumpernickel Rye Bread

A traditional rye bread shaped into traditional loaves. Excellent toasted!

3½ to 4 cups all-purpose flour
2 packages Red Star Instant Blend Dry Yeast
1 tablespoon salt
2 cups water
½ cup dark molasses
2 tablespoons shortening
3 cups pumpernickel rye flour

Oven 375°   2 Loaves

In large mixer bowl, combine 2½ cups all-purpose flour, yeast and salt; mix well. In saucepan, heat water, molasses and shortening until warm (120-130°; shortening does not need to melt). Add to flour mixture. Blend at low speed until moistened; beat 3 minutes at medium speed. By hand, gradually stir in rye flour and enough remaining all-purpose flour to make a firm dough. Knead on floured surface about 5 minutes. Place in greased bowl, turning to grease top. Cover; let rise in warm place until double, about 1 hour.

Punch down dough. Divide into 2 parts. On lightly floured surface, roll or pat each half to a 14x7-inch rectangle. Starting with shorter side, roll up tightly, pressing dough into roll with each turn. Pinch edges and ends to seal. Place in greased 8x4-inch bread pans. Cover; let rise in warm place until almost doubled, about 30 minutes. Bake at 375° for 40 to 45 minutes until loaves sound hollow when tapped. Remove from pans; cool.

Bohemian Rye Bread

A light rye bread with a hint of licorice.

3¾ to 4¼ cups all-purpose flour
2½ cups medium rye flour
2 packages Red Star Instant Blend Dry Yeast
¼ cup sugar
1 tablespoon salt
1 tablespoon fennel seeds
2 teaspoons caraway seeds
2½ cups water
3 tablespoons shortening

Oven 375°   2 Round Loaves

In large mixer bowl, combine 1½ cups all-purpose flour, 1 cup rye flour, yeast, sugar, salt, fennel and caraway seed; mix well. In saucepan, heat water and shortening until warm (120-130°; shortening does not need to melt). Add to flour mixture. Blend at low speed until moistened; beat 3 minutes at medium speed. By hand, gradually stir in remaining rye flour and enough remaining all-purpose flour to make a firm dough. Knead on floured surface about 5 minutes. (Dough will be slightly sticky.) Place in greased bowl, turning to grease top. Cover; let rise in warm place until double, about 1 hour.

Punch down dough. Divide into 2 parts. On lightly floured surface, shape each half into a round loaf. Place on greased cookie sheets. Flatten slightly. Cover; let rise in warm place until almost doubled, about 30 minutes. Bake at 375° for 35 to 40 minutes until loaves sound hollow when tapped. Remove from cookie sheets; cool.

Rye Breads

Old Milwaukee Rye Bread

An old-fashioned sour rye bread with caraway seed. Letting the "Sour" stand for 3 days will give more sour flavor.

1 package Red Star Instant Blend Dry Yeast
1½ cups warm water
2 cups medium rye flour
1 tablespoon caraway seeds
4¾ to 5¼ cups all-purpose flour
1 cup medium rye flour
1 package Red Star Instant Blend Dry Yeast
1 tablespoon salt
1 tablespoon caraway seeds
1 cup water
¼ cup molasses
3 tablespoons shortening
Cornmeal

Oven 375°   2 Round Loaves

Prepare a Sour 2 to 3 days before use: Dissolve 1 package yeast in 1½ cups warm water (110-115°) in 3-quart glass bowl. Stir in 2 cups rye flour and 1 tablespoon caraway seed. Cover loosely with plastic wrap or foil; let stand in warm place. Stir twice a day.

In large mixer bowl, combine 1 cup all-purpose flour, 1 cup rye flour, 1 package yeast, salt and 1 tablespoon caraway seed; mix well. In saucepan, heat water, molasses and shortening until warm (120-130°; shortening does not need to melt). Add to flour mixture. Add Sour. Blend at low speed until moistened; beat 3 minutes at medium speed. By hand, gradually stir in enough remaining all-purpose flour to make a firm dough. Knead on floured surface about 5 minutes. Place in greased bowl, turning to grease top. Cover; let rise in warm place until double, about 1 hour.

Punch down dough. Divide into 2 parts. On lightly floured surface, shape each half into a round loaf. Place on greased cookie sheets sprinkled with cornmeal. Cover; let rise in warm place for 15 minutes. With very sharp knife, make 2 or 3 slashes, ¼ inch deep, on top of each loaf. Let rise about 15 minutes longer until double. Bake at 375° for 40 to 45 minutes until loaves sound hollow when tapped. Remove from cookie sheets; cool.

Delicatessen Black Bread

A dark and delicious rye bread! The cornstarch glaze gives a shiny top to the loaves like the ones available in delicatessens.

2½ to 3 cups all-purpose flour
2 cups rye flour
2 packages Red Star Instant Blend Dry Yeast
2 cups whole bran cereal
1 tablespoon salt
1 tablespoon caraway seeds
2 teaspoons onion powder
1½ cups milk
½ cup water
¼ cup dark molasses
¼ cup oil
1 square (1 oz.) unsweetened chocolate
¼ cup water
½ teaspoon cornstarch
caraway seeds

Cheese 'N Rye Bread

Oven 375° **2 Round Loaves**

In large mixer bowl, combine 1 cup all-purpose flour, 1 cup rye flour, yeast, bran cereal, salt, caraway seed and onion powder; mix well. In saucepan, heat milk, ½ cup water, molasses, oil and chocolate until warm (120-130°; chocolate does not need to melt). Add to flour mixture. Blend at low speed until moistened; beat 3 minutes at medium speed. By hand, gradually stir in remaining rye flour and enough remaining all-purpose flour to make a firm dough. Knead on floured surface until smooth and elastic, about 5 minutes. Place in greased bowl, turning to grease top. Cover; let rise in warm place until double, 1 to 1½ hours.

Punch down dough. Divide into 2 parts. On lightly floured surface, shape each half into a round loaf. Place in greased 8-inch layer cake pans. Cover; let rise in warm place until almost doubled, about 30 minutes. Bake at 375° for 40 to 45 minutes. Combine ¼ cup water and cornstarch for glaze in small saucepan; heat to boiling. Brush on loaves 5 minutes before end of baking. Sprinkle caraway seeds on loaves, if desired. Return loaves to oven for 5 minutes or until glaze is glossy and loaves sound hollow when tapped. Remove from pans; cool.

Loaves of light rye bread with a mild cheese flavor.

4 to 4½ cups all-purpose flour
1 cup rye flour
2 packages Red Star Instant Blend Dry Yeast
2 tablespoons sugar
2 tablespoons Stella grated Parmesan cheese
1 tablespoon salt
1 cup milk
1 cup water
2 tablespoons shortening
2 cups (8 oz.) Stella shredded Cheddar cheese

Oven 375° **2 Loaves**

In large mixer bowl, combine 1 cup all-purpose flour, rye flour, yeast, sugar, Parmesan cheese and salt; mix well. In saucepan, heat milk, water, shortening and Cheddar cheese until warm (120-130°; cheese and shortening do not need to melt). Add to flour mixture. Blend at low speed until moistened; beat 3 minutes at medium speed. By hand, gradually stir in enough remaining all-purpose flour to make a firm dough. Knead on floured surface until smooth and elastic, 5 to 8 minutes. Place in greased bowl, turning to grease top. Cover; let rise in warm place until double, about 1 hour.

Punch down dough. Divide into 2 parts. On lightly floured surface, roll or pat each half to a 14x7-inch rectangle. Starting with shorter side, roll up tightly, pressing dough into roll with each turn. Pinch edges and ends to seal. Place in greased 9x5 or 8x4-inch bread pans. Cover; let rise in warm place until double, about 45 minutes. Bake at 375° for 25 to 30 minutes until loaves sound hollow when tapped. Remove from pans; cool.

Swedish Limpa

A traditional Scandinavian classic!

3¾ to 4¼ cups all-purpose flour
2 packages Red Star Instant
   Blend Dry Yeast
¼ cup sugar
1 to 2 tablespoons grated
   orange rind
1 tablespoon salt
2 cups water
¼ cup molasses
3 tablespoons shortening
2½ cups medium rye flour

Oven 375°   2 Round Loaves

In large mixer bowl, combine 2½ cups all-purpose flour, yeast, sugar, orange rind and salt; mix well. In saucepan, heat water, molasses and shortening until warm (120-130°; shortening does not need to melt). Add to flour mixture. Blend at low speed until moistened; beat 3 minutes at medium speed. By hand, gradually stir in rye flour and enough remaining all-purpose flour to make a firm dough. Knead on floured surface until smooth and elastic, about 5 minutes. (Dough will be slightly sticky.) Place in greased bowl, turning to grease top. Cover; let rise in warm place until double, about 1 hour.

Punch down dough. Divide into 2 parts. On lightly floured surface, shape each half into a round loaf. Place on greased cookie sheets. Flatten slightly. Cover; let rise in warm place until double, about 45 minutes. Bake at 375° for 40 to 45 minutes until loaves sound hollow when tapped. Remove from cookie sheets; cool.

"Wild Fire" Rye Bread

This bread is named "Wild Fire" because it disappears so fast! A delicious whole wheat-rye bread flavored with orange rind, fennel and anise seeds.

2 cups whole wheat flour
2 cups rye flour
2 packages Red Star Instant
   Blend Dry Yeast
2 tablespoons grated orange
   rind
1 tablespoon fennel seed
1 tablespoon anise seed
2 teaspoons salt
1½ cups buttermilk
⅔ cup molasses
½ cup water
¼ cup oil
1¾ to 2 cups all purpose flour

Oven 350°   2 Round Loaves

In large mixer bowl, combine 1¼ cups whole wheat flour, 1¼ cups rye flour, yeast, orange rind, fennel seed, anise seed and salt; mix well. In saucepan, heat buttermilk, molasses and oil until warm (120-130°). Add to flour mixture. Blend at low speed until moistened; beat 3 minutes at medium speed. By hand, gradually stir in remaining rye and whole wheat flours and enough all-purpose flour to make a firm dough. Knead on floured surface about 5 minutes. Place in greased bowl, turning to grease top. Cover; let rise in warm place until double, 1 to 1½ hours.

Punch down dough. Divide into 2 parts. On lightly floured surface, shape each half into a round loaf. Place on greased cookie sheets. Cover; let rise in warm place until almost doubled, about 45 minutes. Bake at 350° for 45 to 50 minutes until loaves sound hollow when tapped. Remove from cookie sheets; cool.

Dilly Caraway Rye Bread

Caraway and dill seeds add a tasty touch to rye bread

2½ to 3 cups all-purpose flour
  2 packages Red Star Instant
    Blend Dry Yeast
  2 tablespoons sugar
  2 teaspoons salt
  2 teaspoons caraway seeds
  2 teaspoons dill seed
  1 cup milk
  ¾ cup water
  2 tablespoons shortening
1½ cups rye flour

Oven 375°   **2 Loaves**

In large mixer bowl, combine 1¾ cups all-purpose flour, yeast, sugar, salt, caraway and dill seed; mix well. In saucepan, heat milk, water, and shortening until warm (120-130°; shortening does not need to melt). Add to flour mixture. Blend at low speed until moistened; beat 3 minutes at medium speed. By hand, gradually stir in rye flour and enough remaining all-purpose flour to make a firm dough. Knead on floured surface about 5 minutes. Place in greased bowl, turning to grease top. Cover; let rise in warm place until double, about 1 hour.

Punch down dough. Divide into 2 parts. On lightly floured surface, roll or pat each half to a 14x7-inch rectangle. Starting with shorter side, roll up tightly, pressing dough into roll with each turn. Pinch edges and ends to seal. Place in greased 8x4-inch bread pans. Cover; let rise in warm place until almost doubled, 20 to 30 minutes. Bake at 375° for 35 to 40 minutes until golden brown. Remove from pans; cool.

Rye-Apple Bread

What could be better than a rye bread made moist with applesauce?

3½ to 4 cups all-purpose flour
  2 cups rye flour
  2 packages Red Star Instant
    Blend Dry Yeast
  1 teaspoon salt
  3 tablespoons caraway seeds
  2 cups sweetened applesauce
  ½ cup water
  ¼ cup molasses
  ¼ cup butter or margarine

Oven 375°   **2 Loaves**

In large mixer bowl, combine 1 cup all-purpose flour, rye flour, yeast, salt and caraway seed; mix well. In saucepan, heat applesauce, water, molasses and butter until warm (120-130°; butter does not need to melt). Add to flour mixture. Blend at low speed until moistened; beat 3 minutes at medium speed. By hand, gradually stir in enough remaining flour to make a firm dough. Knead on floured surface about 5 minutes. (Dough will be slightly sticky.) Place in greased bowl, turning to grease top. Cover; let rise in warm place until double, about 1 hour.

Punch down dough. Divide into 2 parts. On lightly floured surface, roll or pat each half to a 14x7-inch rectangle. Starting with shorter side, roll up tightly, pressing dough into roll with each turn. Pinch edges and ends to seal. Place in greased 8x4-inch bread pans. Cover; let rise in warm place until double, about 1 hour. Bake at 375° for 35 to 40 minutes until loaves sound hollow when tapped. Remove from pans; cool.

Buttermilk Rye Bread

Wonderful flavor! This rye bread also includes whole wheat flour and wheat germ for added nutrition and texture.

2 cups rye flour
2 cups whole wheat flour
2 packages Red Star Instant Blend Dry Yeast
2 tablespoons wheat germ
1½ tablespoons caraway seeds
1 tablespoon salt
1½ cups buttermilk
½ cup water
⅓ cup molasses
¼ cup oil
2 to 2½ cups all-purpose flour

Oven 375°   **2 Loaves**

In large mixer bowl, combine 1½ cups rye flour, 1½ cups whole wheat flour, yeast, wheat germ, caraway seed and salt; mix well. In saucepan, heat buttermilk, water, molasses and oil until warm (120-130°). Add to flour mixture. Blend at low speed until moistened; beat 3 minutes at medium speed. By hand, gradually stir in remaining rye and whole wheat flours and enough all-purpose flour to make a firm dough. Knead on floured surface 5 to 8 minutes. Place in greased bowl, turning to grease top. Cover; let rise in warm place until double, about 1 hour.

Punch down dough. Divide into 2 parts. On lightly floured surface, roll or pat each half to a 14x7-inch rectangle. Starting with shorter side, roll up tightly, pressing dough into roll with each turn. Pinch edges and ends to seal. Place in greased 9x5-inch bread pans. Cover; let rise in warm place until double, 1 to 1½ hours. Bake at 375° for 35 to 40 minutes until loaves sound hollow when tapped. Remove from pans; cool.

Sauerkraut Rye Bread

A light colored rye bread with a slightly sour flavor. With only one rising, it's faster to make!

2½ to 3 cups all-purpose flour
2 cups medium rye flour
2 packages Red Star Instant Blend Dry Yeast
½ cup nonfat dry milk solids
2 tablespoons sugar
1 tablespoon whole caraway seeds
1½ teaspoons salt
¼ teaspoon ginger
1¼ cups warm water
2 tablespoons oil
1 can (8 oz.) undrained sauer-kraut, room temperature

Oven 375°   **2 Loaves**

In large mixer bowl, combine 1 cup all-purpose flour, ¼ cup rye flour, yeast, dry milk, sugar, caraway seed, salt, and ginger; mix well. Add warm water (120-130°) and oil to flour mixture. Blend at low speed until moistened; beat 3 minutes at medium speed. By hand, gradually stir in sauerkraut, remaining rye flour and enough remaining all-purpose flour to make a firm dough. (The amount of flour will depend upon how much juice the sauerkraut has.) Knead on floured surface about 5 minutes.

Divide dough into 2 parts. On lightly floured surface, roll or pat each half to a 14x7-inch rectangle. Starting with shorter side, roll up tightly, pressing dough into roll with each turn. Pinch edges and ends to seal. Place in greased 8x4-inch bread pans. Cover; let rise in warm place until double, about 1 hour. Bake at 375° for 35 to 40 minutes until loaves sound hollow when tapped. If too dark, cover loosely with foil last 5 to 10 minutes of baking. Remove from pans; cool.

Cornmeal Bagels

For the bagel-lover this crunchy cornmeal version will be a special treat.

3 to 3¼ cups all-purpose flour
½ cup cornmeal
1 package Red Star Instant Blend Dry Yeast
2 tablespoons sugar
1½ teaspoons salt
1 cup warm water
2 tablespoons oil
1 egg
2 quarts water
2 tablespoons sugar
1 egg white, slightly beaten
Poppy or sesame seeds

Oven 375°   **12 Bagels**

In large mixer bowl, combine 1 cup flour, cornmeal, yeast, 2 tablespoons sugar and salt; mix well. Add warm water (120-130°) and oil to flour mixture. Add egg. Blend at low speed until moistened; beat 3 minutes at medium speed. By hand, gradually stir in enough remaining flour to make a soft dough. Knead on floured surface until smooth and elastic, 3 to 5 minutes. Place in greased bowl, turning to grease top. Cover; let rise in warm place until doubled, about 1 hour.

Punch down dough. Divide into 4 parts. Divide each part into 3 pieces. On lightly floured surface, shape each piece into a smooth ball. Punch a hole in the center with a finger. Pull dough gently to make a 1 to 2-inch hole.

Heat water and sugar to boiling. Place a few bagels at a time in boiling water. Simmer 3 minutes, turning once. Remove with slotted spoon. Place on greased cookie sheet. Brush tops with egg white; sprinkle with poppy or sesame seed. Bake at 375° for 20 to 25 minutes until golden brown. Remove from cookie sheets; cool.

English Muffins

A wonderful homemade taste! Enjoy with butter and your favorite jam or jelly. These muffins are also excellent for Eggs Benedict; use a 4-inch cutter to make larger.

2¾ to 3¼ cups all-purpose flour
1 package Red Star Instant Blend Dry Yeast
1 tablespoon sugar
1 teaspoon salt
1¼ cups warm water
2 tablespoons shortening
Cornmeal

Electric Griddle 325°   **12 to 14 Muffins**

In large mixer bowl, combine 1¼ cups flour, yeast, sugar and salt; mix well. Add warm water (120-130°) and shortening to flour mixture. Blend at low speed until moistened; beat 3 minutes at medium speed. By hand, gradually stir in enough remaining flour to make a firm dough. Knead on floured surface until smooth and elastic, about 5 minutes. Place in greased bowl, turning to grease top. Cover; let rise in warm place until light and doubled, 45 to 60 minutes.

Punch down dough. On surface sprinkled with cornmeal, roll dough to ¼-inch thickness. With biscuit or cookie cutter, cut into 3 or 4-inch circles. Place muffins on ungreased cookie sheets. Cover; let rise at room temperature until double, about 30 minutes. Bake on lightly oiled electric griddle or fry pan at 325° for about 8 minutes on each side until deep golden brown. Cool. To serve, split and toast.

Crispy Yeast Waffles

 You'll like the difference in these waffles. They can conveniently be made ahead.

2⅔ cups all-purpose flour
1 package Red Star Instant Blend Dry Yeast
2 tablespoons sugar
1 teaspoon salt
1¾ cups milk
¼ cup water
¼ cup butter or margarine
3 eggs

Waffle Iron   6 to 8 Waffles

In large mixer bowl, combine flour, yeast, sugar and salt; mix well. In saucepan, heat milk, water and butter until warm (120-130°; butter does not need to melt). Add to flour mixture. Add eggs. Blend at low speed until moistened; beat 1 minute at medium speed. Cover bowl with plastic wrap and foil; refrigerate several hours or overnight.

Stir down batter. Bake on waffle iron on medium heat. Serve hot with butter and toppings.

My Notes: _____

_____

_____

_____

_____

_____

_____

_____

Yeast Pancakes

Puffy and light pancakes with a subtle flavor and aroma.

2 cups all-purpose flour
1 package Red Star Instant Blend Dry Yeast
2 tablespoons sugar
1¼ cups milk
¼ cup water
2 eggs
¼ cup butter or margarine, melted
1 teaspoon soda
½ teaspoon salt

Griddle 375°   14 to 16 Five-Inch Pancakes

In large mixer bowl, combine 1 cup flour, yeast, and 1 tablespoon sugar; mix well. In saucepan, heat milk and water until warm (120-130°). Add to flour mixture. Stir until combined. Cover with plastic wrap. Set aside for 1 hour.

In small bowl, beat eggs; add butter. Combine remaining flour, sugar, soda and salt.

Stir down yeast mixture; add egg and flour mixtures. Beat until smooth. Bake on hot griddle.

Soft Pretzel

Plan a pretzel making party! Have the dough ready to shape, simmer and bake. Your guests will enjoy the soft, crusty results served warm from the oven with mustard or butter. Soft pretzels are best served the day they are baked.

2½ to 3 cups all-purpose flour
1 package Red Star Instant Blend Dry Yeast
1 tablespoon sugar
½ teaspoon salt
1 cup warm water
2 tablespoons oil
2 quarts water
⅓ cup soda
1 egg white, slightly beaten Coarse salt

Oven 425°   **12 Pretzels**

In large mixer bowl, combine 1¼ cups flour, yeast, sugar and salt; mix well. Add warm water (120-130°) and oil to flour mixture. Blend at low speed until moistened; beat 3 minutes at medium speed. By hand, gradually stir in enough remaining flour to make a firm dough. Knead on floured surface until smooth and elastic, 5 to 8 minutes. Place in greased bowl, turning to grease top. Cover; let rise in warm place until light and doubled, about 1 hour.

Punch down dough. Divide into 4 parts. Divide each fourth into 3 pieces. On lightly floured surface, roll each piece to an 18-inch rope. Shape rope into a circle, overlapping about 4 inches from each end and leaving ends free. Take one end of dough in each hand and twist at the point where dough overlaps. Carefully lift ends across to the opposite edge of circle. Tuck ends under edge to make a pretzel shape; moisten and press ends to seal. Place on greased cookie sheets. Let rise, uncovered, until puffy, about 20 minutes. In a 3-quart stainless or enameled saucepan, bring water and soda to boil. Lower 1 or 2 pretzels into saucepan, simmer for 10 seconds on each side. Lift from water with slotted spoon or spatula; drain. Place on well greased cookie sheet. Let dry briefly. Brush with egg white; sprinkle with coarse salt. Bake at 425° for 12 to 15 minutes until browned. Remove from cookie sheet. Serve warm with butter or mustard, if desired.

 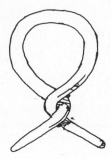 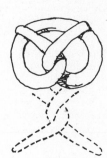

Whole Wheat Banana Bagels

The pleasant blend of whole wheat and bananas will fascinate the bagel-fancier and provide a base for many toppings.

1 cup all-purpose flour
2 to 2½ cups whole wheat flour
1 package Red Star Instant Blend Dry Yeast
1½ teaspoons salt
¾ cup warm water
½ cup mashed banana (about 1 banana)
2 tablespoons oil
1 tablespoon honey
1 egg
2 quarts water
2 tablespoons sugar
1 egg white, slightly beaten
Poppy or sesame seeds

Oven 375°   **12 Bagels**

In large mixer bowl, combine 1 cup all-purpose flour, ½ cup whole wheat flour, yeast and salt; mix well. Add warm water (120-130°), banana, oil and honey to flour mixture. Add egg. Blend at low speed until moistened; beat 3 minutes at medium speed. By hand, gradually stir in enough remaining whole wheat flour to make a soft dough. Knead on floured surface until smooth and elastic, 3 to 5 minutes. Place in greased bowl, turning to grease top. Cover; let rise in warm place until double, about 1 hour.

Punch down dough. Divide dough into 4 parts. Divide each fourth into 3 pieces. On lightly floured surface, shape each piece into a smooth ball. Punch a hole in the center with a finger. Pull dough gently to make a 1 to 2-inch hole.

Heat water and sugar to boiling. Place a few bagels at a time in boiling water. Simmer 3 minutes, turning once. Remove with slotted spoon. Place on greased cookie sheet. Brush tops with egg white; sprinkle with poppy or sesame seed. Bake at 375° for 20 to 25 minutes until golden brown. Remove from cookie sheets; cool.

My Notes: _____

_____

_____

_____

_____

_____

_____

_____

_____

_____

_____

_____

_____

SOURDOUGH

Sourdough, as the name implies, is a dough with a slightly sour or tangy flavor. The flavor is derived from using a "starter"—a mixture of flour, yeast, water and sugar which is allowed to ferment naturally. This produces a fairly thick, bubbly sour-smelling liquid, which can then be used in many kinds of baked products. Once "started," the sourdough starter can be used over and over again. Replenish it each time it is used to nourish the yeast and keep the starter alive and bubbly.

Although historical accounts of the origin of sourdough vary, the old-fashioned art of sourdough cookery is part of our country's heritage. Trappers and prospectors, exploring and settling the Western coast up into Alaska, are said to have carried a pot or crock of sourdough starter with them to make hotcakes, biscuits and breads. They found they could use this mysterious mixture over and over again without it spoiling. Since sourdough was a mainstay of the meals of early pioneers, especially those in Alaska, the men and their breads became synonymous, and these settlers were nicknamed "Sourdoughs."

Sourdough is as much a part of today's baking as it was in those early days. Although the starter serves as part of the leavening, additional yeast is added to breads to produce a light, tender product. The "feel" of doughs made with a sourdough starter is different from other doughs; the dough is slightly sticky.

All of our sourdough recipes are mixed by hand to preserve the historic spirit of sourdough. The flavor is best if the doughs are not hurried and are given enough time to rise; a temperature of 80-85° is ideal. The doughs will take longer to rise at a lower room temperature.

As the starter gets older, the flavor will become more tangy; baked products made with "aged" starters will have more sourdough flavor.

We hope you'll enjoy this collection of sourdough recipes and the opportunity to recreate a bit of the past!

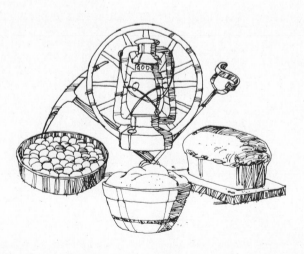

Sourdough Starter

1 package Red Star Instant
Blend Dry Yeast
2 cups warm water
3½ cups all-purpose flour
1 tablespoon sugar

In a 4-quart glass, pottery, plastic or stainless steel bowl, dissolve yeast in warm water (110-115°); let stand 5 minutes. Add flour and sugar. By hand, stir until blended. The mixture will be thick; any remaining lumps will dissolve during the fermentation process. Cover loosely with plastic wrap or foil. Let stand in warm place for 5 days, stirring 2 or 3 times each day. The starter will "rise and fall" during the fermentation period; it becomes thinner as it stands. A temperature of 80-85° is best for the sour flavor to develop. An ideal place is on the counter next to your range. When the starter is developed, it is bubbly and may have a yellow liquid layer on top; stir into the starter before using. The starter can be used for baking or placed in the refrigerator to use later.

To use starter, measure out desired amount as specified in the recipe. When refrigerated, let starter come to room temperature before using; this will take about 4 hours. If you plan to bake in the morning, leave the starter out overnight.

Replenish remaining starter with 3 parts of flour to 2 parts of water and 1 teaspoon sugar. For example, if you take out 1½ cups starter, add 1½ cups flour, 1 cup warm water (110-115°) and 1 teaspoon sugar. Stir until blended; some lumps may remain. Cover loosely and let stand in warm place for 10 to 12 hours or overnight. The starter will rise and become bubbly. Stir, then place in refrigerator to store. A large container such as an apothecary jar can be used for storage. It should be large enough for replenishing and expansion of the starter. Pour remaining starter into a bowl and replenish. Then return to container for refrigerator storage. Never add anything to the remaining starter except flour, water and sugar.

Use a glass, pottery or plastic container for storing the starter in the refrigerator. Cover loosely to allow accumulated gases to escape. During storage, a yellow liquid layer may form on top; stir into starter before using. You will see only small bubbles in the starter during storage.

If you bake about once a week with the starter, it should remain lively and active. Stir in 1 teaspoon sugar to keep it active if the starter is not used every week. If you wish to bake several times a week with a starter, you may want to have two starters. As the starter gets older, the flavor will become more tangy.

Sourdough English Muffins

Delicious with a sourdough taste. They freeze well to use later.

1 package Red Star Instant Blend Dry Yeast
½ cup warm water
2½ to 3 cups all-purpose flour
1 cup sourdough starter, room temperature
2 tablespoons oil
1 tablespoon sugar
1 teaspoon salt
Cornmeal

Griddle 325°   14 to 16 Muffins

In large bowl, dissolve yeast in warm water (110-115°); let stand 5 minutes. Add 2 cups flour, starter, oil, sugar and salt. By hand, stir until smooth. Gradually stir in enough remaining flour to make a firm dough. Knead on floured surface until smooth and elastic, about 5 minutes. Place in greased bowl, turning to grease top. Cover; let rise at room temperature until light and doubled, 1 to 1½ hours.

Punch down dough. On surface sprinkled with cornmeal, roll dough to ¼-inch thickness. With biscuit or cookie cutter, cut into 3 or 4-inch circles. Turn to coat top side with cornmeal. Place on greased cookie sheet. Cover; let rise at room temperature until double, about 30 minutes. With hands, carefully lift muffins from cookie sheet and place on lightly greased electric griddle or frypan. Bake at 325° for about 10 minutes on each side until deep golden brown. Cool. To serve, split and toast.

Sourdough Pancakes

To begin your sourdough adventure, you may wish to make pancakes first as they are so easy. For fun, make the Silver Dollar size—they were a favorite of the Alaskan prospectors.

1¼ cups all-purpose flour
1 cup milk
½ cup sourdough starter, room temperature
1 tablespoon sugar
1 tablespoon oil
1 teaspoon soda
½ teaspoon salt
1 egg

Griddle 450°   12 Four-Inch Pancakes

In large bowl, combine flour, milk and starter. Let stand in warm place for 30 minutes. By hand, stir in remaining ingredients (batter will be slightly lumpy). Pour about ¼ cup batter onto lightly greased, preheated 450° electric griddle or frypan. Bake until golden, turning to bake other side when surface is bubbly and edges are slightly dry.

Silver Dollar Pancakes

Griddle 450°   44 Dollar-size Pancakes

Prepare Sourdough Pancakes as directed. Pour 1 tablespoon batter onto griddle or frypan for each pancake.

Sourdough French Bread

 Reminiscent of the San Francisco Sourdough bread.

1 package Red Star Instant
  Blend Dry Yeast
1 cup warm water
3½ to 4 cups all-purpose flour
1½ cups sourdough starter, room
  temperature
1 tablespoon sugar
2 teaspoons salt
  Cornmeal

Oven 400°   **2 Loaves**

In large bowl, dissolve yeast in warm water (110-115°); let stand 5 minutes. Add 2 cups flour, starter, sugar and salt. By hand, stir until smooth. Gradually stir in enough remaining flour to make a firm dough. Knead on floured surface until smooth and elastic, 5 to 8 minutes. Place in greased bowl, turning to grease top. Cover; let rise at room temperature until light and doubled, 1 to 1½ hours.

Punch down dough. Divide into 2 parts. On lightly floured surface, roll or pat each half to a 12x5-inch rectangle. Starting with longer side, roll up tightly, pressing dough into roll with each turn. Pinch edges and ends to seal. Place on greased cookie sheet sprinkled with cornmeal. Cover; let rise at room temperature until double, 45 to 60 minutes. With very sharp knife, make 2 or 3 diagonal slashes across top of loaf. Spray or brush loaf with cold water. Bake at 400° for 30 to 35 minutes until golden brown. Spray or brush loaves with water several times during baking for a crispier crust. Remove from cookie sheets; cool.

Sourdough Rye Bread

 A tangy sour rye bread flavored with caraway seeds.

1 package Red Star Instant
  Blend Dry Yeast
1 cup warm water
2¼ to 2¾ cups all-purpose flour
1½ cups sourdough starter, room
  temperature
2 tablespoons shortening
1 tablespoon sugar
2 teaspoons salt
2 teaspoons caraway seeds
2 cups medium rye flour

Oven 375°   **2 Loaves**

In large bowl, dissolve yeast in warm water (110-115°); let stand 5 minutes. Add 2 cups all-purpose flour, starter, shortening, sugar, salt and caraway seed. By hand, stir until smooth. Gradually stir in rye flour and enough remaining all-purpose flour to make a firm dough. Knead on floured surface, about 5 minutes. Place in greased bowl, turning to grease top. Cover; let rise at room temperature until double, 1 to 1½ hours.

Punch down dough. Divide into 2 parts. On lightly floured surface, shape each half into a round loaf. Place on greased cookie sheet. Cover; let rise at room temperature until double, 45 to 60 minutes. With very sharp knife, make an "X" on top of each loaf. Bake at 375° for 35 to 40 minutes until loaves sound hollow when tapped. Remove from cookie sheets; cool.

Sourdough Cracked Wheat Rolls

These long rolls, crunchy with cracked wheat, make excellent Hoagie sandwiches.

1 package Red Star Instant Blend Dry Yeast
1 cup warm water
3¾ to 4¼ cups all-purpose flour
1½ cups sourdough starter, room temperature
1 tablespoon sugar
1 tablespoon oil
2 teaspoons salt
½ cup cracked wheat

Oven 400°   **10 Rolls**

In large bowl, dissolve yeast in warm water (110-115°); let stand 5 minutes. Add 2 cups all-purpose flour, starter, sugar, oil and salt. By hand, stir until smooth. Gradually stir in cracked wheat and enough remaining flour to make a firm dough. Knead on floured surface, 5 to 8 minutes. Place in greased bowl, turning to grease top. Cover; let rise at room temperature until double, 1 to 1½ hours.

Punch down dough. Divide into 2 parts. Divide each half into 5 pieces. On lightly floured surface, roll or pat each piece to a 6x4-inch rectangle. Starting with longer side, roll up tightly, pressing dough into roll with each turn. Pinch edges and ends to seal. Place on greased cookie sheet. Cover; let rise at room temperature until double, about 45 minutes. With very sharp knife, make a lengthwise slash down the center of each roll. Spray or brush rolls with cold water. Bake at 400° for 20 to 25 minutes until golden brown. Spray or brush rolls with water several times during the first 10 minutes of baking for a crispier crust. Remove from cookie sheets; cool.

Sourdough Sandwich Rolls

These round rolls make good "burger buns."

1 package Red Star Instant Blend Dry Yeast
1 cup warm water
4¾ to 5¼ cups all-purpose flour
1½ cups sourdough starter, room temperature
1 tablespoon sugar
1 tablespoon oil
2 teaspoons salt
1 egg
1 egg, slightly beaten
1 tablespoon water

Oven 400°   **10 Rolls**

In large bowl, dissolve yeast in warm water (110-115°); let stand 5 minutes. Add 2 cups flour, starter, sugar, oil, salt and 1 egg. By hand, stir until smooth. Gradually stir in enough remaining flour to make a firm dough. Knead on floured surface until smooth and elastic, 5 to 8 minutes. Place in greased bowl, turning to grease top. Cover; let rise at room temperature until light and doubled, 1 to 1½ hours.

Punch down dough. Divide into 2 parts. Divide each half into 5 pieces. On lightly floured surface, shape each piece into a smooth ball. Place on greased cookie sheet. Flatten to a 4-inch diameter. Cover; let rise at room temperature until double, about 30 minutes. With very sharp knife, make an "X" on the top of each roll. Combine egg and 1 tablespoon water. Brush tops of rolls. Bake at 400° for 15 to 20 minutes until golden brown. Remove from cookie sheets; cool.

Batter breads

Herb Onion Batter Bread

Apple Kuchen

Soup To Nuts Pop Up Bread   **Sally Lunn**

Strawberry Coffeecake

BATTER BREADS

All delicious and beautiful breads don't have to be kneaded. In this chapter, you'll find a collection of attractive, easy-to-make breads that are all no-knead or batter breads. The dough is a batter, which is simply mixed, allowed to rise, then baked.

Batter breads have long been a part of Red Star® Yeast baking history—our early Batterway recipes were mixed by hand and given one or two long risings. Since they were not kneaded or shaped, these breads were time-savers for our grandmothers. Today, faster acting yeast and the electric mixer make the batter method even easier and quicker. The mixer is usually used for the first part of the mixing to help develop the gluten. This beating takes the place of kneading. Additional flour is stirred in by hand to make a stiff batter. Because less flour is used, batters are stickier than kneaded doughs. The batter is given one or two risings, depending on the recipe, then baked.

Batter breads are a boon for today's time-conscious bread baker. They are not only easy but fun to make. You'll find all types of breads in this chapter—basic breads, like *Batterway White Bread and Rolls,* coffeecakes and a great classic, *Sally Lunn.* There are batter breads included in some of the other chapters, so check the Index for a complete listing.

Batter breads are usually baked in a standard baking pan, casserole or soufflé dishes; but there are also some breads baked in coffee cans. It is best to spread or spoon the batter into the pan or dish, pushing the batter evenly into corners with a rubber spatula. Occasionally, batter breads may be shaped.

To be successful with these breads, do not let them rise too long or they may fall during baking. Although the batter will rise until double or almost doubled, depending on the recipe, it may not come up to the top of the pan or dish.

Batter breads are more open in texture than kneaded breads and the top may have a rougher appearance rather than a smooth crust. Batter breads are at their best when fresh-baked. To serve warm, slice batter breads a little thicker. They can be reheated to get that fresh-baked taste. They are also great when toasted. Although batter breads can be frozen, they will dry slightly.

If you're just starting to make yeast breads, batter breads may be the best choice for you. They are as easy as mixing a cake. When you haven't the time to make a kneaded bread, choose from this array of batter breads.

Batterway White Bread

A quick and easy white bread with no kneading. It will have a more open texture.

6½ cups all-purpose flour
  2 packages Red Star Instant Blend Dry Yeast
  3 tablespoons sugar
  1 tablespoon salt
  3 cups warm water
  2 tablespoons shortening
  Butter

Oven 375°   **2 Loaves**

In large mixer bowl, combine 3½ cups flour, yeast, sugar and salt; mix well. Add warm water (120-130°) and shortening to flour mixture. Blend at low speed until moistened, beat 3 minutes at medium speed. By hand, gradually stir in remaining flour to make a stiff batter. Cover; let rise in warm place until double, about 30 minutes.

Stir down batter. Spread in greased 9x5 or 8x4-inch bread pans. Cover; let rise in warm place until batter reaches tops of pans, 20 to 30 minutes. Bake at 375° for 35 to 40 minutes until golden brown. Remove from pans; brush with butter. Cool.

Batterway White Rolls

A quick, no knead dinner roll that will add homemade goodness to any meal.

3¾ cups all-purpose flour
  2 packages Red Star Instant Blend Dry Yeast
  ¼ cup sugar
  1½ teaspoons salt
  1½ cups water
  ⅓ cup shortening
  1 egg
  Butter

Oven 400°   **18 Rolls**

In large mixer bowl, combine 1½ cups flour, yeast, sugar and salt; mix well. In saucepan, heat water and shortening until warm (120-130°; shortening does not need to melt). Add to flour mixture. Add egg. Blend at low speed until moistened; beat 3 minutes at medium speed. By hand, gradually stir in remaining flour to make a stiff batter. Cover; let rise in warm place until double, about 30 minutes.

Stir down batter. Spoon into greased muffin pan cups. Cover; let rise in warm place until double, 20 to 30 minutes. Bake at 400° for 10 to 15 minutes until golden brown. Remove from pans; brush with butter. Cool.

Corn-Herb Batter Bread

❀ Cornmeal and herbs make this batter bread special. The loaves are attractive baked in coffee cans.

3½ to 4 cups unbleached flour
1 package Red Star Instant Blend Dry Yeast
3 tablespoons sugar
1½ teaspoons sage
1 teaspoon salt
1 teaspoon celery seeds
⅛ teaspoon ground ginger
⅛ teaspoon marjoram leaves
1 can (13 oz.) evaporated milk
½ cup water
2 tablespoons oil
½ cup yellow cornmeal

Oven 350°   **2 Loaves**

In large mixer bowl, combine 1½ cups flour, yeast, sugar, sage, salt, celery seed, ginger and marjoram; mix well. In saucepan, heat milk, water and oil until warm (120-130°). Add to flour mixture. Blend at low speed until moistened; beat 3 minutes at medium speed. By hand, gradually stir in cornmeal and enough remaining flour to make a stiff batter.

Spoon batter into 2 greased 1-lb. coffee cans. Cover; let rise in warm place, 45 minutes. Bake at 350° for 45 to 50 minutes. Cool 10 minutes in cans; remove from cans. Cool.

Swiss Cheese Bread

❀ A favorite easy batter bread made delicious with Swiss cheese.

5 cups all-purpose flour
2 packages Red Star Instant Blend Dry Yeast
3 tablespoons sugar
1½ tablespoons salt
1 cup water
1 cup milk
2 tablespoons butter or margarine
1 egg
1½ cups shredded Swiss cheese

Oven 375°   **2 Round Loaves**

In large mixer bowl, combine 2½ cups flour, yeast, sugar and salt; mix well. In saucepan, heat water, milk and butter until warm (120-130°; butter does not need to melt). Add to flour mixture. Add egg. Blend at low speed until moistened; beat 3 minutes at medium speed. By hand, gradually stir in cheese and remaining flour to make a soft batter. Cover; let rise in warm place until light and doubled, about 1 hour.

Stir down batter. Spoon into 2 greased 1-quart casseroles. Bake at 375° for 35 to 40 minutes until golden brown. If too dark, cover loosely with foil last 5 to 10 minutes of baking. Remove from casseroles; cool.

Bacon-Onion Batter Bread

A quick and easy batter bread made delicious with bacon-onion dip mix and cottage cheese. This easy casserole bread is perfect with any meal.

3¼ cups all-purpose flour
2 packages Red Star Instant Blend Dry Yeast
1 package (.56 oz.) Bacon-Onion Dip Mix
¼ teaspoon baking soda
1 cup cream style cottage cheese
½ cup water
2 tablespoons shortening
1 egg
Butter
Coarse salt

Oven 375°   **1 Round Loaf**

In large mixer bowl, combine 1½ cups flour, yeast, dip mix and baking soda; mix well. In small saucepan, heat cottage cheese, water and shortening until warm (120-130°; shortening does not need to melt). Add to flour mixture. Add egg. Blend at low speed until moistened; beat 3 minutes at medium speed. By hand, gradually stir in remaining flour to make a stiff batter.

Spoon into greased 2-quart casserole. Cover; let rise in warm place until light and doubled, about 1 hour. Bake at 375° for 35 to 40 minutes until golden brown. Brush with butter; sprinkle with coarse salt. Remove from casserole; serve warm or cold.

Batterway Dill Rolls

Serve these rolls warm to share the tantalizing aroma of dill and onion.

2½ cups all-purpose flour
2 packages Red Star Instant Blend Dry Yeast
2 tablespoons sugar
1 tablespoon instant minced onion
2 teaspoons dill seed
½ teaspoon salt
1 cup small curd cottage cheese, drained
½ cup water
2 tablespoons butter or margarine
1 egg
Butter

Oven 350°   **18 Rolls**

In large mixer bowl, combine 1¼ cups flour, yeast, sugar, onion, dill seed and salt; mix well. In saucepan, heat cottage cheese, water and butter until warm (120-130°; butter does not need to melt). Add to flour mixture. Add egg. Blend at low speed until moistened; beat 3 minutes at medium speed. By hand, gradually stir in remaining flour to make a stiff batter. Cover; let rise in warm place until doubled, about 30 minutes.

Stir down batter. Spoon in greased muffin pan cups. Cover; let rise in warm place until double, 20 to 30 minutes. Bake at 350° for 15 to 20 minutes until golden brown. Remove from pans; brush with butter. Cool.

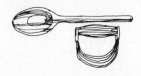

Dilly of a Batter Bread

A casserole bread with the popular flavor combination of onion and dill with a surprise ingredient—yogurt, which gives a unique flavor.

3¼ cups all-purpose flour
2 packages Red Star Instant Blend Dry Yeast
2 tablespoons sugar
1 tablespoon instant minced onion
2 teaspoons dill seed
1 teaspoon salt
1 carton (8 oz.) plain yogurt
½ cup water
2 tablespoons shortening
1 egg

Oven 375°   **1 Round Loaf**

In large mixer bowl, combine 1½ cups flour, yeast, sugar, onion, dill seed and salt; mix well. In small saucepan, heat yogurt, water and shortening until warm (120-130°; shortening does not need to melt). Add to flour mixture. Add egg. Blend at low speed until moistened; beat 3 minutes at medium speed. By hand, gradually stir in remaining flour to make a stiff batter.

Spoon into greased 1½ or 2-quart casserole. Cover; let rise in warm place until light and double, about 1 hour. Bake at 375° for 35 to 40 minutes until golden brown. Remove from casserole; serve warm or cold.

Savory Cheese Rolls

Easy savory cheese rolls for your next barbecue.

3 cups all-purpose flour
2 packages Red Star Instant Blend Dry Yeast
1 tablespoon sugar
1 tablespoon instant minced onion
1 teaspoon salt
½ teaspoon celery seeds
1 cup milk
½ cup water
2 tablespoons shortening
1 egg
1 cup (4 oz.) Stella shredded Fontinella or Cheddar cheese

Oven 400°   **18 Rolls**

In large mixer bowl, combine 2 cups flour, yeast, sugar, onion, salt and celery seed; mix well. In saucepan, heat milk, water and shortening until warm (120-130°; shortening does not need to melt). Add to flour mixture. Add egg. Blend at low speed until moistened; beat 3 minutes at medium speed. By hand, gradually stir in cheese and remaining flour to make a stiff batter. Cover; let rise in warm place until light and double, about 30 minutes.

Stir down batter. Spoon into greased muffin pan cups. Cover; let rise in warm place until double, about 30 minutes. Bake at 400° for 15 to 20 minutes until golden brown. Remove from muffin pan cups. Serve warm.

Easy Cheesy Loaf

An easy batter loaf that bakes with a pizza flavored cheese surprise filling.

2½ cups all-purpose flour
2 packages Red Star Instant Blend Dry Yeast
2 tablespoons sugar
1 teaspoon salt
½ cup milk
½ cup water
¼ cup butter or margarine
1 egg
1 tablespoon sesame seeds

Filling:

¼ cup butter or margarine, softened
½ teaspoon Italian herb seasoning
¼ teaspoon garlic powder
1 cup (4 oz.) Stella shredded Cheddar cheese

Oven 350°   **One 10-inch Bundt® Loaf**

In large mixer bowl, combine 1½ cups flour, yeast, sugar and salt; mix well. In saucepan, heat milk, water and butter until warm (120-130°; butter does not need to melt). Add to flour mixture. Add egg. Blend at low speed until moistened; beat 3 minutes at medium speed. By hand, gradually stir in remaining flour to make a stiff batter.

Prepare Filling: Combine all Filling ingredients; mix well.

Sprinkle sesame seed in well greased 12-cup Bundt® pan or 10-inch tubed cake pan. Spread half of batter in pan. Spoon Filling over batter. Spread remaining batter over Filling. (Batter will cover during baking.) Cover; let rise in warm place until double; about 1 hour. Bake at 350° for 35 to 40 minutes until golden brown. Invert onto serving plate. Cool.

Soup to Nuts Pop Up Bread

✸ A new batter bread recipe idea created by combining dry soup mix, nuts and cheese.

3 to 3½ cups all-purpose flour
2 packages Red Star Instant Blend Dry Yeast
¼ cup sugar
1 package (1⅝ oz.) dry vegetable soup mix, without noodles or meat
1 teaspoon salt
½ cup milk
½ cup water
½ cup oil
2 eggs
1 cup Stella shredded Cheddar cheese
½ cup chopped walnuts

Oven 375°   **2 Loaves**

In large mixer bowl, combine 2 cups flour, yeast, sugar, dry soup mix and salt; mix well. In saucepan, heat milk, water and oil until warm (120-130°). Add to flour mixture. Add eggs. Blend at low speed until moistened; beat 3 minutes at medium speed. By hand, gradually stir in cheese, nuts and enough remaining flour to make a stiff batter.

Spoon batter into 2 greased 1-lb. coffee cans. Cover; let rise in warm place until double, about 1 hour. Bake at 375° for 30 to 35 minutes until golden brown. If too dark, cover loosely with foil last 5 to 10 minutes of baking. Cool 15 minutes in cans; remove from cans. Cool.

Herb Onion Batter Bread

◢ A casserole bread with all the flavor of herb stuffing.

3¼ cups all-purpose flour
2 packages Red Star Instant Blend Dry Yeast
2 tablespoons sugar
1 teaspoon salt
½ teaspoon ground sage
½ teaspoon rosemary leaves, crushed
¼ teaspoon thyme leaves, crushed
1 cup finely chopped onion
¼ cup butter or margarine
1¼ cups warm water
1 egg

Oven 375°   **1 Loaf**

In large mixer bowl, combine 1½ cups flour, yeast, sugar, salt, sage, rosemary and thyme; mix well. In small skillet, sauté onion in butter until golden. Add to flour mixture. Add warm water (120-130°) and egg. Blend at low speed until moistened; beat 3 minutes at medium speed. By hand, gradually stir in remaining flour to make a stiff batter.

Spoon into greased 2-quart casserole. Cover; let rise in warm place until double, about 1 hour. Bake at 375° for 35 to 40 minutes until golden brown. Remove from casserole; serve warm or cold.

Raisin Bran Banana Bread

✹ This batter banana bread has added nutrition with raisin bran cereal. It makes a heavy but good loaf.

5½ to 6 cups all-purpose flour
2 packages Red Star Instant Blend Dry Yeast
⅔ cup sugar
1½ teaspoons salt
1 teaspoon baking soda
1 teaspoon cinnamon
½ cup water
½ cup milk
½ cup butter or margarine
2 eggs
2 cups mashed bananas (about 4 bananas)
2½ cups raisin bran cereal
1 cup coarsely chopped nuts
Powdered sugar

Oven 375°   **2 Loaves**

In large mixer bowl, combine 2 cups flour, yeast, sugar, salt, baking soda and cinnamon; mix well. In saucepan, heat water, milk and butter until warm (120-130°; butter does not need to melt). Add to flour mixture. Add eggs and mashed bananas. Blend at low speed until moistened; beat 3 minutes at medium speed. By hand, gradually stir in raisin bran cereal, nuts and enough remaining flour to make a stiff batter. Cover; let rise in warm place until light and doubled, about 1 hour.

Stir down batter. Spoon into 2 greased 9x5-inch bread pans. Cover; let rise in warm place until double, 1 to 1½ hours. Bake at 375° for 35 to 40 minutes until loaf sounds hollow when tapped. If too dark, cover loosely with foil last 5 to 10 minutes of baking. Remove from pans; cool. Sift powdered sugar over tops.

Apple Crisp Coffeecake

Apple pie lovers will appreciate this moist, rich coffeecake. All the familiar flavors are here—apples, brown sugar, cinnamon, butter and a hint of lemon.

3 cups all-purpose flour
2 packages Red Star Instant Blend Dry Yeast
¼ cup sugar
1 teaspoon salt
½ cup water
½ cup milk
6 tablespoons butter or margarine
4 apples
2 tablespoons lemon juice

Topping:

1 cup all-purpose flour
1 cup packed brown sugar
2 teaspoons cinnamon
2 teaspoons lemon rind
½ cup butter or margarine

Oven 375°   Two 9-inch Coffeecakes

In large mixer bowl, combine 1½ cups flour, yeast, sugar and salt; mix well. In saucepan, heat water, milk and butter until warm (120-130°; butter does not need to melt). Add to flour mixture. Blend at low speed until moistened; beat 3 minutes at medium speed. By hand, gradually stir in remaining flour to make a soft batter. Cover bowl with plastic wrap and foil. Refrigerate 4 to 24 hours.

Peel and slice apples. Sprinkle with lemon juice; toss lightly. Set aside.

Prepare Topping: Combine flour, brown sugar, cinnamon and lemon rind. With pastry blender, cut in butter until consistency of cornmeal.

Spread half of batter evenly into greased 9-inch square cake pan. Arrange apple slices in three rows on batter; pressing in gently. Sprinkle Topping over apples. Cover; let rise in warm place until double, about 1 hour. Bake at 375° for 25 to 30 minutes until golden brown. Cut in squares. Serve warm.

My Notes: _____

_____

_____

_____

_____

_____

_____

_____

_____

_____

_____

_____

_____

_____

Peanut Butter Batter Buns

Perfect for the family—gooey peanut butter rolls for breakfast or anytime.

1½ cups all-purpose flour
1 package Red Star Instant Blend Dry Yeast
2 tablespoons sugar
½ teaspoon salt
½ cup milk
¼ cup water
2 tablespoons butter or margarine
1 egg

Topping:

½ cup sugar
½ cup chopped peanuts
¼ cup peanut butter
2 tablespoons honey
¼ cup butter or margarine, softened

Oven 350°   **12 to 14 Rolls**

In large mixer bowl, combine 1 cup flour, yeast, sugar and salt; mix well. In saucepan, heat milk, water and butter until warm (120-130°; butter does not need to melt). Add to flour mixture. Add egg. Blend at low speed until moistened; beat 3 minutes at medium speed. By hand, gradually stir in remaining flour to make a stiff batter. Cover; let rise in warm place until light and doubled, about 45 minutes.

Prepare Topping: Blend all Topping ingredients until smooth. Spoon Topping into greased muffin pan cups.

Stir down batter. Spoon over Topping in muffin pan cups. Cover; let rise in warm place until double, about 30 minutes. Bake at 350° for 20 to 25 minutes until golden brown. Cover pan with foil and invert onto rack. Serve warm or cold.

Crispy Cinnamon Rounds

Sugary batter rolls stay crisp when stored loosely wrapped.

2¼ cups all-purpose flour
1 package Red Star Instant Blend Dry Yeast
2 tablespoons sugar
½ teaspoon salt
½ teaspoon nutmeg
¾ cup warm water
3 tablespoons shortening
1 egg
¾ cup sugar
½ cup chopped pecans or walnuts
¼ cup packed brown sugar
1 teaspoon cinnamon

Oven 400°   **18 to 22 Rolls**

In large mixer bowl, combine 1 cup flour, yeast, 2 tablespoons sugar, salt and nutmeg; mix well. Add warm water (120-130°), shortening, and egg to flour mixture. Blend at low speed until moistened; beat 3 minutes at medium speed. By hand, gradually stir in remaining flour to make a stiff batter. Cover; let rise in warm place until light and double, about 45 minutes.

Prepare Topping: Combine ¾ cup sugar, pecans, brown sugar and cinnamon; mix well. Pour half of sugar mixture onto wax paper.

Stir down batter. Drop batter by tablespoons into sugar mixture; toss lightly to coat. Flatten each piece to 4 or 5-inch circle, ⅛-inch thick, pressing sugar mixture into both sides. Place on greased foil lined cookie sheets. Bake at 400° for 12 to 15 minutes until light golden brown. (Do not overbake.) Remove from cookie sheets; cool.

Apple Kuchen

A warm butter sauce adds the right touch to this apple-topped kuchen. Melted butter blended into the topping adds to the keeping quality of the sliced apples.

3 cups all-purpose flour
2 packages Red Star Instant
** Blend Dry Yeast**
¼ cup sugar
½ teaspoon salt
½ cup water
¼ cup milk
¾ cup butter or margarine
4 eggs
4 cups apples, sliced (3 large
** apples)**
½ cup chopped pecans
⅓ cup sugar
¼ cup butter, melted
1 teaspoon cinnamon
1 teaspoon grated lemon rind

Butter Sauce:

1 cup sugar
½ cup butter
½ cup Half and Half
1 teaspoon vanilla

Oven 350°   13x9-inch Coffeecake

In large mixer bowl, combine 1¾ cups flour, yeast, ¼ cup sugar and salt; mix well. In saucepan, heat water, milk and butter until warm (120-130°; butter does not need to melt). Add to flour mixture. Add eggs. Blend at low speed until moistened; beat 3 minutes at medium speed. By hand, gradually stir in remaining flour to make a soft batter. Cover; let rise in warm place until double, about 30 minutes.

Prepare Topping: Peel and slice apples. In medium bowl, combine apples, pecans, ⅓ cup sugar, ¼ cup butter, cinnamon and lemon rind.

Stir down batter. Spread in greased 13x9-inch cake pan. Spoon Topping over batter. Cover; let rest 10 minutes. Bake at 350° for 45 to 50 minutes until golden brown. Serve warm with Butter Sauce.

Prepare Butter Sauce: In small saucepan, combine sugar, butter and Half and Half. Bring to a boil; simmer until thickened. Add vanilla.

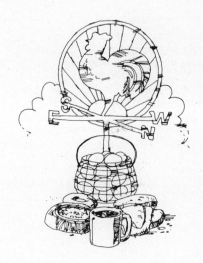

71

Crunchy Cinnamon Coffeecake

A delicious coffeecake, ready to eat in only an hour!

3 cups all-purpose flour
2 packages Red Star Instant Blend Dry Yeast
⅓ cup sugar
½ teaspoon salt
½ cup milk
½ cup water
¼ cup butter or margarine
1 egg
½ cup sugar
½ cup all-purpose flour
½ cup nuts
1 teaspoon cinnamon
½ cup firm butter

Oven 375°   **One 13x9-inch Coffeecake**

In large mixer bowl, combine 1½ cups flour, yeast, ⅓ cup sugar and salt; mix well. In saucepan, heat milk, water and butter until warm (120-130°; butter does not need to melt). Add to flour mixture. Add egg. Blend at low speed until moistened; beat 3 minutes at medium speed. By hand, gradually stir in remaining 1½ cups flour to make a stiff batter. Spread in well greased 13x9-inch cake pan. Cover; let rise in warm oven (Turn oven to lowest setting for 1 minute, turn off.) for 25 minutes.

Prepare Topping: Combine ½ cup sugar, ½ cup flour, nuts and cinnamon. Cut in butter with pastry blender until particles are the size of small peas. Sprinkle Topping over batter. With back of spoon make random indentations in batter. Bake at 375° for 20 to 25 minutes. Serve warm or cold.

Strawberry Coffeecake

Strawberry preserves are tucked under a crunchy topping in this easy coffeecake.

1¾ cups all-purpose flour
1 package Red Star Instant Blend Dry Yeast
¼ cup sugar
½ teaspoon ground nutmeg
¼ teaspoon salt
⅓ cup milk
⅓ cup water
2 tablespoons shortening
1 egg
½ cup strawberry, peach or apricot preserves

Topping:
½ cup sugar
½ cup all-purpose flour
¼ cup flaked coconut
½ teaspoon cinnamon
2 tablespoons butter or margarine, melted

Oven 350°   One 9-inch Coffeecake

In large mixer bowl, combine 1 cup flour, yeast, sugar, nutmeg and salt; mix well. In saucepan, heat milk, water and shortening until warm (120-130°; shortening does not need to melt). Add to flour mixture. Add egg. Blend at low speed until moistened; beat 3 minutes at medium speed. By hand, gradually stir in remaining flour to make a stiff batter. Spread in greased 9-inch square cake pan.

Prepare Topping: Combine all Topping ingredients.

Spread preserves over batter; sprinkle with Topping. Cover; let rise in warm place until double, about 45 minutes. Bake at 350° for 30 to 35 minutes until golden brown. Serve warm.

Caramel Apple Buns

A different kind of sticky bun. Apple juice and cinnamon in a one-rise dough.

3¼ to 3½ cups all-purpose flour
2 packages Red Star Instant Blend Dry Yeast
1 tablespoon sugar
1 tablespoon cinnamon
1 teaspoon salt
¾ cup apple juice
½ cup water
¼ cup butter
1 egg

Topping:
¾ cup packed brown sugar
¼ cup butter
2 tablespoons light corn syrup
¾ cup chopped nuts

Oven 375°   **24 Buns**

In large mixer bowl, combine 1¼ cups flour, yeast, sugar, cinnamon and salt; mix well. In saucepan, heat apple juice, water and butter until warm (120-130°; butter does not need to melt). Add to flour mixture. Add egg. Blend at low speed until moistened; beat 3 minutes at medium speed. By hand, gradually stir in enough remaining flour to make a stiff batter.

Prepare Topping: In saucepan, combine brown sugar, butter and corn syrup; heat and stir until blended. Add nuts. Spoon Topping into greased muffin pan cups.

Spoon batter over Topping. Cover; let rise in warm place until double, about 45 minutes. Bake at 375° for 15 to 20 minutes until golden brown. Cover pans with foil and invert onto rack. Cool 1 minute; remove pans. Cool.

Almond Streusel Coffeecake

A delicious coffeecake with the streusel topping reveled throughout.

3 cups all-purpose flour
2 packages Red Star Instant Blend Dry Yeast
⅓ cup sugar
½ teaspoon salt
¾ cup water
½ cup milk
¼ cup butter or margarine
2 eggs
½ cup sugar
½ cup all-purpose flour
½ cup chopped slivered almonds
¼ cup butter or margarine, melted
1 teaspoon cinnamon

Oven 375°   **One 13x9-inch Coffeecake**

In large mixer bowl, combine 1½ cups flour, yeast, ⅓ cup sugar and salt; mix well. In saucepan, heat water, milk and butter until warm (120-130°; butter does not need to melt). Add to flour mixture. Add eggs. Blend at low speed until moistened; beat 3 minutes at medium speed. By hand, gradually stir in remaining 1½ cups flour to make a stiff batter. Spread in greased 13x9-inch cake pan.

Prepare Topping: Combine ½ cup sugar, ½ cup flour, almonds, ¼ cup melted butter and cinnamon.

Sprinkle Topping over batter. With back of a spoon, make random indentations in batter. Cover; let rise in warm place until double, about 30 minutes. Bake at 375° for 25 to 30 minutes until golden brown. Serve warm or cold.

Sally Lunn

A light, rich batter bread named for an English girl, Sally Lunn, who is said to have baked and sold a similar bread in the town of Bath two centuries ago. Serve warm wedges with coffee or a salad luncheon. Delicious toasted for breakfast.

4¼ cups all-purpose flour
1 package Red Star Instant Blend Dry Yeast
⅓ cup sugar
1 teaspoon salt
¾ cup milk
¼ cup water
½ cup butter or margarine
3 eggs

Oven 350°   One 10-inch Coffeecake

In large mixer bowl, combine 2 cups flour, yeast, sugar and salt; mix well. In saucepan, heat water, milk and butter until warm (120-130°; butter does not need to melt). Add to flour mixture. Add eggs. Blend at low speed until moistened; beat 3 minutes at medium speed. By hand, gradually stir in remaining flour to make a stiff batter. Cover; let rise in warm place until light and doubled, about 1 hour.

Stir down batter. Spoon into greased 10-inch tubed cake pan. Cover; let rise in warm place to within 1½ inches from top of pan, about 30 minutes. Bake at 350° for 40 to 45 minutes until golden brown. If too dark, cover loosely with foil last 5 to 10 minutes of baking. Remove from pan. Serve warm or cold.

Apple-Cinnamon Puffs

A delicious roll with chopped apples inside and cinnamon on top. One rise makes it quick enough for breakfast.

2 cups all-purpose flour
1 package Red Star Instant Blend Dry Yeast
2 tablespoons sugar
½ teaspoon salt
¾ cup warm water
¼ cup oil
1 egg
1 cup chopped apples
3 tablespoons butter, melted
¼ cup sugar
1 teaspoon cinnamon

Oven 375°   12 Rolls

In large mixer bowl, combine 1 cup flour, yeast, 2 tablespoons sugar and salt; mix well. Add warm water (120-130°) and oil to flour mixture. Add egg. Blend at low speed until moistened; beat 3 minutes at medium speed. By hand, gradually stir in apples and remaining flour to make a soft batter.

Spoon into well greased muffin pan cups. Cover; let rise in warm place until double, 45 to 60 minutes. Bake at 375° for 15 to 20 minutes until golden brown.

Combine ¼ cup sugar and cinnamon. Dip tops of hot rolls into melted butter, then into sugar-cinnamon mixture. Serve warm.

Holiday Muffins

These holiday muffins have a delicate almond flavor and a jeweled topping. They're delicious and attractive.

2½ cups all-purpose flour
  1 package Red Star Instant
    Blend Dry Yeast
  ⅓ cup sugar
  1 teaspoon salt
  ½ cup water
  ¼ cup milk
  ¼ cup butter or margarine
  1 egg
  ½ teaspoon almond extract
  ⅓ cup raisins, chopped
  ⅓ cup chopped almonds
  2 tablespoons chopped candied
    cherries
  1 tablespoon corn syrup

Oven 350°   **12 Muffins**

In small mixer bowl, combine 1 cup flour, yeast, sugar and salt; mix well. In saucepan, heat water, milk and butter until warm (120-130°; butter does not need to melt). Add to flour mixture. Add egg and almond extract. Blend at low speed until moistened; beat 3 minutes at medium speed. By hand, gradually stir in remaining flour to make a soft batter.

Prepare Topping: Combine raisins, almonds, cherries and corn syrup; set aside.

Spoon batter into greased muffin pan cups. Cover; let rise in warm place, 1 to 1½ hours. Make an indentation in top of each muffin; fill with 1 teaspoon of Topping. Bake at 350° for 20 to 25 minutes. Cool 3 minutes in pans; remove from pans. Serve warm.

Orange Puffs

A one-rise roll with an orange cinnamon-sugar coating. A batter roll that's quick enough to make for breakfast. They are best served warm right from the oven.

2¼ cups all-purpose flour
  1 package Red Star Instant
    Blend Dry Yeast
  ¼ cup sugar
  ½ teaspoon salt
  ½ cup milk
  ¼ cup water
  3 tablespoons butter or
    margarine
  1 egg
  2 tablespoons frozen orange
    juice concentrate, thawed and
    undiluted
  ⅓ cup sugar
1½ teaspoons cinnamon
  ¼ cup frozen orange juice
    concentrate, thawed and
    undiluted

Oven 375°   **12 Rolls**

In large mixer bowl, combine 1 cup flour, yeast, ¼ cup sugar and salt; mix well. In saucepan, heat milk, water and butter until warm (120-130°; butter does not need to melt). Add to flour mixture. Add egg and 2 tablespoons juice concentrate. Blend at low speed until moistened; beat 2 minutes at medium speed. By hand, gradually stir in remaining flour to make a soft dough.

Spoon dough into greased muffin pan cups. Cover; let rise in warm place until light and doubled, about 30 minutes. Bake at 375° for 15 to 20 minutes until golden brown. Combine ⅓ cup sugar and cinnamon. Dip hot rolls into 4 tablespoons juice concentrate, then into cinnamon-sugar. Serve warm.

Sweet loaves, coffeecakes &

Orange Raisin Butter Bread

Tea Ring with Cranberry
Date Filling

sweet rolls

Calypso Bread

Super Pecan
Caramel Rolls

Chocolate Swirl
Coffeecake

SWEET LOAVES, COFFEECAKES AND SWEET ROLLS

The recipes in this chapter provide a choice of festive sweet loaves, delicious coffeecakes or tempting sweet rolls. These are breads which say, "Come over for coffee . . . " or "You're special . . ." or they will simply satisfy a sweet tooth! The doughs are rich and tender; many have fillings, glazes or toppings which add extra flavor. Some of these breads take their shape from the pan in which they are baked, such as the *Caramel Crown Coffeecake* baked in a Bundt® pan and the *Coffeecake À La Meringue* baked in a tubed cake pan. Others are braided, coiled or rolled into intriguing shapes, such as *My Sunshine Braid, Sweet Whirls* and *Luscious Lemon Brioche Knots.*

You'll find doughnut recipes, including a recipe for *Long John's.* For chocolate lovers there are five breads using chocolate; one is especially for children—they'll love the *Chocolate Cinnamon Crisps* as an after-school snack. The *Seven-Up Refrigerator Dough* is ideal for busy schedules as the dough can be made up ahead of time and refrigerated, then shaped into four different coffeecakes. Several of the coffeecakes use ingredients which you probably have on hand so they could be a weekend family project for family or guests.

The secret to light, tender sweet doughs is to keep the dough soft—as soft as you can handle without it sticking to your hands or the board when kneading. Use the lower protein all-purpose flours for a more tender dough. After the initial mixing step, stir in just enough flour to make a soft dough. Some doughs are richer and don't require as much kneading—3 to 5 minutes is usually sufficient. Knead in only enough flour for easy handling. Shaping the dough on a lightly floured pastry cloth or a lightly oiled board is helpful to prevent too much flour from being worked into the dough.

Many of these breads are best served warm from the oven—or they can be reheated. The microwave oven is ideal for reheating. See the information section in the front part of this book for more tips on reheating breads.

Although these sweet dough breads can be frozen, they don't keep as well as the basic loaves or rolls; they do dry out slightly after freezing.

These are special breads for your family—or to share with friends.

Cream of Orange Bread

Orange and spice complement each other perfectly in this delectable bread.

3 to 3½ cups all-purpose flour
2 packages Red Star Instant Blend Dry Yeast
3 tablespoons packed brown sugar
1 teaspoon salt
2 tablespoons grated orange rind
1 teaspoon grated lemon rind
⅛ teaspoon ground ginger or cardamom
½ cup water
⅔ cup Half and Half
2 tablespoons butter or margarine
¼ cup frozen orange juice concentrate, thawed and undiluted

Oven 375°   **1 Loaf**

In large mixer bowl, combine 1½ cups flour, yeast, brown sugar, salt, grated fruit rinds and ginger; mix well. In saucepan, heat water, Half and Half and butter until warm (120-130°; butter does not need to melt). Add to flour mixture. Add juice concentrate. Blend at low speed until moistened; beat 3 minutes at medium speed. By hand, gradually stir in enough remaining flour to make a firm dough. Knead on floured surface until smooth and elastic, 5 to 8 minutes. Place in greased bowl, turning to grease top. Cover; let rise in warm place until double, about 1 hour.

Punch down dough. On lightly floured surface, roll or pat to a 14x7-inch rectangle. Starting with shorter side, roll up tightly, pressing dough into roll with each turn. Pinch edges and ends to seal. Place in greased 9x5-inch bread pan. Cover; let rise in warm place until double, about 45 minutes. Bake at 375° for 35 to 40 minutes. Remove from pan; cool.

Spiced Pumpkin Bread

An unusual and delicious loaf subtly flavored with pumpkin and cinnamon. An excellent accompaniment for ham.

3¾ to 4¼ cups all-purpose flour
2 packages Red Star Instant Blend Dry Yeast
¼ cup sugar
2 teaspoons salt
1 teaspoon cinnamon
½ cup water
½ cup canned pumpkin
3 tablespoons butter or margarine
2 eggs

Oven 375°   **1 Loaf**

In large mixer bowl, combine 1½ cups flour, yeast, sugar, salt and cinnamon; mix well. In saucepan, heat water, pumpkin and butter until warm (120-130°; butter does not need to melt). Add to flour mixture. Add eggs. Blend at low speed until moistened; beat 3 minutes at medium speed. By hand, gradually stir in enough remaining flour to make a firm dough. Knead on floured surface until smooth and elastic, 5 to 8 minutes. Place in greased bowl, turning to grease top. Cover; let rise in warm place until light and doubled, about 45 minutes.

Punch down dough. On lightly floured surface, roll or pat to a 14x7-inch rectangle. Starting with shorter side, roll up tightly, pressing dough into roll with each turn. Pinch edges and ends to seal. Place in greased 9x5-inch bread pan. Cover; let rise in warm place until double, about 45 minutes. Bake at 375° for 35 to 40 minutes until golden brown. If too dark, cover loosely with foil last 5 to 10 minutes of baking. Remove from pan; cool.

RAISIN VARIATION: Stir in ¾ cup raisins with the flour.

Cinnamon Swirl Loaves

🚂 A nutty sugar-cinnamon filling swirled in rich bread loaves— extra good toasted!

**5 to 5½ cups all-purpose flour
2 packages Red Star Instant Blend Dry Yeast
½ cup sugar
1 teaspoon salt
¾ cup milk
½ cup water
½ cup butter or margarine
2 eggs
½ cup packed brown sugar
¼ cup chopped pecans or walnuts
1 tablespoon cinnamon
2 tablespoons butter or margarine, melted**

Oven 350°   **2 Loaves**

In large mixer bowl, combine 2½ cups flour, yeast, sugar and salt; mix well. In saucepan, heat milk, water and butter until warm (120-130°; butter does not need to melt). Add to flour mixture. Add eggs. Blend at low speed until moistened; beat 3 minutes at medium speed. By hand, gradually stir in enough remaining flour to make a firm dough. Knead on floured surface until smooth and elastic, 5 to 8 minutes. Place in greased bowl, turning to grease top. Cover; let rise in warm place until light and doubled, about 1 hour.

Prepare Filling: Combine brown sugar, nuts and cinnamon; set aside.

Punch down dough. Divide into 2 parts. On lightly floured surface, roll or pat each half to a 14x7-inch rectangle. Brush with half of melted butter; sprinkle half of Filling over dough. Starting with shorter side, roll up tightly, pressing dough into roll with each turn. Pinch edges and ends to seal. Place in greased 9x5 or 8x4-inch bread pans. Cover; let rise in warm place until double, about 45 minutes. Bake at 350° for 40 to 45 minutes until golden brown. Remove from pans; cool.

Cinnamon Custard Swirl

🎀 A new twist for cinnamon bread —cinnamon sugar is swirled in a custard flavored dough. It's a marvelous loaf!

**5 to 5½ cups all-purpose flour
2 packages Red Star Instant Blend Dry Yeast
1 package (3 oz.) egg custard mix
2 teaspoons salt
1 cup milk
½ cup water
¼ cup butter or margarine
2 eggs
½ cup sugar
4 teaspoons cinnamon
2 tablespoons butter or margarine, softened
Butter, melted
1½ tablespoons sugar
1 tablespoon cinnamon**

Oven 375°   **2 Loaves**

In large mixer bowl, combine 2 cups flour, yeast, custard mix and salt; mix well. In saucepan, heat milk, water and butter until warm (120-130°; butter does not need to melt). Add to flour mixture. Add eggs. Blend at low speed until moistened; beat 3 minutes at medium speed. By hand, gradually stir in enough remaining flour to make a firm dough. Knead on floured surface until smooth and elastic, 5 to 8 minutes. Place in greased bowl, turning to grease top. Cover; let rise in warm place until light and doubled, about 1 hour.

Prepare Filling: Combine ½ cup sugar and 4 teaspoons cinnamon; set aside.

Punch down dough. Divide into 2 parts. On lightly floured surface, roll each half to a 14x7-inch rectangle. Spread with 1 tablespoon softened butter; sprinkle half of Filling over dough. Starting with shorter side, roll up tightly, pressing dough into roll with each turn. Pinch edges and ends to seal. Place in greased 9x5-inch bread pans. Cover; let rise in warm place until double, about 1 hour. Bake at 375° for 35 to 40 minutes. Brush tops of loaves with melted butter; sprinkle with mixture of 1½ tablespoons sugar and 1 tablespoon cinnamon. Remove from pans; cool.

Orange Raisin Butter Bread

A sweet version of "buttercrust" bread—melted butter soaks into the dough during baking. Serve this delicious orange-flavored golden raisin bread for a holiday breakfast or brunch. Good toasted—simply omit the glaze.

- 7 to 7½ cups all-purpose flour
- 2 packages Red Star Instant Blend Dry Yeast
- 1 tablespoon salt
- 1 tablespoon grated orange rind
- ⅛ teaspoon mace
- 1¼ cups water
- 1 cup milk
- ½ cup honey
- ¼ cup butter or margarine
- 2 eggs
- ¾ cup golden raisins
- ⅔ cup coarsely chopped pecans
- 1 tablespoon butter or margarine, melted

Glaze:
- ½ cup powdered sugar
- 2 to 3 teaspoons orange juice
- 1 teaspoon grated orange rind

Oven 375°   **2 Loaves**

In large mixer bowl, combine 3½ cups flour, yeast, salt, orange rind and mace; mix well. In saucepan, heat water, milk, honey and butter until warm (120-130°; butter does not need to melt). Add to flour mixture. Add eggs. Blend at low speed until moistened; beat 3 minutes at medium speed. By hand, gradually stir in raisins, pecans and enough remaining flour to make a firm dough. Knead on floured surface 5 to 8 minutes. Place in greased bowl, turning to grease top. Cover; let rise in warm place until double, about 1 hour.

Punch down dough. Divide into 2 parts. On lightly floured surface, roll or pat each half to a 14x7-inch rectangle. Starting with shorter side, roll up tightly, pressing dough into roll with each turn. Pinch edges and ends to seal. Place in greased 9x5-inch bread pans. With very sharp knife, make a slash 1 inch deep lengthwise down center of each loaf. Pour melted butter into each slash. Cover; let rise in warm place until double, about 45 minutes. Bake at 375° for 35 to 40 minutes until golden brown. If too dark, cover loosely with foil last 5 to 10 minutes of baking. Remove from pans. Drizzle Glaze on loaves; cool.

Prepare Glaze: Combine all Glaze ingredients; blend until smooth.

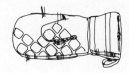

Apple Cinnamon Raisin Bread

🏵 Apple juice, cinnamon, and raisins—a subtle blend of flavors, a marvelous loaf of bread!

3 to 3½ cups all-purpose flour
1 package Red Star Instant Blend Dry Yeast
1 tablespoon sugar
1 tablespoon cinnamon
1 teaspoon salt
¾ cup apple juice
½ cup water
1 tablespoon oil
¾ cup raisins

Oven 375°   **1 Loaf**

In large mixer bowl, combine 1½ cups flour, yeast, sugar, cinnamon, and salt; mix well. In saucepan, heat apple juice, water, and oil until warm (120-130°). Add to flour mixture. Blend at low speed until moistened; beat 3 minutes at medium speed. By hand, gradually stir in raisins and enough remaining flour to make a firm dough. Knead on floured surface, 5 to 8 minutes. Place in greased bowl, turning to grease top. Cover; let rise in warm place until double, about 1 hour.

Punch down dough. On lightly floured surface, roll or pat to a 14x7-inch rectangle. Starting with shorter side, roll up tightly, pressing dough into roll with each turn. Pinch edges and ends to seal. Place in greased 9x5-inch bread pan. Cover; let rise in warm place until double, about 1 hour. Bake at 375° for 35 to 40 minutes until loaf sounds hollow when tapped. Remove from pan; cool.

My Sunshine Braid

🏵 Attractive, nutritious braids rich with raisins, carrots and eggs.

7 to 7½ cups all-purpose flour
2 packages Red Star Instant Blend Dry Yeast
1 tablespoon salt
1 cup milk
½ cup water
¼ cup butter or margarine
⅓ cup honey
3 eggs
2 cups coarsely shredded carrots
1½ cups raisins
2 tablespoons grated orange rind
1 egg, slightly beaten
1 teaspoon water

Oven 375°   **2 Braids**

In large mixer bowl, combine 2½ cups flour, yeast and salt; mix well. In saucepan, heat milk, ½ cup water and butter until warm (120-130°; butter does not need to melt). Add to flour mixture. Add honey and 3 eggs. Blend at low speed until moistened; beat 3 minutes at medium speed. By hand, gradually stir in carrots, raisins, orange rind and enough remaining flour to make a soft dough. Knead on floured surface until smooth and elastic, 5 to 8 minutes. Place in greased bowl, turning to grease top. Cover; let rise in warm place until double, about 1 hour.

Punch down dough. Divide into 2 parts. Divide each half into 3 pieces. On lightly floured surface, roll each piece to a 15-inch rope. On greased cookie sheet, loosely braid 3 ropes from center to ends. Pinch ends and tuck under to seal. Cover; let rise in warm place until almost doubled, about 45 minutes. Combine egg and 1 teaspoon water; brush braid. Bake at 375° for 35 to 40 minutes until golden brown. Remove from cookie sheets; cool.

Calypso Bread

An interesting coffee can bread with flavors popular in the Caribbean. Ginger, coffee and mashed banana make it a special bread.

5 to 5½ cups all-purpose flour
2 packages Red Star Instant
Blend Dry Yeast
½ cup sugar
1 tablespoon instant coffee
powder
1½ teaspoons salt
½ teaspoon ground ginger
½ cup milk
½ cup water
¼ cup butter or margarine
1 egg
¾ to 1 cup mashed bananas
(about 2 bananas)
½ cup chopped walnuts
Butter, softened

Oven 375°   2 Loaves

In large mixer bowl, combine 2 cups flour, yeast, sugar, salt, ginger and coffee; mix well. In saucepan, heat milk, water and butter until warm (120-130°; butter does not need to melt). Add to flour mixture. Add egg. Blend at low speed until moistened; beat 3 minutes at medium speed. By hand, gradually stir in bananas, nuts and enough remaining flour to make a firm dough. Knead on floured surface until smooth and elastic, 5 to 8 minutes. Place in greased bowl, turning to grease top. Cover; let rise in warm place until double, 1 to 1½ hours.

Punch down dough. Divide into 2 parts. Shape each half into a round ball. Place in well-greased 1-lb. coffee cans or on greased cookie sheet. Cover; let rise in warm place until double, about 30 minutes. Bake at 375° for 30 to 35 minutes until golden brown. If too dark, cover loosely with foil last 5 to 10 minutes of baking. Remove from cans; brush with butter. Cool.

Star Spangled Banana Bread

Perfect for a church bake sale. The special touch of ginger and orange rind add to this delicious banana bread.

5½ to 6 cups all-purpose flour
2 packages Red Star Instant
Blend Dry Yeast
½ cup sugar
1 teaspoon salt
1 teaspoon grated orange rind
½ teaspoon ground ginger
½ cup milk
½ cup water
½ cup butter or margarine
1 egg
1 cup mashed bananas
(about 2 bananas)
Butter

Oven 400°   2 Round Loaves

In large mixer bowl, combine 2 cups flour, yeast, sugar, salt, orange rind and ginger; mix well. In saucepan, heat milk, water and butter until warm (120-130°; butter does not need to melt). Add to flour mixture. Add egg and mashed bananas. Blend at low speed until moistened; beat 3 minutes at medium speed. By hand, gradually stir in enough remaining flour to make a firm dough. Knead on floured surface until smooth and elastic, 5 to 8 minutes. Place in greased bowl, turning to grease top. Cover; let rise in warm place until double, about 1 hour.

Punch down dough. Divide into 2 parts. Shape each half into a round loaf. Place in greased 8-inch layer cake pans. Cover; let rise in warm place until double, about 45 minutes. Bake at 400° for 25 to 30 minutes until golden brown. Remove from pans; brush butter. Cool.

Fruit-Nut Wheat Bread

Shredded apple makes this whole wheat bread moist. Nuts and raisins add variety.

5 to 5½ cups all-purpose flour
2 packages Red Star Instant Blend Dry Yeast
1 tablespoon salt
1¾ cups water
½ cup honey
¼ cup oil
1 cup coarsely shredded peeled apple
½ cup chopped walnuts
½ cup raisins
2 cups whole wheat flour
Butter

Oven 375°   2 Round Loaves

In large mixer bowl, combine 2½ cups flour, yeast, and salt; mix well. In saucepan, heat water, honey, and oil until warm (120-130°). Add to flour mixture. Blend at low speed until moistened; beat 3 minutes at medium speed. By hand, stir in apple, nuts, raisins, and whole wheat flour. Gradually stir in enough remaining all-purpose flour to make a firm dough. Knead on floured surface 5 to 8 minutes. Place in greased bowl, turning to grease top. Cover; let rise in warm place until double, about 1 hour.

Punch down dough. Divide into 2 parts. On lightly floured surface, shape each half into a round loaf. Place in greased 9-inch layer cake pans. Cover; let rise in warm place until double, 30 to 45 minutes. Bake at 375° for 40 to 45 minutes until loaves sound hollow when tapped. Remove from pans; brush with butter. Cool.

Orange Raisin Salt-Free Bread

A versatile bread for those on a salt-free diet—delicious for ham sandwiches or toasted for breakfast. For a salt-free white bread, use French bread.

2½ to 3 cups all-purpose flour
1 package Red Star Instant Blend Dry Yeast
1 teaspoon sugar
1 tablespoon grated orange rind
1 cup warm water
2 tablespoons oil
½ cup raisins
Salt-free butter

Oven 375°   1 Loaf

In large mixer bowl, combine flour, yeast, sugar and orange rind; mix well. Add warm water (120-130°) and oil to flour mixture. Blend at low speed until moistened; beat 3 minutes at medium speed. By hand, gradually stir in raisins and enough remaining flour to make a firm dough. Knead on floured surface, about 5 minutes. Place in greased bowl, turning to grease top. Cover; let rise at room temperature until double, about 1 hour.

Punch down dough. On lightly floured surface, roll or pat dough to a 14x7-inch rectangle. Starting with shorter side, roll up tightly, pressing dough into roll with each turn. Pinch edge and ends to seal. Place in greased 8x4-inch bread pan. Cover; let rise at room temperature until almost doubled, about 20 minutes. (The dough rises faster without salt. Let the loaf rise only until it comes slightly above the pan.) Bake at 375° for 35 to 40 minutes until golden brown. Remove from pan; brush with butter. Cool.

Apricot Nut Loaves

These attractive loaves present a subtle blend of flavors, apricots, pecans, nutmeg, and ginger. A perfect choice for gift giving any time of the year.

4½ to 5 cups all-purpose flour
2 packages Red Star Instant Blend Dry Yeast
⅓ cup sugar
2 teaspoons salt
½ teaspoon ground ginger
½ teaspoon ground nutmeg
1 cup milk
½ cup water
¼ cup butter or margarine
1 egg
¾ cup dried apricots, finely cut up
¾ cup chopped pecans
Butter, softened
Sugar

Oven 375°   **2 Loaves**

In large mixer bowl, combine 2 cups flour, yeast, sugar, salt, ginger and nutmeg; mix well. In saucepan, heat milk, water and butter until warm (120-130°; butter does not need to melt). Add to flour mixture. Add egg. Beat at low speed until moistened; beat 3 minutes at medium speed. By hand, gradually stir in fruit and nuts and enough remaining flour to make a firm dough. Knead on well-floured surface until smooth and elastic, 5 to 8 minutes. Place in greased bowl, turning to grease top. Cover; let rise in warm place until double, about 1 hour.

Punch down dough. Divide into 2 parts. On lightly floured surface, roll or pat each half to a 14x7-inch rectangle. Starting with the shorter side, roll up tightly, pressing dough into roll with each turn. Pinch edges and ends to seal. Place in greased 8x4 or 9x5-inch bread pans. Cover; let rise in warm place until double, 30 to 45 minutes. Bake at 375° for 25 to 30 minutes until golden brown. Remove from pans; brush with butter and sprinkle with sugar. Cool.

My Notes: _____

_____

_____

_____

_____

_____

_____

_____

_____

_____

Tea Ring

A Tea Ring is one of the most traditional yeast breads. It is versatile, allowing a choice of filling. It is attractive with a distinctive shape and perfect for any occasion.

5¼ to 5¾ cups all-purpose flour
  2 packages Red Star Instant Blend Dry Yeast
  ½ cup sugar
  1 teaspoon salt
  1 cup milk
  ½ cup water
  ¼ cup butter or margarine
  2 eggs

Oven 350°   2 Tea Rings

Prepare Filling or Fillings. In large mixer bowl, combine 2½ cups flour, yeast, sugar, and salt; mix well. In saucepan, heat milk, water, and butter until warm (120-130°; butter does not need to melt). Add to flour mixture. Add eggs. Blend at low speed until moistened; beat 3 minutes at medium speed. By hand, gradually stir in enough remaining flour to make a soft dough. Knead on floured surface until smooth and elastic, 5 to 8 minutes. Place in greased bowl, turning to grease top. Cover; let rise in warm place until double, about 1 hour.

Punch down dough. Divide into 2 parts. On lightly floured surface, roll each half to a 15x12-inch rectangle. Spread with Filling. Starting with longer side, roll up tightly. Pinch edges to seal. Form ring, pinch ends to seal. Place each ring, seam side down on a greased cookie sheet. With scissors, make cuts 1 inch apart through top of ring to 1 inch from center. Turn each slice on its side. Cover; let rise in warm place until almost doubled, about 20 minutes. Bake at 350° for 20 to 25 minutes until golden brown. Remove from cookie sheets; cool. Drizzle with powdered sugar Glaze, if desired.

Cinnamon Pecan Filling

½ cup packed brown sugar
2 teaspoons cinnamon
½ cup finely chopped pecans
2 tablespoons butter, softened
Filling for 1 Tea Ring

In small bowl, combine brown sugar, cinnamon, and nuts; mix well. Spread rectangle with butter. Sprinkle with Filling.

Poppy Seed Filling

½ cup whole poppy seeds
⅓ cup milk
⅓ cup sugar
1 egg
½ cup chopped walnuts
¼ teaspoon almond flavoring
Filling for 1 Tea Ring

In small saucepan, combine poppy seeds and milk. Bring to a boil. Simmer about 5 minutes until milk is absorbed; stirring constantly. Add sugar; cook 5 minutes longer. Beat egg slightly. Stir a little of the hot mixture into the egg; add to the poppy seed. Cook until thickened. Do not boil. Remove from heat. Stir in nuts and almond flavoring; cool completely.

Date Orange Filling

1 cup whole dates, chopped
¼ cup orange juice
1 tablespoon grated orange rind
1 tablespoon sugar
Filling for 1 Tea Ring

In small saucepan, combine all ingredients. Bring to a boil. Simmer about 3 minutes, until thickened; cool completely. If Filling is too thick to spread, add orange juice to thin.

Lemon Crunch Coffeecake

Cranberry Date Filling

¼ cup sugar
¼ cup corn syrup
⅓ cup water
1 cup cranberries
½ cup whole dates, chopped
¼ cup chopped nuts
2 teaspoons lemon juice

Filling for 1 Tea Ring

In medium saucepan, boil sugar, corn syrup, and water 5 minutes. Add cranberries. Cover and cook 4 minutes, stirring occasionally. Add chopped dates; cook 1 minute. Remove from heat; stir in nuts and lemon juice. Cool completely.

TIP: If using frozen cranberries, increase cooking time.

Maple Nut Filling

½ cup packed brown sugar
½ cup chopped walnuts
1 teaspoon cinnamon
½ teaspoon maple flavoring
¼ cup maple syrup

Filling for 2 Tea Rings

In small bowl, combine brown sugar, walnuts, and cinnamon. Brush maple syrup over each half of dough. Sprinkle with sugar and nut mixture.

A tender yeast cake with a super topping—crunchy and lemony!

1½ to 2 cups all-purpose flour
1 package Red Star Instant Blend Dry Yeast
2 tablespoons sugar
½ teaspoon salt
½ cup buttermilk
¼ cup water
2 tablespoons shortening
1 egg

Topping:

⅓ cup all-purpose flour
⅓ cup sugar
¼ cup chopped almonds
¼ cup butter or margarine, melted
1 teaspoon lemon rind
¼ teaspoon vanilla

Oven 375°   One 9-inch Coffeecake

In large mixer bowl, combine 1¼ cups flour, yeast, sugar and salt; mix well. In saucepan, heat buttermilk, water and shortening until warm (120-130°; shortening does not need to melt). Add to flour mixture. Add egg. Blend at low speed until moistened; beat 3 minutes at medium speed. By hand, gradually stir in enough remaining flour to make a soft dough. Knead on floured surface until smooth and elastic, about 3 minutes. Cover; let rest 5 minutes.

Prepare Topping: Combine all Topping ingredients; set aside.

Press dough in a greased 9-inch square cake pan. Sprinkle Topping over dough. With back of spoon, make random indentations in dough. Cover; let rise in warm place until double, about 30 minutes. Bake at 375° for 25 to 30 minutes until golden brown. Serve warm or cold.

Seven-Up Refrigerator Dough

A convenient refrigerator dough that can be made one day and shaped and baked the next day, if desired. The 7-Up makes the dough more tender. Shape dough into any of the four coffeecakes which follow.

**5 to 5½ cups all-purpose flour
2 packages Red Star Instant Blend Dry Yeast
¼ cup sugar
1 teaspoon salt
1 cup 7-Up
½ cup water
¼ cup butter or margarine
1 egg
3 egg yolks**

In large mixer bowl, combine 2 cups flour, yeast, sugar and salt; mix well. In saucepan, heat 7-Up, water, and butter until warm (120-130°; butter does not need to melt). Add to flour mixture. Add egg and yolks. Blend at low speed until moistened; beat 3 minutes at medium speed. By hand, gradually stir in enough remaining flour to make a soft dough. Knead on floured surface until smooth and elastic, 3 to 5 minutes. Place in greased bowl, turning to grease top. Cover with plastic wrap and foil. Refrigerate 4 to 24 hours. While dough is chilling, punch down several times. Remove desired amount of dough; refrigerate remaining dough until ready to use. Shape into coffeecakes as follows.

Apricot and Cream Cheese Coffeecake

**¼ Recipe Seven-Up Refrigerator Dough
¾ cup apricot preserves
1 package (3 oz.) cream cheese, softened
2 tablespoons sugar
1 tablespoon orange juice
¼ cup sliced or slivered almonds**

Oven 375°   One 9-inch Coffeecake

Press dough into greased 9-inch square cake pan. Spread preserves evenly on dough. In small bowl, blend cream cheese, sugar and orange juice until smooth; spread over preserves. Cover; let rise in warm place until double, about 30 minutes. Sprinkle almonds on top. Bake at 375° for 20 to 25 minutes until lightly browned. Serve warm or cold.

Pineapple Coconut Coffeecake

**½ Recipe Seven-Up Refrigerator Dough
1½ cups (15 oz.) pineapple preserves
1 cup flaked coconut**

Oven 375°   One 13x9-inch Coffeecake

Press dough into greased 13x9-inch cake pan. Spread preserves evenly on dough. Sprinkle coconut on top. Cover; let rise in warm place until double, about 30 minutes. Bake at 375° for 25 to 30 minutes. If coconut gets too brown, cover loosely with foil last 5 to 10 minutes of baking. Cool 10 minutes in pan. Remove from pan. Serve warm or cold.

TIP: Any flavor preserves or jam may be used.

Raspberry Coil Coffeecake

¼ Recipe Seven-Up Refrigerator
  Dough
⅓ cup raspberry preserves
½ cup powdered sugar
2 to 3 teaspoons milk

Oven 375°   1 Coffeecake

Divide dough into 6 pieces. On lightly floured suface, roll each piece
to an 18-inch rope. Beginning at the
center of greased large cookie
sheet, make a loose swirl with the
first rope. Add a second rope,
overlapping about one inch of the
first one; coil second rope around
the first rope. Continue adding the
remaining ropes in the same man-
ner. Spread preserves evenly on
dough. Cover loosely with wax
paper; let rise in warm place until
double, about 30 minutes. Bake
at 375° for 20 to 25 minutes until
golden brown. Remove from cookie
sheet. Drizzle Glaze on warm coffeecake. Serve warm.

Prepare Glaze: Blend powdered
sugar and milk until smooth.

Cinnamon Nut Bubble Loaf

⅓ cup sugar
¼ cup finely chopped nuts
1 teaspoon cinnamon
½ Recipe Seven-Up Refrigerator
  Dough
¼ cup butter or margarine,
  melted

Oven 375°   One 9x5-inch
                    Bubble Loaf

In medium bowl, combine sugar,
nuts and cinnamon. Divide dough
into 4 parts. Divide each fourth into
6 pieces. Shape each piece into a
smooth ball. Dip in melted butter;
roll in sugar-nut mixture. Place
in greased 9x5-inch bread pan, making 2 layers. Pour any remaining
butter on balls in pan; sprinkle any
remaining sugar-nut mixture on
top. Cover; let rise in warm place
until double, about 30 minutes.
Bake at 375° for 30 to 35 minutes.
Cool 10 minutes in pan. Remove
from pan. Serve warm or cold.

My Notes: _____

_____

_____

_____

_____

_____

_____

_____

Maple Nut Twist

A delicious maple nut coffeecake in a popular braid shape. Maple syrup and chopped walnuts in the dough and maple flavoring in the delicious Glaze make this large loaf perfect for any coffeecake occasion.

4½ to 5 cups all-purpose flour
2 packages Red Star Instant Blend Dry Yeast
¼ cup packed brown sugar
1 teaspoon salt
½ cup milk
½ cup water
¼ cup maple syrup
¼ cup butter or margarine
2 eggs
¾ cup chopped walnuts

Glaze:

1 cup powdered sugar
¼ teaspoon maple flavoring
2 to 3 tablespoons milk

Oven 400°   **1 Braid**

In large mixer bowl, combine 2 cups flour, yeast, brown sugar and salt; mix well. In saucepan, heat milk, water, maple syrup and butter until warm (120-130°; butter does not need to melt). Add to flour mixture. Add eggs. Blend at low speed until moistened; beat 3 minutes at medium speed. By hand, gradually stir in walnuts and enough remaining flour to make a soft dough. Knead on floured surface until smooth and elastic, 5 to 8 minutes. Place in greased bowl, turning to grease top. Cover; let rise in warm place until double, about 1 hour.

Punch down dough. Divide into 3 parts. On lightly floured surface, roll each third to a 15-inch rope. On greased large cookie sheet, loosely braid 3 ropes from center to ends. Pinch ends and tuck under to seal. Cover; let rise in warm place until almost doubled, about 30 minutes. Bake at 400° for 25 to 30 minutes until golden brown. Remove from cookie sheet; cool. Drizzle Glaze over Braid.

Prepare Glaze: Combine all Glaze ingredients; blend until smooth.

My Notes: _____

_____

_____

_____

_____

_____

_____

_____

_____

_____

Tropical Butterfly Stollen

This recipe not only has a delicious pineapple-coconut filling, but an attractive butterfly shape.

3 to 3½ cups all-purpose flour
2 packages Red Star Instant Blend Dry Yeast
¼ cup sugar
1 teaspoon salt
½ cup water
½ cup milk
¼ cup butter or margarine
1 egg
1 can (20 oz.) crushed pineapple in heavy syrup, undrained, reserve 1 tablespoon juice
1 cup sugar
1 cup chopped pecans
¾ cup flaked coconut
2 tablespoons light corn syrup

Oven 375°   1 Large Stollen

In large mixer bowl, combine 1½ cups flour, yeast, ¼ cup sugar and salt; mix well. In saucepan, heat water, milk and butter until warm (120-130°; butter does not need to melt). Add to flour mixture. Add egg. Blend at low speed until moistened; beat 3 minutes at medium speed. By hand, gradually stir in enough remaining flour to make a soft dough. Place in greased bowl. Cover; let rise in warm place until light and doubled, about 1 hour.

Prepare Filling: In heavy saucepan or skillet, combine pineapple and 1 cup sugar. Bring to a boil. Simmer 15 to 20 minutes over medium heat, stirring constantly, until all the juice is absorbed; cool.

Punch down dough. On floured surface, knead 30 seconds. Roll to a 15x12-inch rectangle. Spread with Filling. Sprinkle pecans and coconut over pineapple. Starting with longer side, roll up tightly. Pinch edge and ends to seal. Fold under each end ⅓ of the way to meet. Place folded side down on greased large cookie sheet. With scissors, cut folded ends to within two inches of meeting point. Lay cut ends flat to form butterfly wings. Cover; let rise in warm place until almost doubled, about 30 minutes. Bake at 375° for 20 minutes. Brush with pineapple syrup glaze made of reserved pineapple juice and corn syrup; bake 5 to 10 minutes longer until golden brown. Cool. Drizzle with Glaze, if desired.

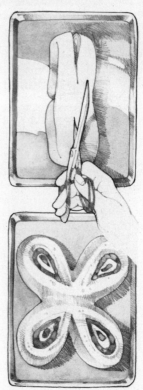

A Honey of a Cake

A rich coffeecake with a delicious honey flavored coconut topping that sinks into the dough slightly during baking to give flavor throughout.

1¼ to 1¾ cups all-purpose flour
1 package Red Star Instant
  Blend Dry Yeast
2 tablespoons sugar
1 teaspoon grated lemon rind
¼ teaspoon salt
⅓ cup milk
¼ cup water
2 tablespoons butter or
  margarine
1 egg

Topping:
⅔ cup flaked coconut
¼ cup sugar
¼ cup butter or margarine
3 tablespoons honey
1 tablespoon milk
1 tablespoon chopped toasted
  almonds
⅛ teaspoon vanilla

Oven 350°   One Coffeecake

In small mixer bowl, combine ½ cup flour, yeast, sugar, lemon rind and salt; mix well. In saucepan, heat milk, water and butter until warm (120-130°; butter does not need to melt). Add to flour mixture. Add egg. Blend at low speed until moistened; beat 3 minutes at medium speed. By hand, gradually stir in enough remaining flour to make a stiff batter. Cover; let rise in warm place until double, about 30 minutes.

Prepare Topping: In small saucepan, combine Topping ingredients. Simmer 1 minute over medium heat. Cool.

Stir down batter. Spread in greased 1½-quart casserole. Cover; let rise in warm place until double, about 30 minutes. Drop Topping by spoonfuls onto batter, carefully spreading to within 1 inch of edges. Bake at 350° for 30 to 35 minutes until edges are golden brown. Serve warm or cold.

Caramel Crown Coffeecake

A moist caramel "crown" tops this delicious bubble coffeecake.

4½ to 5 cups all-purpose flour
2 packages Red Star Instant
  Blend Dry Yeast
½ cup sugar
1 teaspoon salt
¾ cup milk
½ cup water
½ cup shortening
2 eggs
1½ cups packed brown sugar
⅓ cup evaporated milk
⅓ cup butter or margarine
2 tablespoons corn syrup
1 cup flaked coconut
½ cup chopped walnuts or pecans

**Oven 375°   One 10-inch
                      Bundt® Coffeecake**

In large mixer bowl, combine 2 cups flour, yeast, sugar and salt; mix well. In saucepan, heat milk, water and shortening until warm (120-130°; shortening does not need to melt). Add to flour mixture. Add eggs. Blend at low speed until moistened; beat 3 minutes at medium speed. By hand, gradually stir in enough remaining flour to make a firm dough. Knead on floured surface until smooth and elastic, 5 to 8 minutes. Place in greased bowl, turning to grease top. Cover; let rise in warm place until light and double, about 1 hour.

Prepare Filling: In medium saucepan, combine brown sugar, evaporated milk, butter and corn syrup. Cook over low heat, stirring occasionally, until sugar has dissolved and butter has melted; set aside.

Punch down dough. Divide into pieces the size of a walnut; shape each piece into a smooth ball. Pour one third of Filling into well greased 12-cup Bundt® pan. Sprinkle with half of coconut and walnuts. Place half of the balls in pan. Pour one third of Filling over balls; sprinkle with remaining coconut and walnuts. Add remaining balls; pour remaining Filling on top. Cover; let rise in warm place until double, about 30 minutes. Bake at 375° for 45 to 50 minutes until golden brown. Cool 10 minutes in pan; invert onto serving plate. Serve warm or cold.

Coffeecake à la Meringue

An unusual combination of a meringue, cinnamon-nut-raisin filling in a sweet dough. Using a tubed pan with a loose bottom makes this coffeecake easier to remove from the pan.

3½ to 4 cups all-purpose flour
2 packages Red Star Instant Blend Dry Yeast
¼ cup sugar
1 teaspoon salt
½ cup sour cream
½ cup water
1 cup butter or margarine
3 eggs, separated
½ teaspoon vanilla
½ cup raisins
½ cup chopped nuts
2 tablespoons cinnamon
¾ cup sugar

Oven 350° **One 10-inch Coffeecake**

In large mixer bowl, combine 1 cup flour, yeast, ¼ cup sugar and salt; mix well. In saucepan, heat sour cream, water and butter until warm (120-130°; butter does not need to melt). Add to flour mixture. Add egg yolks and vanilla. Blend at low speed until moistened; beat 3 minutes at medium speed. By hand, gradually stir in enough remaining flour to make a soft dough. Cover; let rise in warm place until light and doubled, about 1 hour.

Prepare Filling: Combine raisins, nuts and cinnamon; set aside.

Punch down dough. On lightly floured surface, roll to a 15x12-inch rectangle. In small mixer bowl, beat egg whites until soft peaks form. Gradually add ¾ cup sugar and continue beating until whites are stiff. Spread meringue over dough. Sprinkle Filling over meringue. Starting with longer side, carefully roll up tightly. Seal edge. Cut into 6 parts. Place cut side up in greased loose-bottom tubed cake pan. Cover; let rise in warm place about 45 minutes. Bake at 350° for 45 to 50 minutes until golden brown. Cool 10 minutes in pan; invert onto serving plate.

Pineapple-Cheese Kuchen

A delicate pineapple filling tops an especially light and good yeast kuchen.

2½ to 3 cups all-purpose flour
2 packages Red Star Instant Blend Dry Yeast
¼ cup sugar
1 teaspoon salt
½ cup water
¼ cup milk
¼ cup shortening
1 egg

Topping:

⅓ cup sugar
1 tablespoon all-purpose flour
1½ cups (12 oz.) creamed small curd cottage cheese, drained
1½ cups canned crushed pineapple in heavy syrup, drained
2 tablespoons sugar
½ teaspoon cinnamon
¼ cup chopped nuts

Oven 375°   Two 9-inch Kuchen

In large mixer bowl, combine 1 cup flour, yeast, sugar and salt; mix well. In saucepan, heat water, milk and shortening until warm (120-130°; shortening does not need to melt). Add to flour mixture. Add egg. Blend at low speed until moistened; beat 3 minutes at medium speed. By hand, gradually stir in enough remaining flour to make a soft dough. Knead on floured surface until smooth and elastic, 3 to 5 minutes. Place in greased bowl, turning to grease top. Cover; let rise in warm place until double, about 1 hour.

Prepare Topping: In small bowl, combine ⅓ cup sugar, flour, cottage cheese and pineapple. In another small bowl, combine remaining Topping ingredients.

Punch down dough. Divide into 2 parts. Spread each half into a greased 9-inch round cake pan, forming a narrow rim around edge. Spread half of pineapple-cottage cheese mixture over dough. Sprinkle with half of sugar-cinnamon mixture. Cover; let rise in warm place until double, about 30 minutes. Bake at 375° for 20 to 25 minutes until edges are golden brown. Cool.

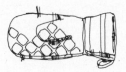

Cream Cheese Dessert Coffeecake

A very rich coffeecake that makes an excellent dessert! A cream cheese filling is sandwiched between a yeast-raised pastry like dough.

1 package Red Star Instant Blend Dry Yeast
¼ cup warm water
2½ cups all-purpose flour
1 tablespoon sugar
1 teaspoon salt
1 cup butter or margarine, cut into pieces
2 packages (8 oz. each) cream cheese, softened
1 cup sugar
1 egg yolk
1 egg white, slightly beaten
½ cup finely chopped nuts

Glaze:

1 cup powdered sugar
1 teaspoon vanilla
2 to 3 tablespoons water

Cardamom Cake

Oven 350° **One 15x10-inch Coffeecake**

In small bowl, dissolve yeast in warm water (110-115°); let stand 5 minutes. In large bowl, combine flour, 1 tablespoon sugar and salt; mix well. With pastry blender, cut in butter until the consistency of cornmeal. Add dissolved yeast to flour mixture; mix lightly with fork. Shape dough into a ball. Cover bowl with plastic wrap and foil; refrigerate 2 hours. (This is a rich dough; it rises very little.)

Prepare Filling: Beat cream cheese, 1 cup sugar and egg yolk until smooth; set aside.

Divide dough into 2 parts. On lightly floured surface, roll each half to a 15x10-inch rectangle. Roll rectangle onto rolling pin to transfer to greased 15x10-inch jelly roll pan. Spread Filling over dough. Carefully place remaining 15x10-inch rectangle over Filling. Brush dough with egg white. Sprinkle nuts over dough. Cover; let rise in warm place 1 hour. Bake at 350° for 25 to 30 minutes. Drizzle Glaze over warm coffeecake. Cut into squares or bars. Store in refrigerator.

Prepare Glaze: Combine Glaze ingredients; blend until smooth.

This delicious coffeecake can be served whenever a good cup of coffee is brewed. An unusual blend of cardamom and spices.

4 to 4½ cups all-purpose flour
2 packages Red Star Instant Blend Dry Yeast
¾ cup sugar
2 teaspoons ground cardamom
1 teaspoon salt
½ teaspoon cinnamon
¼ teaspoon ground cloves
¼ teaspoon ground ginger
½ cup water
½ cup milk
½ cup butter or margarine
4 eggs
Powdered sugar

Oven 375° **One 10-inch Bundt® Coffeecake**

In large mixer bowl, combine 1½ cups flour, yeast, sugar, cardamom, salt, cinnamon, cloves and ginger; mix well. In saucepan, heat water, milk and butter until warm (120-130°; butter does not need to melt). Add to flour mixture. Add eggs. Blend at low speed until moistened; beat 3 minutes at medium speed. By hand, gradually stir in enough remaining flour to make a stiff batter.

Spoon batter into well greased 12-cup Bundt® pan. Cover; let rise in warm place until light and double, about 1½ hours. Bake at 375° for 30 to 35 minutes until golden brown. Remove from pan; cool. Drizzle with powdered sugar Glaze, or sift powdered sugar over top before serving.

Gold Rush Treat

🏵 A bubble coffeecake with a
surprise—inside each ball of
dough is a chunk of "golden" pineapple. A treat to serve family and
friends.

3 to 3½ cups all-purpose flour
1 package Red Star Instant
Blend Dry Yeast
3 tablespoons sugar
1½ teaspoons salt
½ cup milk
½ cup water
3 tablespoons butter or
margarine
1 egg
1 cup sugar
½ cup finely chopped pecans
1 teaspoon cinnamon
¼ cup butter or margarine,
melted
1 cup (about 32) pineapple
chunks in heavy syrup,
well drained

Oven 350°   **One 10-inch**
Bundt® Coffeecake

In large mixer bowl, combine 1½
cups flour, yeast, 3 tablespoons
sugar and salt; mix well. In saucepan, heat milk, water, and butter
until warm (120-130°; butter does
not need to melt). Add to flour
mixture. Add egg. Blend at low
speed until moistened; beat at medium speed for 3 minutes. By hand,
gradually stir in enough remaining
flour to make a soft dough. Knead
on floured surface until smooth and
elastic, 5 to 8 minutes. Place in
greased bowl, turning to grease top.
Cover; let rise in warm place until
light and doubled, about 45 minutes.
Combine 1 cup sugar, nuts and
cinnamon.

Punch down dough. Divide into
pieces the size of a walnut (about
32 pieces). Flatten each piece of
dough; wrap around a pineapple
chunk. Dip in melted butter; roll
in sugar-cinnamon mixture to coat.
Layer balls in well-greased 12-cup
Bundt® pan. Cover; let rise in
warm place until double, about 30
minutes. Bake at 350° for 35 to
40 minutes until golden brown. Cool
10 minutes in pan, invert onto
serving plate.

Orange Almond Bubble Loaf

Cinnamon sugar with toasted almonds coat balls of orange flavored dough in this attractive bubble coffeecake.

4½ to 5 cups all-purpose flour
2 packages Red Star Instant Blend Dry Yeast
1 tablespoon grated orange rind
1 teaspoon salt
½ cup water
½ cup milk
¼ cup honey
½ cup butter or margarine
2 eggs
½ cup sugar
½ cup toasted almonds, chopped
1 tablespoon cinnamon
¼ cup butter or margarine, melted

Oven 350°   **One 10-inch Bundt® Coffeecake**

In large mixer bowl, combine 2 cups flour, yeast, orange rind and salt; mix well. In saucepan, heat water, milk, honey and butter until warm (120-130°; butter does not need to melt). Add to flour mixture. Add eggs. Blend at low speed until moistened; beat 3 minutes at medium speed. By hand, gradually stir in enough remaining flour to make a soft dough. Knead on floured surface until smooth and elastic, 3 to 5 minutes. Place in greased bowl, turning to grease top. Cover; let rise in warm place until light and doubled, about 1 hour. In medium bowl, combine sugar, almonds and cinnamon.

Punch down dough. Divide into 4 parts. Divide each fourth into 6 pieces. Shape each piece into a smooth ball. Dip in melted butter; roll in sugar-cinnamon mixture to coat. Layer balls in greased 12-cup Bundt® pan. Cover; let rise in warm place until double, about 30 minutes. Bake at 350° for 30 to 35 minutes until golden brown. Cool 10 minutes in pan; invert onto serving plate. Drizzle with Almond Glaze, if desired.

TIP: To toast almonds, place on cookie sheet in 300° oven for about 15 minutes; stir occasionally.

My Notes: _____

_____

_____

_____

_____

_____

_____

_____

_____

_____

Coffeecakes

Rich Pecan Filled Coffeecake

A butter rich yeast dough that bakes up almost like pastry and is filled with pecans. Slight breaks in the pastry during baking are typical of a coffeecake this rich. You'll want to serve slices with coffee any time of the day.

1 package Red Star Instant Blend Dry Yeast
1 tablespoon sugar
⅓ cup warm water
2½ cups all-purpose flour
½ teaspoon salt
1 cup cold butter or margarine, cut in pieces
2 eggs, beaten
1 cup finely chopped pecans
¾ cup packed brown sugar
¼ cup butter, melted

Oven 325°   **Two 12-inch Coffeecakes**

In small bowl, dissolve yeast and sugar in warm water (110-115°). Let stand 5 minutes. In large bowl, combine flour and salt; mix well. With pastry blender, cut in butter until the consistency of cornmeal. Add dissolved yeast and eggs to flour mixture. Mix lightly with fork. Shape dough into a ball. Cover bowl with plastic wrap and foil. Refrigerate for 1 to 3 hours. (This is a rich dough; it rises very little.)

Prepare Filling: Combine pecans and brown sugar. Gradually stir in butter until combined.

Divide dough into 2 parts. On lightly floured surface, roll or pat each half to a 12x10-inch rectangle. Sprinkle half of Filling over dough. Starting with longer side, roll up. Pinch edge and ends to seal. Place on greased cookie sheet, seam-side down. With very sharp knife, make five slashes across the top of each coffeecake. Bake at 325° for 20 to 25 minutes until light brown. Remove from cookie sheets; cool. Cut into slices.

Lemon Bubble Roll

A refreshing lemon flavored bubble coffeecake topped with a Lemon Glaze. Perfect for spring and summer brunches and buffets.

3½ to 4 cups all-purpose flour
2 packages Red Star Instant Blend Dry Yeast
⅓ cup sugar
2 teaspoons grated lemon rind
1 teaspoon salt
½ cup milk
½ cup water
¼ cup butter or margarine
2 eggs
1 teaspoon vanilla

Glaze:
⅓ cup sugar
¼ cup sour cream
2 tablespoons butter or margarine
1 tablespoon lemon juice

Oven 350°   **One 10-inch Bundt® Coffeecake**

In large mixer bowl, combine 2 cups flour, yeast, sugar, lemon rind and salt; mix well. In saucepan, heat milk, water and butter until warm (120-130°; butter does not need to melt). Add to flour mixture. Add eggs and vanilla. Blend at low speed until moistened; beat 3 minutes at medium speed. By hand, gradually stir in enough remaining flour to make a soft dough. Knead on floured surface until smooth and elastic, 5 to 8 minutes. Place in greased bowl, turning to grease top. Cover; let rise in warm place until light and doubled, about 45 minutes.

Punch down dough. Divide into pieces the size of a walnut; shape each piece into a smooth ball. Layer balls in greased 12-cup Bundt® pan. Cover; let rise in warm place until double, about 30 minutes. Bake at 350° for 30 to 35 minutes until golden brown. Cool 10 minutes in pan; invert onto serving plate. Drizzle Glaze over coffeecake.

Prepare Glaze: In saucepan, combine all Glaze ingredients. Boil 3 minutes, stirring occasionally. Cool slightly.

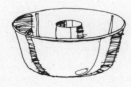

Honey Swirled Coffeecake

A unique but easy shaping makes this tasty coffeecake very attractive.

3½ to 4 cups all-purpose flour
2 packages Red Star Instant Blend Dry Yeast
¼ cup sugar
1 teaspoon salt
½ cup buttermilk
½ cup water
¼ cup shortening
2 eggs
⅓ cup honey
¼ cup chopped walnuts or pecans
¼ cup raisins
1 tablespoon frozen orange juice concentrate, thawed and undiluted
¾ teaspoon cinnamon
1 tablespoon butter or margarine, softened

Oven 350°   **One 10-inch Bundt® Coffeecake**

In large mixer bowl, combine 1½ cups flour, yeast, sugar and salt; mix well. In saucepan, heat buttermilk, water and shortening until warm (120-130°; shortening does not need to melt). Add to flour mixture. Add eggs. Blend at low speed until moistened; beat 3 minutes at medium speed. By hand, gradually stir in enough remaining flour to make a firm dough. Knead on floured surface until smooth and elastic, 5 to 8 minutes. Place in greased bowl, turning to grease top. Cover; let rise in warm place until light and doubled, about 1 hour.

Prepare Filling: Combine honey, nuts, raisins, juice concentrate and cinnamon; mix well. Set aside.

Punch down dough. Divide into 2 parts. On lightly floured surface, roll each half to a 12-inch square; spread with half the softened butter, then half the Filling. Roll up tightly; pinch edges to seal. Cut into 1-inch slices. Place slices horizontally in 4 layers in generously greased Bundt® or tubed cake pan, allowing 6 slices per layer. Alternate position of slices in each layer. Cover; let rise in warm place until double, about 45 minutes. Bake at 350° for 35 to 40 minutes until golden brown. Invert immediately onto cooling rack. Serve warm or cold. Drizzle with powdered sugar Glaze, if desired.

Fruit Filled Lattice Coffeecake

The combination of prune and poppy seed fillings are unique in this light and tender coffeecake. Overlapping strips of dough creating a lattice look are topped with pearl sugar.

5¼ to 5¾ cups all-purpose flour
2 packages Red Star Instant Blend Dry Yeast
½ cup sugar
2 teaspoons salt
1 cup milk
½ cup water
⅓ cup butter or margarine
2 eggs
1 can (12 oz.) prepared poppy seed filling
1 can (12 oz.) prepared prune filling
1 egg white, slightly beaten
1 tablespoon water
Pearl sugar

Oven 350°   **3 Coffeecakes**

In large mixer bowl, combine 2½ cups flour, yeast, sugar and salt; mix well. In saucepan, heat milk, water and butter until warm (120-130°; butter does not need to melt). Add to flour mixture. Add eggs. Blend at low speed until moistened; beat 3 minutes at medium speed. By hand, gradually stir in enough remaining flour to make a soft dough. Knead on floured surface until smooth and elastic, 5 to 8 minutes. Place in greased bowl, turning to grease top. Cover; let rise in warm place until light and doubled, about 1 hour.

Prepare Filling: Combine poppy seed and prune fillings.

Punch down dough. Divide into 3 parts. On lightly floured surface, roll each third to a 12x7-inch rectangle. Spread one third of Filling (about ¾ cup) over the center third of dough. On each long side, cut 1-inch strips, 2 inches long. Starting at one end, fold strips at an angle across Filling, alternating from side to side. Place coffeecake on greased cookie sheet. Combine egg white and water; gently brush top of coffeecake. Sprinkle with pearl sugar. Cover; let rise in warm place until almost doubled, 15 to 20 minutes. Bake at 350° for 20 to 25 minutes until golden brown. Remove from cookie sheets; cool.

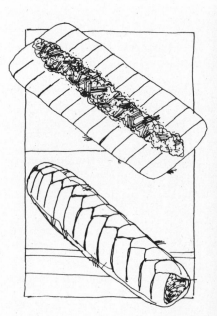

Raised Doughnuts

A bit richer than raised dough-nuts from the bakery, this recipe is worth the time and effort. Fill the Bismarcks with a favorite jam or jelly.

3 to 3½ cups all-purpose flour
1 package Red Star Instant Blend Dry Yeast
¼ cup sugar
1 teaspoon salt
¾ cup milk
¼ cup water
¼ cup shortening
1 egg
Oil

Oil 400°   **24 Doughnuts or Bismarcks**

In large mixer bowl, combine 1½ cups flour, yeast, sugar and salt; mix well. In saucepan, heat milk, water and shortening until warm (120-130°; shortening does not need to melt). Add to flour mixture. Add egg. Blend at low speed until moistened; beat 3 minutes at medium speed. By hand, gradually stir in enough remaining flour to make a soft dough. Knead on floured surface until smooth and elastic, 5 to 8 minutes. Place in greased bowl, turning to grease top. Cover; let rise in warm place until light and doubled, about 1 hour.

Punch down dough. Divide into 2 parts. On lightly floured surface, roll each half to a 12x6-inch rectangle. Cut with 2½-inch doughnut cutter. Place on floured cookie sheets and let rise until double, about 30 minutes. Heat oil to 400°. Fry until golden brown. Drain on absorbent paper towels. Shake in a sack with sugar or Glaze, if desired.

VARIATION: For Bismarcks, cut with 2½-inch cutter. Place on floured cookie sheets and let rise until double, about 30 minutes. Heat oil to 400°. Fry until golden brown. Drain on absorbent paper towels. Cool. Cut 1-inch slit in side of each Bismarck. Spoon ½ teaspoon jam or jelly into slit. Close.

My Notes: _____

_____

_____

_____

_____

_____

_____

_____

_____

_____

_____

_____

_____

_____

Long Johns

A yeast raised doughnut variation. A pleasant blend of nutmeg in the dough and maple flavored frosting make it a winner.

4 to 4½ cups all-purpose flour
2 packages Red Star Instant
    Blend Dry Yeast
¼ cup sugar
1 teaspoon salt
½ teaspoon ground nutmeg
½ cup water
½ cup evaporated milk or
    Half and Half
¼ cup shortening
1 egg
    Oil

Frosting:

½ cup packed brown sugar
¼ cup butter or margarine
¼ teaspoon maple flavoring
2 tablespoons Half and Half
1 cup powdered sugar

Oil 425°   **24 Doughnuts**

In large mixer bowl, combine 1½ cups flour, yeast, sugar, salt and nutmeg; mix well. In saucepan, heat water, milk and shortening until warm (120-130°; shortening does not need to melt). Add to flour mixture. Add egg. Blend at low speed until moistened; beat 3 minutes at medium speed. By hand, gradually stir in enough remaining flour to make a soft dough. Knead on floured surface until smooth and elastic, 5 to 8 minutes. Place in greased bowl, turning to grease top. Cover; let rise in warm place until light and doubled, about 1 hour.

Punch down dough. Divide into 2 parts. Roll or pat each half to a 12x6-inch rectangle. Cut into 1-inch strips. Cover; let rise until double, about 30 minutes. Heat oil to 425°. Fry until golden brown. Drain on absorbent paper towels. Cool; frost.

Prepare Frosting: In small saucepan, combine butter and brown sugar. Boil 2 minutes, stirring constantly. Add maple flavoring and Half and Half. Stir in enough powdered sugar until of spreading consistency.

Deep-Fried Cinnamon Puffs

A perfect recipe for the amateur. In minutes serve warm cinnamon-sugar doughnut puffs.

2½ cups all-purpose flour
1 package Red Star Instant
    Blend Dry Yeast
¼ cup sugar
½ teaspoon salt
½ teaspoon cinnamon
½ cup milk
¼ cup water
¼ cup butter or margarine
2 eggs
    Oil
½ cup sugar
½ teaspoon cinnamon

Oil 400°   **About 42 Puffs**

In large mixer bowl, combine flour, yeast, ¼ cup sugar, salt and ½ teaspoon cinnamon; mix well. In saucepan, heat milk, water and butter until warm (120-130°; butter does not need to melt). Add to flour mixture. Add eggs. Beat at low speed until moistened; beat 3 minutes at medium speed. Cover; let rise in warm oven (Turn oven to lowest setting for 1 minute, turn off.) for 20 minutes.

Heat oil to 400°. Drop batter by tablespoonfuls into oil; fry until golden brown. Drain on absorbent paper towels. Combine ½ cup sugar and ½ teaspoon cinnamon. Roll warm puffs in cinnamon-sugar mixture.

Sour Cream Raised Doughnuts

A rich and delicately flavored dough puffs into delicious raised doughnuts.

3¼ to 3½ cups all-purpose flour
2 packages Red Star Instant Blend Dry Yeast
¼ cup sugar
1 teaspoon salt
⅛ teaspoon cinnamon
⅛ teaspoon ground nutmeg
1 cup sour cream
½ cup water
1 egg
1 teaspoon vanilla
Oil

Oil 400°   **About 30 Raised Doughnuts**

In large mixer bowl, combine 1¼ cups flour, yeast, sugar, salt and spices; mix well. In saucepan, heat sour cream and water until warm (120-130°). Add to flour mixture. Add egg and vanilla. Blend at low speed until moistened; beat 3 minutes at medium speed. By hand, gradually stir in enough remaining flour to form a soft dough. Knead on floured surface until smooth and elastic, 5 to 8 minutes. Place in greased bowl, turning to grease top. Cover; let rise in warm place until light and doubled, about 45 minutes.

Punch down dough. On lightly floured surface, roll to ¼-inch thickness. Cut with 2½-inch doughnut cutter. Place on floured cookie sheets and let rise until double, about 30 minutes. Heat oil to 400°. Fry until golden brown. Drain on absorbent paper towels. Shake in a sack with sugar or Glaze, if desired.

Frosting and Glazes for Doughnuts

Chocolate Frosting for Long Johns

In small saucepan, melt 2 squares (2 oz.) semi-sweet chocolate and 2 tablespoons butter or margarine over low heat. Add 2 cups sifted powdered sugar, 2 tablespoons boiling water and 1 teaspoon vanilla. Blend until smooth. Spread on cooled doughnuts.

To make Chocolate Glaze: Add more boiling water until of dipping consistency. Dip tops of doughnuts in Glaze.

Powdered Sugar Glaze

In small bowl, combine 1 cup sifted powdered sugar, 2 tablespoons boiling water and ¼ teaspoon vanilla. Blend until smooth. Dip warm doughnuts into Glaze. Place on racks for Glaze to harden.

Lemon Glaze

In small bowl, combine 1 cup sifted powdered sugar, 1 tablespoon hot water or milk, 1 teaspoon lemon juice and ½ teaspoon grated lemon rind. Blend until smooth. Dip tops of doughnuts in Glaze.

Tip: After dipping tops of doughnuts in Glaze, dip in finely chopped nuts or shredded coconut.

To coat with sugar: Shake warm doughnuts in a paper bag containing granulated sugar, powdered sugar or a mixture of ½ cup granulated sugar and 1 teaspoon cinnamon.

Chocolate Swirl Coffeecake

For chocolate lovers! A rich chocolate nut filling swirls through a tender sweet dough, topped with a chocolate glaze.

4½ to 5 cups all-purpose flour
2 packages Red Star Instant Blend Dry Yeast
¾ cup sugar
½ teaspoon salt
⅔ cup water
½ cup butter or margarine
⅓ cup Half and Half
2 eggs

Filling:

¾ cup semi-sweet chocolate pieces
¼ cup Half and Half
2 tablespoons sugar
½ teaspoon cinnamon
¼ cup finely chopped nuts

Glaze:

¼ cup semi-sweet chocolate pieces
1 tablespoon butter or margarine
⅓ cup powdered sugar
3 to 4 teaspoons water

Oven 350°   **One 10-inch Coffeecake**

In large mixer bowl, combine 2 cups flour, yeast, sugar and salt; mix well. In saucepan, heat water, butter and Half and Half until warm (120-130°; butter does not need to melt). Add to flour mixture. Add eggs. Blend at low speed until moistened; beat 3 minutes at medium speed. By hand, gradually stir in enough remaining flour to make a soft dough. Knead on floured surface until smooth and elastic, 3 to 5 minutes. Cover; let rise in warm place until light and double, about 1 hour.

Prepare Filling: In small saucepan, combine chocolate pieces, Half and Half, sugar and cinnamon. Cook and stir over low heat until chocolate melts. Stir in nuts. Cool.

On lightly floured surface, roll dough to an 18x10-inch rectangle. Spread with Filling. Starting with longer side, roll up tightly. Pinch edge to seal. Place seam side down in greased 10-inch tubed cake pan. Pinch ends to seal. Cover; let rise in warm place until almost doubled, 30 to 45 minutes. Bake at 350° for 45 to 50 minutes until golden brown. If too dark, cover loosely with foil last 5 to 10 minutes of baking. Cool 15 minutes in pan; remove from pan. Turn right side up. Drizzle with warm Glaze. Cool.

Prepare Glaze: In small saucepan, melt chocolate pieces and butter over low heat. Remove from heat. Stir in powdered sugar and enough water until of Glaze consistency.

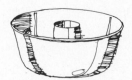

Chocolate Cinnamon Crisps

These large crisp rolls, also known as elephant ears, are sure to be a hit as an after-school snack. They include two childrens' favorite flavors— chocolate and cinnamon. To keep their crispness, store loosely covered or wrap in foil or freezer wrap.

3½ to 4 cups all-purpose flour
1 package Red Star Instant Blend Dry Yeast
⅓ cup nonfat dry milk solids
¼ cup sugar
½ teaspoon salt
1 cup water
¼ cup shortening
2 squares (1 oz. each) semi-sweet chocolate
1 egg
⅓ cup sugar
1 teaspoon cinnamon
2 tablespoons butter or margarine, melted

Topping:

½ cup sugar
¼ cup finely chopped pecans or walnuts
1 teaspoon cinnamon
2 tablespoons butter or margarine, melted

Oven 400°   12 Large Rolls

In large mixer bowl, combine 1½ cups flour, yeast, dry milk, ¼ cup sugar and salt; mix well. In saucepan, heat water, shortening and chocolate pieces until warm (120-130°; shortening and chocolate do not need to melt). Add to flour mixture. Add egg. Blend at low speed until moistened; beat 3 minutes at medium speed. By hand, gradually stir in enough remaining flour to make a soft dough. Knead on floured surface, 3 to 5 minutes. Place in greased bowl, turning to grease top. Cover; let rise in warm place until double, 1 to 1½ hours.

Prepare Filling: Combine ⅓ cup sugar and cinnamon; set aside.

Punch down dough. On lightly floured surface, roll dough to a 12-inch square. Brush dough with butter. Sprinkle Filling over dough. Roll up tightly. Pinch edge to seal. Cut into 12 slices. Place on greased cookie sheets 3 to 4 inches apart. Flatten each slice to a 4-inch diameter. Cover; let rise in warm place until almost double, about 15 minutes.

Prepare Topping: Combine sugar, nuts and cinnamon; set aside.

Cover roll with wax paper. With rolling pin, flatten to ⅛-inch thickness. Brush rolls with butter. Sprinkle Topping over rolls. Cover with wax paper again. With rolling pin, roll Topping into rolls. Bake at 400° for 15 to 18 minutes until crisp around edges. Remove from cookie sheets; cool.

My Notes: _____

_____

_____

_____

_____

_____

_____

_____

_____

Chocolate Yeast Cake

🚂 A moist light chocolate cake topped with a rich brown butter frosting.

**3 cups all-purpose flour
1 package Red Star Instant Blend Dry Yeast
1 cup packed brown sugar
1 cup sugar
1 teaspoon soda
½ teaspoon salt
1¼ cups milk
¼ cup water
1 cup shortening
3 eggs
1 teaspoon vanilla
2 squares (2 oz.) unsweetened chocolate, melted**

Brown Butter Frosting:
**¼ cup butter or margarine
2 cups powdered sugar
½ teaspoon vanilla
3 to 4 tablespoons milk**

Oven 350°   One 13x9-inch cake

In large mixer bowl, combine flour, yeast, brown sugar, sugar, soda and salt; mix well. In saucepan, heat milk and water until warm (120-130°). Add to flour mixture. Add shortening, eggs, vanilla and chocolate. Blend at low speed until moistened; beat 2 minutes at medium speed. Pour into 13x9-inch cake pan which has been greased on the bottom only. Cover; let rise in warm place 30 minutes. Bake at 350° for 45 to 50 minutes until top springs back when touched lightly in center. Cool. Frost with Brown Butter Frosting.

Prepare Frosting: Melt butter until golden brown. Add to powdered sugar and vanilla. Mix in milk until of spreading consistency.

French Mocha Ring

An attractive coffeecake topped with a coffee icing.

**3½ cups all-purpose flour
2 packages Red Star Instant Blend Dry Yeast
½ cup water
½ cup milk
3 eggs
¾ cup sugar
½ cup butter or margarine, softened
1 tablespoon grated orange rind
1 teaspoon salt
1 teaspoon vanilla
1 cup golden raisins
½ cup chopped nuts**

Mocha Glaze:
**1 cup powdered sugar
¼ cup butter or margarine, softened
2 tablespoons strong coffee
1 teaspoon vanilla**

Oven 350°   One 10-inch Bundt® Coffeecake

In large mixer bowl, combine 1 cup flour and yeast; mix well. In saucepan, heat water and milk until warm (120-130°). Add to flour mixture. Blend at low speed until moistened; beat 3 minutes at medium speed. Cover; let rise in warm place for about 30 minutes. Beat in eggs, sugar, butter, orange rind, salt and vanilla until smooth. By hand, gradually stir in raisins and remaining flour to make a soft dough. Sprinkle nuts on bottom of well greased 12-cup Bundt® pan. Spoon dough into pan. Cover; let rise in warm place about 1 hour. Bake at 350° for 40 to 45 minutes until golden brown. Cool 10 minutes in pan; invert onto serving plate. Drizzle with Mocha Glaze when cool.

Prepare Glaze: In small mixer bowl, combine all Glaze ingredients; beat until smooth.

Gay Nineties Self-Frosted Cake

The German chocolate topping bakes right with this coffeecake. It's easy to make with only one rise.

1 bar (4 oz.) German's sweet chocolate
1½ tablespoons water
½ teaspoon vanilla
½ cup sweetened condensed milk
1⅓ cups all-purpose flour
1 package Red Star Instant Blend Dry Yeast
¼ cup sugar
½ teaspoon salt
½ cup water
¼ cup milk
2 tablespoons butter or margarine
1 egg
2 tablespoons butter or margarine, melted
½ cup chopped pecans

Oven 375°   **One 9-inch Coffeecake**

In double boiler, break chocolate into pieces. Add 1½ tablespoons water and vanilla; melt over hot water. Remove from heat; stir in sweetened condensed milk. Line bottom of 9-inch square cake pan with two layers of wax paper; lightly grease. Pour in chocolate mixture.

In small mixer bowl, combine flour, yeast, sugar and salt; mix well. In saucepan, heat ½ cup water, milk and 2 tablespoons butter until warm (120-130°; butter does not need to melt). Add to flour mixture. Add egg. Blend at low speed until moistened; beat 3 minutes at medium speed. Spoon over chocolate mixture. Brush melted butter over top of batter. Let rise in warm place until double, 30 to 45 minutes.

Bake at 375° for 20 to 25 minutes until golden brown. Run knife around edge of cake; invert onto serving plate and lift off pan. Let stand 2 minutes before carefully pulling off wax paper. Sprinkle pecans over top and lightly press into chocolate frosting. Serve warm or cold.

My Notes: _____

_____

_____

_____

_____

_____

_____

_____

_____

_____

_____

_____

_____

_____

_____

_____

Cinnamon Rolls ✓

⬛ 🚂 An old-fashioned cinnamon roll! A combination of brown and granulated sugar in the filling adds more flavor.

3¼ to 3¾ cups all-purpose flour
1 package Red Star Instant
  Blend Dry Yeast
¼ cup sugar
1 teaspoon salt
½ cup milk
½ cup water
¼ cup butter or margarine
1 egg
¼ cup packed brown sugar
2 tablespoons sugar
2 teaspoons cinnamon
2 tablespoons butter, softened

Oven 375°   **12 Rolls**

In large mixer bowl, combine 1½ cups flour, yeast, ¼ cup sugar and salt; mix well. In saucepan, heat milk, water and ¼ cup butter until warm (120-130°; butter does not need to melt). Add to flour mixture. Add egg. Blend at low speed until moistened; beat 3 minutes at medium speed. By hand, gradually stir in enough remaining flour to make a soft dough. Knead on floured surface until smooth and elastic, 5 to 8 minutes. Place in greased bowl, turning to grease top. Cover; let rise in warm place until double, about 1 hour.

Prepare Filling: Combine brown sugar, 2 tablespoon sugar and cinnamon; set aside.

Punch down dough. On lightly floured surface, roll to a 15x12-inch rectangle. Spread with softened butter. Sprinkle Filling over dough. Starting with shorter side, roll up tightly. Pinch edge to seal. Cut into 12 slices. Place in greased 13x9-inch cake pan. Cover; let rise in warm place until almost doubled, about 30 minutes. Bake at 375° for 20 to 25 minutes until golden brown. Remove from pan; cool.

Super Pecan Caramel Rolls ✓

🚂 These rolls are super in flavor and lightness! The sugar-cinnamon filling compliments the glazed caramel topping. For an extra-special occasion, use pecan halves.

6½ to 7 cups all-purpose flour
2 packages Red Star Instant
  Blend Dry Yeast
½ cup sugar
1½ teaspoons salt
1 cup milk
1 cup water
½ cup butter or margarine
2 eggs
¼ cup sugar
¼ cup packed brown sugar
1 tablespoon cinnamon
¼ cup butter or margarine,
  softened

Topping:
⅔ cup butter or margarine
⅔ cup packed brown sugar
6 tablespoons light corn syrup
⅔ cup coarsely chopped pecans

Oven 375°   **24 Rolls**

In large mixer bowl, combine 3 cups flour, yeast, ½ cup sugar and salt; mix well. In saucepan, heat milk, water and butter until warm (120-130°; butter does not need to melt). Add to flour mixture. Add eggs. Blend at low speed until moistened; beat 3 minutes at medium speed. By hand, gradually stir in enough remaining flour to make a soft dough. Knead on floured surface until smooth and elastic, 5 to 8 minutes. Place in greased bowl, turning to grease top. Cover; let rise in warm place until double, about 1 hour.

Prepare Filling: Combine ¼ cup sugar, brown sugar and cinnamon; set aside.

Prepare Topping: In small saucepan, combine butter, brown sugar and corn syrup. Heat and stir until blended. Divide Topping between 2 greased 13x9-inch cake pans. Sprinkle with nuts.

Punch down dough. Divide into 2 parts. On lightly floured surface, roll each half to a 15x12-inch rectangle. Spread with 2 tablespoons softened butter; sprinkle half of Filling over dough. Starting with shorter side, roll up tightly. Pinch edge to seal. Cut into 12 slices. Place on Topping in pan. Cover; let rise in warm place until almost doubled, about 30 minutes. Bake at 375° for 20 to 25 minutes until golden brown. Cover pans with foil; invert onto racks. Cool 1 minute; remove pans. Cool.

Pineapple Pecan Rolls

🎗 A caramel pecan roll flavored with pineapple preserves in the dough and the filling. For variety, use peach or apricot preserves.

3¾ to 4¼ cups all-purpose flour
1 package Red Star Instant Blend Dry Yeast
2 tablespoons sugar
1 teaspoon salt
¾ cup milk
¼ cup water
¼ cup shortening
1 egg
½ cup pineapple preserves
2 tablespoons butter, softened
3 tablespoons pineapple preserves
¼ cup packed brown sugar
⅓ cup chopped pecans

Topping:
½ cup packed brown sugar
⅓ cup butter or margarine
2 tablespoons corn syrup
½ cup chopped pecans

Oven 350°   **18 Rolls**

In large mixer bowl, combine 1½ cups flour, yeast, sugar and salt; mix well. In saucepan, heat milk, water and shortening until warm (120-130°; shortening does not need to melt). Add to flour mixture. Add egg. Blend at low speed until moistened; beat 3 minutes at medium speed. By hand, gradually stir in ½ cup preserves and enough remaining flour to make a soft dough. Knead on floured surface 5 to 8 minutes. Place in greased bowl, turning to grease top. Cover; let rise in warm place until double, about 45 minutes.

Prepare Topping: In small saucepan, combine brown sugar, butter and corn syrup. Heat and stir until blended. Spread Topping in ungreased 13x9-inch cake pan. Sprinkle with nuts.

Punch down dough. On lightly floured surface, roll dough to an 18x9-inch rectangle. Spread with 2 tablespoons butter and 3 tablespoons preserves. Sprinkle ¼ cup brown sugar and ⅓ cup pecans over dough. Starting with longer side, roll up tightly. Pinch edge to seal. Cut into 18 slices. Place on Topping in pan. Cover; let rise in warm place until double, about 45 minutes. Bake at 350° for 25 to 30 minutes. Cover pan with foil; invert onto rack. Cool 1 minute; remove pan. Cool.

Grandma's Cinnamon Rolls

Cinnamon rolls like grandma used to make! Hot coffee and maple flavor give the glaze an extra-special flavor.

5½ to 6 cups all-purpose flour
2 packages Red Star Instant Blend Dry Yeast
½ cup sugar
1½ teaspoons salt
1 cup milk
1 cup water
¼ cup butter or margarine
2 eggs
¾ cup sugar
½ cup chopped nuts
1½ teaspoons cinnamon
⅓ butter or margarine, melted

Glaze:
2 cups powdered sugar
3 tablespoons butter or margarine, melted
½ teaspoon maple flavor
3 to 4 tablespoons hot coffee

Oven 375°   24 Rolls

In large mixer bowl, combine 2 cups flour, yeast, ½ cup sugar and salt; mix well. In saucepan, heat milk, water and butter until warm (120-130°; butter does not need to melt). Add to flour mixture. Add eggs. Blend at low speed until moistened; beat 3 minutes at medium speed. By hand, gradually stir in enough remaining flour to make a soft dough. Knead on floured surface until smooth and elastic, 5 to 8 minutes. Place in greased bowl, turning to grease top. Cover; let rise in warm place until light and doubled, about 1 hour.

Prepare Filling: Combine ¾ cup sugar, nuts and cinnamon; set aside.

Punch down dough. Divide into 2 parts. On lightly floured surface, roll or pat each half to a 12x9-inch rectangle. Brush each part with half of melted butter; sprinkle half of Filling over dough. Starting with shorter side, roll up tightly. Pinch edge to seal. Cut into 12 slices. Place in greased 13x9-inch cake pans. Cover; let rise in warm place until almost doubled, about 30 minutes. Bake at 375° for 20 to 25 minutes until golden brown. Drizzle Glaze over hot rolls; cool.

Prepare Glaze: Combine all Glaze ingredients; blend until smooth.

My Notes: _____

_____

_____

_____

_____

_____

_____

_____

_____

_____

_____

Orange Coconut Rolls

A quick, one rise orange roll topped with almonds and coconut. Part of the orange honey topping is used to brush the dough before sprinkling with coconut.

4½ to 5 cups all-purpose flour
2 packages Red Star Instant Blend Dry Yeast
⅓ **cup sugar**
1 tablespoon grated orange rind
1 teaspoon salt
1 cup milk
½ **cup water**
⅓ **cup butter or margarine**
1 egg

Topping:
1½ cups sugar
⅓ **cup butter**
¼ **cup orange juice**
2 tablespoons honey
1 cup coconut
½ **cup sliced almonds**

Oven 400°   **24 Rolls**

In large mixer bowl, combine 2 cups flour, yeast, sugar, orange rind and salt; mix well. In saucepan, heat milk, water and butter until warm (120-130°; butter does not need to melt). Add to flour mixture. Add egg. Blend at low speed until moistened; beat 3 minutes at medium speed. By hand, gradually stir in enough remaining flour to make a soft dough. Knead on floured surface until smooth and elastic, 5 to 8 minutes. Cover dough; let rest 10 minutes.

Prepare Topping: In small saucepan, combine sugar, butter, orange juice and honey. Heat and stir until blended. Reserve 6 tablespoons. Divide remaining Topping between 2 greased 9-inch square cake pans. Sprinkle ⅓ cup coconut and ¼ cup almonds over Topping. Return reserved 6 tablespoons of Topping to saucepan to keep warm over low heat.

Divide dough into 2 parts. On lightly floured surface, roll or pat each half to a 12x9-inch rectangle. Brush with 3 tablespoons warm Topping. Sprinkle 3 tablespoons coconut over dough. Starting with longer side, roll up tightly. Pinch edges to seal. Cut into 12 slices. Place on Topping in pans. Cover; let rise in warm place until almost doubled, about 30 minutes. Bake at 400° for 15 to 20 minutes until golden brown. Cover pans with foil; invert onto rack. Cool 1 minute; remove pans. Cool.

Easy Orange-Pineapple Rolls

Buttery, pineapple upside down rolls ideal to make and serve warm for a morning coffee.

4½ to 5 cups all-purpose flour
2 packages Red Star Instant Blend Dry Yeast
⅓ cup sugar
1 teaspoon salt
1 tablespoon grated orange rind
1 cup milk
½ cup water
⅓ cup butter or margarine
1 egg
¼ cup butter or margarine
⅔ cup packed brown sugar
¼ cup orange juice
1 can (20¼ oz.) sweetened crushed pineapple, drained

Oven 350°   **24 Rolls**

In large mixer bowl, combine 2 cups flour, yeast, sugar, salt and orange rind; mix well. In saucepan, heat milk, water and ⅓ cup butter until warm (120-130°; butter does not need to melt). Add to flour mixture. Add egg. Blend at low speed until moistened; beat 3 minutes at medium speed. By hand, gradually stir in enough remaining flour to make a soft dough. Knead on floured surface until smooth and elastic, 3 to 5 minutes. Cover; let rise in warm oven (Turn oven to lowest setting for 1 minute, turn off.) for 15 minutes.

Melt ¼ cup butter in 13x9-inch cake pan. Add brown sugar, orange juice and pineapple; mix well. Divide dough into 4 parts. Divide each fourth into 6 pieces. Shape each piece into a smooth ball; place on topping in pan. Cover; place in warm oven to rise for 10 minutes. Bake at 350° for 25 to 30 minutes until golden brown. Cover pan with foil; invert onto rack. Cool 1 minute; remove pan. Serve warm or cold.

Orange Cinnamon Butterflies

These sweet rolls have an unusual shape and combine favorite flavors of orange and raisins.

2½ to 3 cups all-purpose flour
1 package Red Star Instant Blend Dry Yeast
¼ cup sugar
1 teaspoon salt
1 tablespoon grated orange rind
1½ teaspoons cinnamon
¼ cup water
½ cup milk
2 tablespoons butter or margarine
1 egg
½ cup chopped raisins
1 tablespoon butter, melted
3 tablespoons sugar
1 teaspoon cinnamon

Glaze:
½ cup powdered sugar
2 teaspoons orange juice
1 tablespoon butter or margarine, softened

Oven 350°   **18 Rolls**

In large mixer bowl, combine 1½ cups flour, yeast, ¼ cup sugar, salt, orange rind and 1½ teaspoons cinnamon; mix well. In saucepan, heat water, milk and 2 tablespoons butter until warm (120-130°; butter does not need to melt). Add to flour mixture. Add egg. Blend at low speed until moistened; beat 3 minutes at medium speed. By hand, gradually stir in raisins and enough remaining flour to make a soft dough. Knead on floured surface until smooth and elastic, 5 to 8 minutes. Place in greased bowl, turning to grease top. Cover; let rise in warm place until double, about 1½ hours.

Punch down dough. On lightly floured surface, roll to an 18x9-inch rectangle. Brush with 1 tablespoon melted butter. Combine 3 tablespoons sugar and 1 teaspoon cinnamon; sprinkle over dough. Starting with longer side, roll up tightly. Pinch edge to seal. Cut into 1-inch slices. Place slices 1 inch apart on greased cookie sheets. Press center of each slice with the back of a knife to form butterfly shape. Cover; let rise in warm place until double, about 30 minutes. Bake at 350° for 20 to 25 minutes. Remove from cookie sheets. Drizzle Glaze over warm rolls; cool.

Prepare Glaze: Combine all Glaze ingredients; blend until smooth.

Sour Cream Banana Rolls

🌟 A delicious sweet roll for those who truly love bananas. Banana in the roll and in the Glaze gives double flavor.

2¾ to 3¼ cups all-purpose flour
1 package Red Star Instant Blend Dry Yeast
2 tablespoons sugar
1 teaspoon salt
½ cup warm water
2 tablespoons butter or margarine, softened
1 egg
½ cup mashed banana (about 1 banana)
1 tablespoon butter or margarine, softened
2 tablespoons sugar
¼ teaspoon cinnamon
¼ cup chopped walnuts

Glaze:
¼ cup sugar
¼ cup sour cream
2 tablespoons mashed banana
1 tablespoon butter or margarine
1 teaspoon lemon juice
¼ cup chopped walnuts

Oven 375°   **15 Rolls**

In large mixer bowl, combine 1½ cups flour, yeast, 2 tablespoons sugar and salt; mix well. Add warm water (120-130°), 2 tablespoons butter, egg and banana. Blend at low speed until moistened; beat 3 minutes at medium speed. By hand, gradually stir in enough remaining flour to form a soft dough. Knead on floured surface until smooth and elastic, 5 to 8 minutes. Place in greased bowl, turning to grease top. Cover; let rise in warm place until light and doubled, about 1 hour.

Punch down dough. On lightly floured surface, roll to a 15x10-inch rectangle. Spread with 1 tablespoon butter. Combine 2 tablespoons sugar, cinnamon and walnuts; sprinkle over dough. Starting with longer side, roll up tightly. Pinch edge to seal. Cut into 1-inch slices. Place slices in greased 13x9-inch cake pan. Cover; let rise in warm place until double, about 1 hour. Bake at 375° for 20 to 25 minutes until golden brown. Pour Glaze over warm rolls. Sprinkle with nuts.

Prepare Glaze: In saucepan combine all Glaze ingredients, except nuts. Boil 3 minutes, stirring occasionally. Cool slightly.

Pumpkin Orange Spice Rolls

Delicately spiced pumpkin rolls filled with sugar, cinnamon, almonds and raisins. A hint of orange in the dough and glaze.

5¼ to 5¾ cups all-purpose flour
2 packages Red Star Instant Blend Dry Yeast
½ cup sugar
1½ teaspoons salt
1 teaspoon grated orange rind
1 teaspoon cinnamon
½ teaspoon ground cloves
¼ teaspoon ground ginger
⅛ teaspoon ground nutmeg
½ cup water
¼ cup milk
½ cup butter or margarine
1 cup canned pumpkin
2 eggs
6 tablespoons sugar
6 tablespoons packed brown sugar
1 teaspoon cinnamon
¾ cup sliced almonds
¾ cup raisins
3 tablespoons butter or margarine, softened

Glaze:
1 cup powdered sugar
2 to 3 tablespoons orange juice

Oven 350°   30 Rolls

In large mixer bowl, combine 2 cups flour, yeast, ½ cup sugar, salt, orange rind, 1 teaspoon cinnamon, cloves, ginger and nutmeg; mix well. In saucepan, heat water, milk, ½ cup butter and pumpkin until warm (120-130°; butter does not need to melt). Add to flour mixture. Add eggs. Blend at low speed until moistened; beat 3 minutes at medium speed. By hand, gradually stir in enough remaining flour to make a soft dough. Knead on floured surface until smooth and elastic, 5 to 8 minutes. Place in greased bowl, turning to grease top. Cover; let rise in warm place until double, about 1 hour.

Prepare Filling: Combine 6 tablespoons sugar, brown sugar, 1 teaspoon cinnamon, almonds and raisins; set aside.

Punch down dough. Divide into 3 parts. On lightly floured surface, roll or pat each third to a 12x10-inch rectangle. Spread with 1 tablespoon softened butter. Sprinkle one third Filling over dough. Starting with shorter side, roll up tightly. Pinch edge to seal. Cut into 10 slices. Place 1 inch apart on greased cookie sheets. Cover; let rise in warm place until double, 30 to 45 minutes. Bake at 350° for 15 to 20 minutes until golden brown. Remove from cookie sheets. Drizzle Glaze over warm rolls; cool.

Prepare Glaze: Blend Glaze ingredients until smooth.

My Notes: _____

_____

_____

_____

_____

_____

_____

_____

_____

_____

_____

_____

Sugar Layered Rolls

🎖 This unusual recipe makes very delicious cinnamon rolls with a new shaping that is worth the effort.

7½ to 8 cups all-purpose flour
2 packages Red Star Instant Blend Dry Yeast
½ cup sugar
2 teaspoons salt
1⅔ cups milk
½ cup water
½ cup butter or margarine
2 eggs
1½ cups sugar
2 teaspoons cinnamon

Oven 350°   **24 Rolls**

In large mixer bowl, combine 3 cups flour, yeast, ½ cup sugar and salt; mix well. In saucepan, heat milk, water and butter until warm (120-130°; butter does not need to melt). Add to flour mixture. Add eggs. Blend at low speed until moistened; beat 3 minutes at medium speed. By hand, gradually stir in enough remaining flour to make a soft dough. Knead on floured surface until smooth and elastic, 5 to 8 minutes. Place in greased bowl, turning to grease top. Cover; let rise in warm place until light and doubled, about 1 hour.

Punch down dough. Divide into 2 parts. Combine 1½ cups sugar and cinnamon. On lightly floured surface, roll each half to a 16x8-inch rectangle. Sprinkle 2 tablespoons cinnamon-sugar mixture on half of dough lengthwise; fold dough over cinnamon-sugar. Roll dough again into rectangle. Repeat; sprinkling of 2 tablespoons cinnamon-sugar, folding the dough, and rolling out 3 more times. Each time the dough is rolled out, the rectangle will become slightly longer and narrower. The last time the dough is rolled out, roll to a 24x2-inch rectangle.

Cut rectangle in half lengthwise (1-inch wide strips). Cut each strip in 4-inch long pieces. Place 12 pieces, cut-side up, in greased 13x9-inch cake pan (2 rows of 6 pieces). Sprinkle ¼ cup cinnamon-sugar mixture over top of rolls in each pan. Cover; let rise in warm place until double, about 30 minutes. Bake at 350° for 30 to 35 minutes until golden brown. Remove from pans; cool.

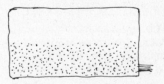

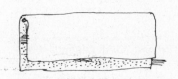

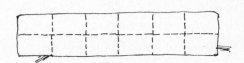

Butterscotch Rum Rolls

An unusual oatmeal roll with a butterscotch flavor. Rum flavoring highlights the filling and glaze.

4 to 4½ cups all-purpose flour
2 packages Red Star Instant
 Blend Dry Yeast
½ cup packed brown sugar
1 teaspoon salt
½ cup water
½ cup milk
½ cup butter or margarine
1 egg
1 teaspoon vanilla
1 cup quick rolled oats
½ cup butterscotch pieces
¼ cup packed brown sugar
2 tablespoons butter, softened
½ teaspoon rum flavoring
½ teaspoon cinnamon

Glaze:

1¼ cups powdered sugar
 ¼ teaspoon rum flavoring
 2 to 3 tablespoons water

Oven 350°   **24 Rolls**

In large mixer bowl, combine 2 cups flour, yeast, ½ cup brown sugar and salt; mix well. In saucepan, heat water, milk and ½ cup butter until warm (120-130°; butter does not need to melt). Add to flour mixture. Add egg and vanilla. Blend at low speed until moistened; beat 3 minutes at medium speed. By hand, gradually stir in oats, butterscotch pieces and enough remaining flour to make a soft dough. Knead on floured surface, 5 to 8 minutes. Place in greased bowl, turning to grease top. Cover; let rise in warm place until double, about 1 hour.

Prepare Filling: Combine ¼ cup brown sugar, softened butter, rum flavoring and cinnamon; set aside.

Punch down dough. Divide into 2 parts. On lightly floured surface, roll each half to a 14x12-inch rectangle. Spread half of Filling over dough. Starting with longer side, roll up tightly. Pinch edge to seal. Cut into 12 slices. Place on greased cookie sheet. Cover; let rise in warm place until almost doubled, 50 to 60 minutes. Bake at 350° for 18 to 20 minutes. Remove from cookie sheets. Drizzle Glaze over warm rolls.

Prepare Glaze: Combine Glaze ingredients; blend until smooth.

Luscious Lemon Brioche Knots

Although the shape is not the same, these rolls are like brioche rolls in that they are very rich and just melt in your mouth! The delicate lemon flavor makes them a year-round favorite.

6 to 6½ cups all-purpose flour
2 packages Red Star Instant
 Blend Dry Yeast
½ cup sugar
1½ teaspoons salt
½ cup milk
½ cup water
⅔ cup butter or margarine
5 eggs
1 teaspoon lemon extract
2 tablespoons butter, melted

Glaze:

½ cup powdered sugar
1 tablespoon hot water
⅛ teaspoon vanilla

Oven 375°   **24 Rolls**

In large mixer bowl, combine 2 cups flour, yeast, sugar and salt; mix well. In saucepan, heat milk, water and butter until warm (120-130°; butter does not need to melt). Add to flour mixture. Add eggs and lemon extract. Blend at low speed until moistened; beat 3 minutes at medium speed. By hand, gradually stir in enough remaining flour to make a very soft dough. Cover; let rise in warm place until light and doubled, about 1 hour.

Stir down dough. Cover; let rise again until doubled, about 30 minutes. Divide dough into 2 parts. On lightly floured surface, roll each half to a 14x12-inch rectangle. Brush with 1 tablespoon melted butter. Starting with shorter side, fold one third of dough over center third of dough; fold other one third of dough over the 2 layers. Cut into 1-inch strips. Twist ends of each piece in opposite directions. Stretch piece slightly; tie in a loose knot. Tuck ends under to make a rosette. Place on greased cookie sheets. Cover; refrigerate 4 hours. Remove from refrigerator; let set at room temperature for 15 minutes. Bake at 375° for 20 to 25 minutes until golden brown. Cool slightly. Brush rolls with Glaze.

Prepare Glaze: Blend Glaze ingredients until smooth.

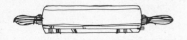

Spicy Buns

A delicious yeast biscuit developed from a Scottish recipe.

3½ to 4 cups all-purpose flour
2 packages Red Star Instant
  Blend Dry Yeast
⅓ cup sugar
1 teaspoon salt
½ teaspoon cinnamon
½ teaspoon ground nutmeg
¼ teaspoon mace
⅛ teaspoon ground ginger
⅔ cup water
½ cup butter or margarine
3 eggs
1 cup raisins or currants
1 egg white, slightly beaten

Oven 350°   **24 to 30 Buns**

In large mixer bowl, combine 2 cups flour, yeast, sugar, salt and spices; mix well. In saucepan, heat water and butter until warm (120-130°; butter does not need to melt). Add to flour mixture. Add eggs. Blend at low speed until moistened; beat 3 minutes at medium speed. By hand, gradually stir in raisins and enough remaining flour to make a soft dough. Knead on floured surface, 5 to 8 minutes. Place in greased bowl, turning to grease top. Cover; let rise in warm place until double, about 1 hour.

Punch down dough. On lightly floured surface, roll dough to ½-inch thickness. Cut out buns with a 1½ to 2-inch round cutter. Place on greased cookie sheets, 1½ inches apart. Cover; let rise in warm place until double, about 30 minutes. Gently brush tops with egg white. Bake at 350° for 10 to 12 minutes until golden brown. Remove from cookie sheets. Drizzle with powdered sugar Glaze, if desired. Serve warm.

Star-Light Delights

A different variation of a butterhorn roll—coiled rolls have an apricot filling.

1 package Red Star Instant Blend Dry Yeast
½ cup warm water
2 cups all-purpose flour
1½ tablespoons sugar
¼ teaspoon salt
½ cup cold butter or margarine, cut into pieces
¼ cup milk
2 egg yolks
⅔ cup apricot preserves
⅓ cup fine dry bread crumbs

Glaze:
½ cup powdered sugar
1 tablespoon milk
¼ teaspoon vanilla

Oven 350°   **12 Rolls**

Dissolve yeast in warm water (110-115°); let stand 5 minutes. In medium mixer bowl, combine flour, sugar, salt and butter. With mixer or pastry blender, combine until the consistency of cornmeal. By hand, gradually stir in milk, egg yolks and yeast to make a soft dough. Cover bowl with plastic wrap and foil; refrigerate several hours.

Prepare Filling: Combine preserves and bread crumbs. Let stand while dough is chilling.

On lightly floured surface, roll dough to a 12-inch rope. Cut into 12 pieces. Roll or pat each piece to an 8x3-inch rectangle. Spoon Filling down the center of each piece. Fold sides of dough to center; pinch edge and ends to seal. On greased cookie sheets, coil each strip loosely. Flatten to a 3 to 4-inch diameter. Cover; let rise in warm place until almost doubled, about 1 hour. Bake at 350° for 15 to 18 minutes. Remove from cookie sheets. Drizzle Glaze over warm rolls.

Prepare Glaze: Combine all Glaze ingredients; blend until smooth.

Sweet Whirls

A coiled sweet roll filled with either your favorite jam or preserves or a cream cheese filling. These rolls are easy to make. Refrigerate the dough, then shape; let rise 10 to 15 minutes and bake. Serve warm from the oven or reheat in oven or microwave.

4½ to 5 cups all-purpose flour
2 packages Red Star Instant Blend Dry Yeast
½ cup sugar
2 teaspoons salt
¾ cup milk
½ cup water
½ cup butter or margarine
2 eggs
1½ cups jam or preserves or Cream Cheese Filling

Danish Yeast Rolls

Oven 375°	24 Rolls

In large mixer bowl, combine 2 cups flour, yeast, sugar and salt; mix well. In saucepan, heat milk, water and butter until warm (120-130°; butter does not need to melt). Add to flour mixture. Add eggs. Blend at low speed until moistened; beat 3 minutes at medium speed. By hand, gradually stir in enough remaining flour to make a soft dough. Cover bowl with plastic wrap and foil; refrigerate 4 hours.

Punch down dough. Divide into 4 parts. Refrigerate remaining dough until ready to shape. Divide each fourth into 6 pieces. On lightly floured surface, roll each piece to a 16-inch rope. On greased cookie sheet, coil rope loosely, tucking end under; place rolls about 2 inches apart. Cover; let rise at room temperature until almost doubled, 10 to 15 minutes. Make a deep indentation in the center of each roll; fill with 1 tablespoon jam or Cream Cheese Filling. Bake at 375° for 15 to 17 minutes until golden brown. Remove from cookie sheets. Serve warm.

Cream Cheese Filling:

1 package (8 oz.) cream cheese, softened
1 egg
¼ cup sugar
2 tablespoons all-purpose flour
½ teaspoon lemon juice
½ teaspoon vanilla
½ teaspoon almond extract

**1½ Cups
Filling for 24 Rolls**

In small mixer bowl, combine all ingredients; blend until smooth.

☽ ✹ Typically Danish, rich and flaky! Milk and egg yolks add richness, butter the flakiness. A sprinkling of sugar and coconut adds a sweet touch.

2 packages Red Star Instant Blend Dry Yeast
½ cup warm water
4 cups all-purpose flour
⅓ cup sugar
2 teaspoons salt
1 cup cold butter or margarine, cut into pieces
1 cup milk
4 egg yolks
2 tablespoons butter or margarine, melted
¼ cup sugar
½ cup flaked coconut

Oven 350°	28 Rolls

Dissolve yeast in warm water (110-115°); let stand 5 minutes. In large mixer bowl, combine flour, ⅓ cup sugar, salt and butter. With mixer or pastry blender, combine until the consistency of cornmeal. By hand, gradually stir in milk, egg yolks and yeast to make a soft dough. Cover bowl with plastic wrap and foil; refrigerate overnight.

Punch down dough. Divide into 2 parts. Refrigerate half of dough until ready to use. On lightly floured pastry cloth or surface, roll each half to a 14x9-inch rectangle. Brush with half of melted butter. Sprinkle 2 tablespoons sugar and ¼ cup of coconut over dough. Starting with longer side, roll up tightly. Pinch edge to seal. Cut into 14 slices. Place on greased cookie sheets. Cover; let rise in warm place until almost doubled, about 30 minutes. Bake at 350° for 20 to 22 minutes until golden brown. Remove from cookie sheets. Drizzle powdered sugar Glaze over warm rolls, if desired. Serve warm.

Speedy Orange Rolls

Serve these quick-to-make orange rolls warm from the oven for breakfast or brunch. The same powdered sugar-orange mixture is used for the filling and the frosting.

1 package Red Star Instant Blend Dry Yeast
¾ cup warm water
2 to 2¼ cups all-purpose flour
2 tablespoons sugar
2 tablespoons butter or margarine, softened
1 teaspoon salt
1 egg

Filling and Frosting:
1 cup powdered sugar
1 teaspoon orange rind
1 tablespoon butter or margarine, softened
4 teaspoons orange juice

Oven 400°   **14 Rolls**

In large bowl, dissolve yeast in warm water (110-115°); let stand 5 minutes. Add 1 cup flour, sugar, butter, salt and egg; stir until smooth. Gradually stir in enough remaining flour to make a soft dough. Knead on floured surface for 1 minute. Cover; let rest 15 minutes.

Prepare Filling and Frosting: Blend all Filling ingredients until smooth.

On lightly floured surface, roll or pat dough to a 14x7-inch rectangle. Spread half of Filling and Frosting over dough. Starting with longer side, roll up tightly. Pinch edge to seal. Cut into 14 slices. Place in greased 9-inch layer cake pan (10 around outer edge, 4 in center). Cover; let rise in warm place until double, about 30 minutes. Bake at 400° for 20 to 25 minutes until golden brown. Cover pan with wax paper; invert onto rack. Cool 1 minute; remove pan. Let rolls stand about 3 minutes for filling to "set." Cover rolls with wax paper; turn right side up. Place on rack. Spread remaining Filling and Frosting on rolls. Serve warm.

Maltese Sesame Rings

A recipe from the island of Malta known as "Kaghak," with a unique blend of cloves, orange and anise.

3½ to 4 cups all-purpose flour
2 packages Red Star Instant Blend Dry Yeast
½ cup sugar
1 teaspoon salt
¼ teaspoon ground cloves
1 tablespoon grated orange rind
1 cup water
2 tablespoons butter or margarine
2 teaspoons vanilla
2 teaspoons anise extract
1 egg white, slightly beaten
¼ teaspoon water
¼ cup sesame seeds

Speedy One Hour Sticky Buns

Oven 400°　　　　**16 Rolls**

In large mixer bowl, combine 1½ cups flour, yeast, sugar, salt, cloves and orange rind; mix well. In saucepan, heat water and butter until warm (120-130°; butter does not need to melt). Add to flour mixture. Blend at low speed until moistened; beat 3 minutes at medium speed. By hand, gradually stir in vanilla, anise extract and enough remaining flour to make a soft dough. Knead on floured surface until smooth and elastic, 5 to 8 minutes. Place in greased bowl, turning to grease top. Cover; let rise in warm place about 45 minutes.

Punch down dough. Divide into 4 parts. Divide each fourth into 4 pieces. On lightly floured surface, roll each piece to an 8-inch rope. Form a ring and pinch ends together. Place each ring 1½ inches apart on greased cookie sheet. Combine egg and water; brush ring. Sprinkle with about ½ teaspoon sesame seed. Let rise uncovered in warm place for about 30 minutes. Bake at 400° for 12 to 15 minutes until golden brown. Remove from cookie sheets; cool.

⏱ A quick and easy recipe that produces all the favorite flavors of caramel rolls in an hour.

4½ to 5 cups all-purpose flour
2 packages Red Star Instant Blend Dry Yeast
⅓ cup sugar
1 teaspoon salt
1 cup milk
½ cup water
⅓ cup butter or margarine
1 egg

Topping:
⅓ cup butter
⅓ cup packed brown sugar
½ cup chopped nuts

Oven 400°　　　　**24 Rolls**

In large mixer bowl, combine 2 cups flour, yeast, sugar and salt; mix well. In saucepan, heat milk, water and butter until warm (120-130°; butter does not need to melt). Add to flour mixture. Add egg. Blend at low speed until moistened; beat 3 minutes at medium speed. By hand, gradually stir in enough remaining flour to make a soft dough. Knead on floured surface until smooth and elastic, 3 to 5 minutes. Place in greased bowl, turning to grease top. Cover; let rise in warm oven (Turn oven to lowest setting for one minute, turn off.) for 15 minutes.

Prepare Topping: In small saucepan, combine butter and brown sugar; heat and stir until blended. Add nuts. Spoon Topping into greased muffin pan cups.

Divide dough into 4 parts. Divide each fourth into 6 pieces. Shape each piece into a smooth ball; place in cups. Cover; let rise in warm oven 10 minutes. Bake at 400° for 10 minutes. Cover pans with foil and invert onto rack. Cool 1 minute; remove pans. Cool.

GLAZES

Some of the coffeecakes and sweet rolls in this book include a recipe for a glaze or frosting; other recipes suggest glazing if desired. A glaze is appropriate on many yeast breads and does add a special touch. Coffeecakes and sweet rolls look more "finished" with a shiny glaze—a simple way to make them look picture-perfect.

A glaze can add flavor and color. Choose a flavor for the glaze which compliments the flavor in the bread. Tinted or white glazes add eye appeal as well as flavor. Adding yellow food color to a lemon or orange glaze visually emphasizes the flavor. The *Sweetheart Coffeecake* could be glazed with an almond glaze tinted pink.

Glazes and frostings usually both start with powdered sugar. Frostings are thicker and more creamy and are spread on the baked product; frostings are also called Icings. Glazes are thin enough to drizzle over the tops of coffeecakes or rolls; the breads should be cool enough so that the glaze holds its shape.

A basic glaze can be used on many coffeecakes or rolls. Vary the glaze by adding other ingredients as listed below.

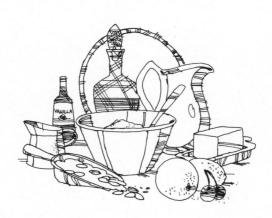

Basic Glaze

1 cup sifted powdered sugar
1 teaspoon softened butter or
margarine
1 to 2 tablespoons hot water
or milk

In small bowl, blend ingredients
until smooth.

Flavor Variations:

Vanilla

Add ½ teaspoon vanilla.

Almond

Add ¼ teaspoon almond extract.

Rum

Add ¼ teaspoon rum flavor OR
1 teaspoon rum.

Brandy

Add ¼ teaspoon brandy flavor
OR 1 teaspoon brandy.

Maple

Add ¼ teaspoon maple flavor.

Pineapple

Substitute pineapple juice for the
water or milk.

Coffee

Substitute hot coffee for the water
or milk.

Orange or Lemon

Add 1 teaspoon grated orange or
lemon rind, if desired; substitute orange or lemon juice for the
water or milk.

Mocha

Add 1 tablespoon cocoa and ½
teaspoon instant coffee.

Cherry

Substitute maraschino cherry
juice for the water or milk.

Cider

Add ¼ teaspoon cinnamon and
dash of nutmeg; substitute apple
cider for the water or milk.

Chocolate

Add 1 tablespoon cocoa OR
½ square (½ oz.) unsweetened chocolate, melted.

Cream Cheese

Beat 1 pkg. (3 oz.) cream cheese,
softened, with ½ teaspoon vanilla,
½ teaspoon lemon juice and ½
teaspoon almond extract until
smooth. Add 1 cup sifted powdered sugar and 1 to 2 teaspoons
milk. Blend until smooth.

Brown Butter

In small saucepan, melt 2 tablespoons butter until golden brown.
Add 1 cup sifted powdered sugar,
½ teaspoon vanilla and 1 to 2 teaspoons water or milk. Blend
until smooth. Glaze thickens as it
cools. Add more water or milk
if necessary to obtain desired
consistency.

Holiday & ethnic

Potica

Christmas Morning Rolls

Guglehupf

breads

Sweetheart Coffeecake

Kolache

125

HOLIDAY AND ETHNIC BREADS

Almost every country claims a bread that is all its own. In this chapter, we've grouped holiday and ethnic breads because most holiday breads are ethnic in origin. America is a great blending of nationalities, so all of these breads have come together for our enjoyment. Since we've included as many ethnic breads as possible, we hope you'll think of this chapter as a little bread tour of the world. Each recipe will indicate the country of its origin and a pronunciation guide for difficult names.

You'll find many breads for two of our major holidays—Easter and Christmas—most of them ethnic in origin, but they don't need to be limited to holidays. Many of these breads are so beautiful they could be used as a centerpiece before serving.

Recipes such as *Brioche, Grecian Sweet Braid* and *Finnish Pulla* are very versatile and would be ideal for any occasion such as a special brunch, bridal shower, anniversary or graduation party. Celebrate Valentine's Day, an anniversary, Mother's Day, Father's Day or just surprise your loved one with *Sweetheart Coffeecake.*

Most of these breads are made from rich, sweet doughs, but two that could accompany any meal are *Hungarian White Bread* and *Armenian Cracker Bread.*

Remember that special breads baked in your kitchen make beautiful gifts for family and friends.

Armenian Cracker Bread

A whole wheat version of the popular crisp Middle Eastern flatbread. Store loosely covered to retain crispness. Break off pieces for munching out of hand. Top with cheese and melt in the oven for a delicious snack.

1¾ to 2¼ cups all-purpose flour
1 package Red Star Instant Blend Dry Yeast
1½ teaspoons salt
1 cup water
¼ cup butter or margarine
1 tablespoon honey
1 cup whole wheat flour
3 to 4 tablespoons sesame seeds

Oven 350°   **8 Thin Breads**

In large mixer bowl, combine 1 cup all-purpose flour, yeast and salt; mix well. In saucepan, heat water, butter and honey until warm (120-130°; butter does not need to melt). Add to flour mixture. Blend at low speed until moistened; beat 3 minutes at medium speed. By hand, gradually stir in whole wheat flour and enough remaining all-purpose flour to make a firm dough. Knead on floured surface, 5 to 8 minutes. Place in greased bowl, turning to grease top. Cover; let rise in warm place until double, about 1 hour.

Punch down dough. Divide into 8 parts. Sprinkle lightly floured surface with sesame seed. Roll and stretch each part to an 8-inch circle. Place on ungreased cookie sheet. Bake at 350° for 15 to 17 minutes until light brown with darker brown spots. Remove from cookie sheets; cool.

Christmas Morning Rolls

A soft and delicious bread. Different with honey and candied fruit and glazed warm with honey for that Christmas sparkle. Do them ahead for Christmas morning, warm them and brush with honey just before serving.

4 to 4½ cups all-purpose flour
2 packages Red Star Instant Blend Dry Yeast
1 teaspoon salt
½ cup water
½ cup milk
½ cup butter or margarine
⅓ cup honey
1 egg
1 cup chopped candied fruit
3 tablespoons honey

Oven 350°   **24 Rolls**

In large mixer bowl, combine 2 cups flour, yeast and salt; mix well. In saucepan, heat water, milk, butter and ⅓ cup honey until warm (120-130°; butter does not need to melt). Add to flour mixture. Add egg. Beat at low speed until moistened; beat 3 minutes at medium speed. By hand, gradually stir in fruit and enough remaining flour to make a soft dough. Knead on floured surface until smooth and elastic, 5 to 8 minutes. Place in greased bowl, turning to grease top. Cover; let rise in warm place until light and double, about 1½ hours.

Divide dough into 4 parts. Divide each fourth into 6 pieces. On lightly floured surface, roll each piece into an 8-inch rope. On greased cookie sheets, coil each rope loosely; pinching ends. Flatten to a 3 to 4-inch diameter. Cover; let rise in warm place until double, about 45 minutes. Bake at 350° for 15 to 18 minutes. Remove from cookie sheets. Brush with honey while warm.

TIP: If preparing rolls ahead and freezing, wait to brush with honey after reheating just before serving.

Baba Au Rhum

This French yeast bread, adapted from the Austrian Guglehupf, was originally named Ali Baba, after a hero in the book, "The Thousand and One Nights." An attractive no-knead coffee bread made extra moist with rum syrup spooned over. Could also be served for dessert.

3 cups all-purpose flour
2 packages Red Star Instant
  Blend Dry Yeast
¼ cup sugar
½ teaspoon salt
¼ cup milk
½ cup water
½ cup butter or margarine
4 eggs
1 cup raisins or currants
½ teaspoon almond extract
¼ cup slivered almonds

Rum Syrup:

1 cup water
½ cup water
½ cup rum

Oven 350°   One 10-inch
               Bundt® Coffeecake

In large mixer bowl, combine 1½ cups flour, yeast, sugar and salt; mix well. In saucepan, heat milk, water and butter until warm (120-130°; butter does not need to melt). Add to flour mixture. Add eggs. Blend at low speed until moistened; beat 3 minutes at medium speed. By hand, gradually stir in raisins, almond extract and remaining flour to make a stiff batter. Cover; let rise in warm place until double, about 45 minutes.

Stir down batter. Generously grease 12-cup Bundt® pan; sprinkle bottom of pan with almonds. Spoon batter into pan. Cover; let rise in warm place until double, about 30 minutes. Bake at 350° for 40 to 45 minutes until deep golden brown. Cool 10 minutes in pan; invert onto serving plate.

Prepare Syrup: In small saucepan, bring sugar and water to a boil, stirring occasionally. Remove from heat; add rum. Spoon over warm bread. (For more penetration, puncture bread with fork.) Serve warm or cold.

Bohemian Christmas Braid

An attractive bread to decorate your holiday table, filled with raisins, nuts and a hint of lemon.

4½ to 5 cups all-purpose flour
2 packages Red Star Instant
  Blend Dry Yeast
½ cup sugar
2 teaspoons salt
2 teaspoons grated lemon rind
⅛ teaspoon mace
¾ cup milk
½ cup water
¼ cup shortening
2 eggs
½ to 1 cup raisins
½ cup chopped almonds

Oven 350°   1 Large Braid

In large mixer bowl, combine 2 cups flour, yeast, sugar, salt, lemon rind and mace; mix well. In saucepan, heat milk, water and shortening until warm (120-130°; shortening does not need to melt). Add to flour mixture. Add eggs. Blend at low speed until moistened; beat 3 minutes at medium speed. By hand, gradually stir in raisins, almonds and enough remaining flour to make a firm dough. Knead on floured surface until smooth and elastic, 5 to 8 minutes. Place in greased bowl, turning to grease top. Cover; let rise in warm place until double, about 1½ hours.

Punch down dough. Divide into 4 parts. On lightly floured surface, roll each of three parts to a 14-inch rope. On greased large cookie sheet, loosely braid from center to ends. Seal ends and tuck under loaf. With very sharp knife, make a ½-inch deep slash down the center of braid. Divide remaining dough into 3 pieces. Roll each piece to a 12-inch rope. Braid loosely from center to ends. Seal ends. Place in cut on larger braid. Press in lightly.

Cover; let rise in warm place until double, about 45 minutes. Bake at 350° for 40 to 45 minutes until golden brown. Remove from cookie sheet; cool. Drizzle with powdered sugar Glaze and Garnish with candied cherries and almonds, if desired.

Brioche (bree-ohsh)

) These elegant top knotted rolls are said to have originated in the district of Brie in France. Light and delicate, they are rich in butter and eggs. Serve warm from the oven for breakfast as the French do—or reheat before serving. These rolls are also delicious to serve for a brunch or luncheon. As the dough is very soft, chilling makes it firm enough to handle.

3½ cups all-purpose flour
1 package Red Star Instant Blend Dry Yeast
⅓ cup sugar
1 teaspoon salt
½ cup water
½ cup butter, softened
4 eggs
1 egg yolk
1 tablespoon milk

Oven 350°   **18 Rolls**

In large bowl, combine 2 cups flour, yeast, sugar and salt; mix well. In saucepan, heat water and butter until warm (120-130°). Add to flour mixture. Add eggs. By hand, stir until smooth. Gradually stir in remaining flour to make a very soft dough. Cover bowl with plastic wrap and foil; refrigerate 6 to 12 hours.

Punch down dough. Divide into 3 parts. Refrigerate two thirds of dough until ready to shape. Divide each third into 6 pieces. Cut off one-fourth of the dough from each piece. On well-floured surface, shape each large and small piece into a smooth ball. Place large balls into greased muffin pan cups or individual brioche pans. Press ball to fill cup; make a deep indentation in the center of dough. Press small ball into indentation. Cover; let rise in warm place until double, about 30 minutes. Combine egg yolk and milk; gently brush tops of rolls. Bake at 350° for 15 to 20 minutes until golden brown. Remove from muffin pan cups; cool.

My Notes: _____
_____
_____
_____
_____
_____
_____
_____

Cranberry Nut Bread

Cranberries and spices add the festive touch, oatmeal adds the moistness. Especially good toasted.

5½ to 6 cups all-purpose flour
2 packages Red Star Instant Blend Dry Yeast
1 cup rolled oats
½ cup sugar
1½ teaspoons salt
1 teaspoon ground allspice
1 teaspoon mace
1½ cups milk
½ cup water
¼ cup shortening
1 egg
2 cups coarsely chopped cranberries
½ cup raisins
½ cup chopped nuts

Oven 350°   **2 Loaves**

In large mixer bowl, combine 2½ cups flour, yeast, rolled oats, sugar, salt, allspice and mace; mix well. In saucepan, heat milk, water and shortening until warm (120-130°; shortening does not need to melt). Add to flour mixture. Add egg. Blend at low speed until moistened; beat 3 minutes at medium speed. By hand, gradually stir in cranberries, raisins, nuts and enough remaining flour to make a firm dough. Knead on floured surface 5 to 8 minutes. Place in greased bowl, turning to grease top. Cover; let rise in warm place until double, about 1 hour.

Punch down dough, divide into 2 parts. On lightly floured surface, roll or pat each half to a 14x7-inch rectangle. Starting with shorter side, roll up tightly, pressing dough into roll with each turn. Pinch edges and ends to seal. Place in greased 9x5-inch bread pans. Cover; let rise in warm place until double, about 1 hour. Bake at 350° for 40 to 45 minutes until deep golden brown. Remove from pans; cool.

TIP: Cranberries can be easily chopped in a blender or food processor.

Finnish Easter Bread

A wonderful "old world" bread—rich enough to serve as dessert. To serve as dessert, spoon Cream Cheese Topping over slices of warm or cold bread.

2½ to 3 cups all-purpose flour
2 packages Red Star Instant Blend Dry Yeast
2 tablespoons sugar
¼ teaspoon salt
½ cup warm water
¼ cup butter or margarine, softened
3 eggs, separated
1 teaspoon grated lemon rind
1 teaspoon grated orange rind
½ cup raisins
½ cup finely chopped almonds
¼ cup sugar

Cream Cheese Topping:
1 package (8 oz.) cream cheese, softened
2 tablespoons milk
½ teaspoon vanilla
⅛ teaspoon salt
2 cups powdered sugar

Holiday Batter Bread

Oven 350°   **1 Loaf**

In large mixer bowl, combine 1 cup flour, yeast, 2 tablespoons sugar and salt; mix well. Add water (120-130°), butter and egg yolks. Blend at low speed until moistened; beat 3 minutes at medium speed. By hand, stir in rind, raisins and almonds. In small mixer bowl, beat egg whites until stiff; gradually add ¼ cup sugar. Fold into flour mixture. Gradually stir in enough remaining flour to make a soft dough. Knead on floured surface, 3 to 5 minutes. Place in greased bowl, turning to grease top. Cover; let rise in warm place until almost double, about 1½ hours.

Punch down dough. On lightly floured surface, roll or pat to a 14x7-inch rectangle. Starting with shorter side, roll up tightly, pressing dough into roll with each turn. Pinch edge and ends to seal. Place in greased 9x5-inch bread pan. With very sharp knife, make a lengthwise slash, ¼ inch deep, down center of loaf. Cover; let rise in warm place until double, about 45 minutes. Bake at 350° for 35 to 40 minutes until golden brown. Remove from pan. Serve warm or cold.

Prepare Cream Cheese Topping: In small mixer bowl, blend cream cheese, milk, vanilla and salt; beat until smooth. Gradually add powdered sugar; beat until fluffy.

Festive fruit bread—especially attractive in "can pans"!

3 cups all-purpose flour
2 packages Red Star Instant Blend Dry Yeast
¼ cup sugar
1 teaspoon salt
¾ cup milk
½ cup water
2 tablespoons shortening
½ cup chopped candied fruits
½ cup chopped walnuts or pecans

Oven 375°   **1 Large Loaf or 4 Small Loaves**

In large mixer bowl, combine 1½ cups flour, yeast, sugar and salt; mix well. In saucepan, heat milk, water and shortening until warm (120-130°; shortening does not need to melt). Add to flour mixture. Blend at low speed until moistened; beat 3 minutes at medium speed. By hand, gradually stir in candied fruits, nuts, and remaining flour to make a stiff batter. Cover; let rise in warm place until light and double, about 30 minutes.

Stir down batter. Spoon into one greased 9x5-inch bread pan or four greased 20-ounce cans. Cover; let rise in warm place until double, about 30 minutes. Bake at 375° for 30 to 35 minutes until golden brown. Remove from pan or cans; cool. Drizzle with favorite powdered sugar Glaze and Garnish with additional fruit and nuts, if desired.

Hot Cross Buns

A traditional Easter bread, these buns date back to early England where they were originally served on Good Friday. Enjoy the homemade goodness of these delicately spiced buns flavored with currants and lemon rind.

3¼ to 3¾ cups all-purpose flour
1 package Red Star Instant Blend Dry Yeast
¼ cup sugar
1 teaspoon cinnamon
1 teaspoon salt
¼ teaspoon ground cloves
¼ teaspoon ground nutmeg
½ cup milk
½ cup water
¼ cup butter or margarine
1 egg
¾ cup currants
2 tablespoons grated lemon rind
1 egg yolk
1 tablespoon water

Frosting:
1 cup powdered sugar
½ teaspoon vanilla
3 to 4 teaspoons water

Oven 375°   **18 Buns**

In large mixer bowl, combine 1½ cups flour, yeast, sugar, cinnamon, salt, cloves and nutmeg; mix well. In saucepan, heat milk, water and butter until warm (120-130°; butter does not need to melt). Add to flour mixture. Add egg. Blend at low speed until moistened; beat 3 minutes at medium speed. By hand, gradually stir in currants, lemon rind and enough remaining flour to make a soft dough. Knead on floured surface until smooth and elastic, 5 to 8 minutes. Place in greased bowl, turning to grease top. Cover; let rise in warm place until double, about 1 hour.

Punch down dough. Divide into 3 parts. Divide each third into 6 pieces. Shape each piece into a smooth ball. Place on greased cookie sheet, sides touching. Cover; let rise in warm place until double, about 30 minutes. Combine egg yolk and water; brush buns. Bake at 375° for 10 to 12 minutes until golden brown. Remove from cookie sheet; cool. Frost.

Prepare Frosting: Combine powdered sugar, vanilla and enough water to make a thick frosting.

Eggnog Stollen (shtawl-len)

A traditional Christmas bread with dry egg custard mix and nutmeg for the eggnog taste, and golden raisins and pecans sprinkled through. We think this will become one of your favorite Christmas breads.

4 to 4½ cups all-purpose flour
2 packages Red Star Instant Blend Dry Yeast
1 package (3 oz.) egg custard mix
1 teaspoon salt
½ teaspoon ground nutmeg
½ cup milk
½ cup water
⅓ cup butter or margarine
2 eggs
1 cup golden raisins
½ cup chopped pecans
2 tablespoons butter, softened
Powdered sugar

Oven 350° **2 Stollen**

In large mixer bowl, combine 1¾ cups flour, yeast, custard mix, salt and nutmeg; mix well. In saucepan, heat milk, water and butter until warm (120-130°; butter does not need to melt). Add to flour mixture. Add eggs. Blend at low speed until moistened; beat 3 minutes at medium speed. By hand, gradually stir in raisins, pecans and enough remaining flour to make a soft dough. Knead on floured surface until smooth and elastic, 5 to 8 minutes. Place in greased bowl, turning to grease top. Cover; let rise in warm place until light and doubled, about 1½ hours.

Punch down dough. Divide into 2 parts. On lightly floured surface, roll or pat each half to a 14x8-inch oval; spread with softened butter. Fold in half lengthwise and curve into a crescent. Press folded edge firmly to partially seal. Place on greased cookie sheet. Cover; let rise in warm place until double, about 30 minutes. Bake at 350° for 20 to 25 minutes until golden brown. Remove from cookie sheet; cool. Sift powdered sugar over tops.

Stollen (shtawl-len)

A German Christmas bread shaped as a folded oval—like a giant Parker House roll. Traditionally, it is full of candied fruit and nuts for the holidays.

4 to 4½ cups all-purpose flour
2 packages Red Star Instant Blend Dry Yeast
⅓ cup sugar
1 teaspoon salt
½ cup milk
½ cup water
⅓ cup butter or margarine
2 eggs
½ cup chopped candied cherries
¼ cup chopped citron
¼ cup raisins
¼ cup chopped walnuts or pecans
1 tablespoon butter or margarine, softened

Oven 350° **2 Small Stollen**

In large mixer bowl, combine 2 cups flour, yeast, sugar and salt; mix well. In saucepan, heat milk, water and butter until warm (120-130°; butter does not need to melt). Add to flour mixture. Add eggs. Blend at low speed until moistened; beat 3 minutes at medium speed. By hand, gradually stir in cherries, citron, raisins, walnuts and enough remaining flour to make a firm dough. Knead on floured surface until smooth and elastic, 5 to 8 minutes. Place in greased bowl, turning to grease top. Cover; let rise in warm place until light and double, about 1 hour.

Punch down dough. Divide into 2 parts. On lightly floured surface, roll or pat each half to a 14x8-inch oval. Spread with softened butter. Fold in half lengthwise and curve into a crescent. Press folded edge firmly to partially seal. Place on greased cookie sheet. Cover; let rise in warm place until double, about 30 minutes. Bake at 350° for 25 to 30 minutes until golden brown. Remove from cookie sheets; cool. Drizzle with your favorite powdered sugar Glaze and Garnish with additional cherries and nuts, if desired.

Grecian Sweet Braid

A hint of anise and a topping of sesame seed and almonds adds a festive touch to this Greek braid. It is almost as tender and rich as cake and keeps well.

5¼ to 5¾ cups all-purpose flour
  2 packages Red Star Instant Blend Dry Yeast
  ½ cup sugar
  1 teaspoon salt
  1 teaspoon anise seeds, ground
  ½ cup milk
  ½ cup water
  ½ cup butter or margarine
  3 eggs
  2 tablespoons chopped almonds
  2 tablespoons sesame seeds
  2 tablespoons sugar
  1 egg, slightly beaten
  1 tablespoon milk

Oven 350°   **2 Braids**

In large mixer bowl, combine 1¾ cups flour, yeast, ½ cup sugar, salt and anise seed; mix well. In saucepan, heat ½ cup milk, water and butter until warm (120-130°; butter does not need to melt). Add to flour mixture. Add eggs. Blend at low speed until moistened; beat 3 minutes at medium speed. By hand, gradually stir in enough remaining flour to make a soft dough. Knead on floured surface until smooth and elastic, 5 to 8 minutes. Place in greased bowl, turning to grease top. Cover; let rise in warm place until light and doubled, about 1 hour.

Prepare Topping: Combine almonds, sesame seed and 2 tablespoons sugar; set aside.

Punch down dough. Divide into 2 parts. Divide each half into 3 pieces. Roll each piece to a 15-inch rope. On greased large cookie sheet, loosely braid 3 ropes from center to ends. Seal ends and tuck under loaf. Cover; let rise in warm place until double, about 30 minutes. Combine egg and milk; gently brush braids. Sprinkle Topping over dough. Bake at 350° for 25 to 30 minutes until golden brown. Remove from cookie sheets; cool.

Finnish Pulla

A must on the Finnish coffee table! So light and delicious, the cardamom flavored slices are traditionally served unbuttered.

20 cardamom pods (1 teaspoon, crushed) or 1 teaspoon ground cardamom
6½ to 7 cups all-purpose flour
  2 packages Red Star Instant Blend Dry Yeast
  ⅔ cup sugar
  2 teaspoons salt
1½ cups milk
  ½ cup water
  ½ cup butter
  2 eggs
  1 egg, slightly beaten
  3 tablespoons sliced almonds or
  3 tablespoons pearl sugar

Oven 350°   **3 Braids**

Crack open cardamom pods; grind or pound seeds. In large mixer bowl, combine 2½ cups flour, yeast, sugar, salt and cardamom; mix well. In saucepan, heat milk, water and butter until warm (120-130°; butter does not need to melt). Add to flour mixture. Add 2 eggs. Blend at low speed until moistened; beat 3 minutes at medium speed. By hand, gradually stir in enough remaining flour to make a soft dough. Knead on floured surface until smooth and elastic, 5 to 8 minutes. Place in greased bowl, turning to grease top. Cover; let rise in warm place until light and doubled, about 1 hour.

Punch down dough. Divide into 3 parts. Divide each third into 3 pieces. On lightly floured surface, roll each piece to a 16-inch rope. On greased cookie sheet, loosely braid 3 ropes from center to ends. Pinch ends and tuck under to seal. Cover; let rise in warm place until almost doubled, 20 to 30 minutes. Gently brush braids with egg; sprinkle with almonds or pearl sugar. Bake at 350° for 20 to 25 minutes until golden brown. Remove from cookie sheets; cool.

Perfect for gift-giving—these pretty braids will flatter any hostess.

5½ to 6 cups all-purpose flour
2 packages Red Star Instant Blend Dry Yeast
½ cup sugar
1 teaspoon salt
1 teaspoon ground cardamom
1 cup milk
½ cup water
⅓ cup butter
2 eggs
½ cup candied cherries, chopped
½ cup mixed candied fruit

Oven 350°   **2 Wreaths**

In large mixer bowl, combine 2½ cups flour, yeast, sugar, salt and cardamom; mix well. In saucepan, heat milk, water and butter until warm (120-130°; butter does not need to melt). Add to flour mixture. Add eggs. Blend at low speed until moistened; beat 3 minutes at medium speed. By hand, gradually stir in fruits and enough remaining flour to make a soft dough. Knead on floured surface until smooth and elastic, 5 to 8 minutes. Place in greased bowl, turning to grease top. Cover; let rise in warm place until double, about 1 hour.

Punch down dough. Divide into 2 parts. Divide each half into 3 pieces. On lightly floured surface, roll each piece to a 24-inch rope. On greased cookie sheet, loosely braid 3 ropes from center to ends. Form into a circle; pinch ends to seal. Cover; let rise in warm place until almost doubled, 20 to 30 minutes. Bake at 350° for 20 to 25 minutes until golden brown. Remove from cookie sheets; cool. Drizzle with powdered sugar Glaze and Garnish with candied cherries, if desired.

Holiday Kringle

The famous rich Danish Kringle! We have included two versions for making the dough — one that can be made more quickly by using the mixer method, and the other is the traditional method of dissolving the yeast separately and cutting the butter into the flour mixture. The traditional method makes a more flaky dough. Choose from two holiday fillings and a Butter Pecan Filling, which is a year-round favorite.

2 cups all-purpose flour
1 package Red Star Instant
  Blend Dry Yeast
2 tablespoons sugar
½ teaspoon salt
½ cup milk
¼ cup water
½ cup butter or margarine
1 egg yolk
1 egg white, slightly beaten

Oven 400°   **2 Kringles**

In large mixer bowl, combine 1 cup flour, yeast, sugar and salt; mix well. In saucepan, heat milk, water and butter until warm (120-130°; butter does not need to melt). Add to flour mixture. Add egg yolk. Blend at low speed until moistened; beat 3 minutes at medium speed. By hand, gradually stir in remaining flour to make a soft dough. Cover with plastic wrap and foil; refrigerate 2 to 24 hours.

Prepare desired Filling.

Punch down dough. Divide into 2 parts. On lightly floured surface, roll each half to an 18x6-inch rectangle. For Cranberry or Candied Fruit Filling: brush 3-inch center strip with egg white; sprinkle half of Filling over dough brushed with egg white. For Butter Pecan Filling: omit brushing with egg white. Spread 3-inch center strip with half of sugar-butter mixture; sprinkle half of nuts over dough which has been spread with the sugar-butter mixture. Fold one long side of dough over Filling, then fold the other side, overlapping dough about 1½ inches. Pinch edge and ends to seal. Place seam side down on greased cookie sheet. Form into a horseshoe shape or a circle; pinch ends together to make the circle. Cover; let rise in warm place until light and puffy, 15 to 20 minutes. Bake at 400° for 15 to 20 minutes until golden brown. Remove from cookie sheets; cool. Sift powdered sugar over top before serving, if desired.

Traditional Method

1 package Red Star Instant
  Blend Dry Yeast
¼ cup warm water
2 cups all-purpose flour
1½ tablespoons sugar
½ teaspoon salt
½ cup butter or margarine,
  cut into pieces
½ cup milk
1 egg yolk
1 egg white, slightly beaten

Oven 400°   2 Kringles

In small bowl, dissolve yeast in warm water (110-115°); let stand 5 minutes. In large bowl, combine flour, sugar and salt; mix well. With pastry blender, cut in butter until the consistency of cornmeal. In saucepan, heat milk to lukewarm; blend in egg yolk. Pour into bowl with yeast. Gradually add milk-yeast mixture to flour mixture; blend lightly with a fork until all particles are moistened. Cover with plastic wrap and foil; refrigerate 2 to 24 hours.

Prepare desired Filling.

Punch down dough. Divide into 2 parts. On lightly floured surface, roll each half to an 18x6-inch rectangle. For Cranberry or Candied Fruit Filling: brush 3-inch center strip with egg white; sprinkle half of Filling over dough brushed with egg white. For Butter Pecan Filling: omit brushing with egg white. Spread 3-inch center strip with half of sugar-butter mixture; sprinkle half of nuts over dough which has been spread with the sugar-butter mixture. Fold one long side of dough over Filling, then fold the other side, overlapping dough about 1½ inches. Pinch edge and ends to seal. Place seam side down on greased cookie sheet. Form into a horseshoe shape or in a circle; pinch ends together to make the circle. Cover; let rise in warm place until light and puffy, 15 to 20 minutes. Bake at 400° for 15 to 20 minutes until golden brown. Remove from cookie sheets; cool. Sift powdered sugar over top before serving, if desired.

Cranberry Filling

1 cup chopped cranberries
½ cup chopped nuts
½ cup raisins, chopped
½ cup sugar
½ teaspoon ground mace
½ teaspoon ground allspice

In small bowl, combine all ingredients. Filling for two Kringles.

Candied Fruit Filling

1 cup chopped red and green candied cherries or candied fruit
1 cup chopped nuts

In small bowl, combine fruit and nuts. Filling for two Kringles.

Butter Pecan Filling

½ cup packed brown sugar
¼ cup butter or margarine
½ teaspoon cinnamon
1 cup chopped pecans

In small mixer bowl, cream sugar, butter and cinnamon until fluffy. Set creamed mixture and pecans aside. Filling for two Kringles.

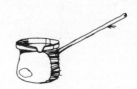

Hungarian White Bread

This light bread features anise seed and fennel seed, traditional spices of Hungary.

6 to 6½ cups all-purpose flour
2 packages Red Star Instant Blend Dry Yeast
3 tablespoons sugar
2 teaspoons salt
¼ to ½ teaspoon anise seeds
½ teaspoon fennel seeds
2 cups water
2 tablespoons oil
Butter

Oven 375°   2 Round Loaves

In large mixer bowl, combine 2 cups flour, yeast, sugar, salt, anise seed and fennel seed; mix well. In saucepan, heat water and oil until warm (120-130°). Add to flour mixture. Blend at low speed until moistened; beat 3 minutes at medium speed. By hand, gradually stir in enough remaining flour to make a soft dough. Knead on floured surface until smooth and elastic, 5 to 8 minutes. Place in greased bowl, turning to grease top. Cover; let rise in warm place until double, about 1 hour.

Punch down dough. Divide into 2 parts. On lightly floured surface, shape each half into a round loaf. Place on greased large cookie sheet. With very sharp knife, make 3 slashes across the top of each loaf. Cover; let rise in warm place until almost doubled, about 30 minutes. Bake at 375° for 25 to 30 minutes until golden brown. Remove from cookie sheets; brush with butter. Cool.

Julekage (yoo-leh-kay-yeh)

A popular Norwegian bread for the Christmas holidays. Serve this traditional rich sweet fruit bread frosted or unfrosted.

6 to 6½ cups all-purpose flour
2 packages Red Star Instant Blend Dry Yeast
¾ cup sugar
1 teaspoon salt
1 teaspoon ground cardamom
1½ cups milk
½ cup water
¼ cup shortening
1 egg
1 cup raisins
½ cup finely chopped citron or candied peel
Butter

Oven 350°   2 Round Loaves

In large mixer bowl, combine 3 cups flour, yeast, sugar, salt and cardamom; mix well. In saucepan, heat milk, water and shortening until warm (120-130°; shortening does not need to melt). Add to flour mixture. Add egg. Blend at low speed until moistened; beat 3 minutes at medium speed. By hand, gradually stir in raisins, citron and enough remaining flour to make a firm dough. Knead on floured surface until smooth and elastic, 5 to 8 minutes. Place in greased bowl, turning to grease top. Cover; let rise in warm place until double, 1 to 1½ hours.

Punch down dough. Divide into 2 parts. Shape each half into a round loaf. Place on greased cookie sheets. Cover; let rise in warm place until double, about 45 minutes. Bake at 350° for 45 to 50 minutes until golden brown. If too dark, cover loosely with foil last 5 to 10 minutes of baking. Remove from cookie sheet. Brush with butter; cool. Drizzle with powdered sugar Glaze, if desired.

Kulich
(koo-lickh)

A traditional Russian Easter bread—tall and round, decorated with a powdered sugar glaze and candies. The loaves are baked in coffee cans to get the unique shape.

5¾ to 6¼ cups all-purpose flour
  2 packages Red Star Instant
    Blend Dry Yeast
  ½ cup sugar
  2 teaspoons salt
1¼ cups buttermilk
  ½ cup water
  ½ cup butter or margarine
  1 teaspoon vanilla
  2 eggs
  ⅔ cup raisins
  ⅔ cup chopped almonds

Oven 375°   **3 Loaves**

In large mixer bowl, combine 2½ cups flour, yeast, sugar and salt; mix well. In saucepan, heat buttermilk, water and butter until warm (120-130°; butter does not need to melt). Add to flour mixture. Add vanilla and eggs. Blend at low speed until moistened; beat 3 minutes at medium speed. By hand, gradually stir in raisins, chopped almonds and enough remaining flour to make a soft dough. Knead on floured surface until smooth and elastic, 5 to 8 minutes.

Divide dough into 3 parts. Shape each third into a smooth ball. Place in greased 1-lb. coffee cans. Cover; let rise in warm place until double, about 1 hour. Bake at 375° for 30 to 35 minutes until golden brown. If too dark, cover loosely with foil last 5 to 10 minutes of baking. Remove from cans; cool. Drizzle with powdered sugar Glaze and Garnish with candies, if desired.

Norwegian
Almond Muffins

A perfect Scandinavian "coffee bread." When warm, the flavor of almonds and cardamom compliments a cup of good coffee.

2 cups all-purpose flour
1 package Red Star Instant
  Blend Dry Yeast
¼ cup sugar
1 teaspoon salt
1 teaspoon ground cardamom
½ cup water
¼ cup milk
¼ cup butter or margarine
¼ cup almond paste
1 egg
½ teaspoon almond extract
⅛ cup cherry preserves
1 tablespoon sugar
¼ cup chopped almonds

Oven 350°   **12 Muffins**

In small mixer bowl, combine 1 cup flour, yeast, sugar, salt and cardamom; mix well. In saucepan, heat water, milk, butter and almond paste until warm (120-130°; butter does not need to melt). Add to flour mixture. Add egg and almond extract. Blend at low speed until moistened; beat 3 minutes at medium speed. By hand, gradually stir in remaining flour to make a soft batter.

Spoon batter into well-greased muffin pan cups. Cover; let rise in warm place 1 to 1½ hours. Before baking, make an indentation in the top of each muffin; spoon about ½ teaspoon cherry preserves into each. Combine 1 tablespoon sugar and almonds; sprinkle over muffins. Bake at 350° for 20 to 25 minutes until golden brown. Cool in pans 3 minutes; remove from pans. Serve warm or cold.

Kolache
(koh-lotch-eh)

A luscious fruit-filled roll native to Czechoslovakia. These are an old world favorite with a new shape and four delicious flavor variations. Traditional prune and apricot fillings have a new twist. Cream cheese and cranberry orange fillings will become favorites.

3 to 3½ cups all-purpose flour
1 package Red Star Instant Blend Dry Yeast
¼ cup sugar
1 teaspoon salt
¾ cup milk
¼ cup water
¼ cup butter or margarine
1 egg
1 tablespoon butter

Oven 375°   **18 Kolaches**

In large mixer bowl, combine 1½ cups flour, yeast, sugar and salt; mix well. In saucepan, heat milk, water and butter until warm (120-130°; butter does not need to melt). Add to flour mixture. Add egg. Blend at low speed until moistened; beat 3 minutes at medium speed. By hand, gradually stir in enough remaining flour to make a soft dough. Knead on floured surface until smooth and elastic, about 3 minutes. Place in greased bowl, turning to grease top. Cover; let rise in warm place until light and doubled, about 1 hour.

Punch down dough. Divide into 2 parts. On lightly floured surface, roll each half to a 12-inch square. Cut each square into nine 4-inch squares. Spoon Filling in center of each square. Fold one corner to the center. Moisten corner of dough with water. Fold opposite corner over and seal. Place on greased cookie sheets. Cover; let rise in warm place until almost double, about 15 minutes. Brush with butter. Bake at 375° for 12 to 15 minutes until golden brown. Remove from cookie sheets. Serve warm or cold.

Prune Orange Filling

1 cup prunes (¾ cup puréed)
⅓ cup orange marmalade
⅓ cup chopped nuts
1 teaspoon lemon juice

Filling for 18 Kolaches
Makes 1½ cups

In small saucepan, cover prunes with water. Cook until tender. Remove seeds. Purée prunes in blender. In small bowl, blend prunes, marmalade and nuts. Add lemon juice. Use about 1 tablespoon Filling for each Kolache.

Cream Cheese Raisin Filling

2 packages (3 oz. each) cream cheese, softened
2 tablespoons sugar
1 egg
1 teaspoon lemon rind
¼ cup golden raisins, chopped

Filling for 18 Kolaches
Makes 1 cup

In small mixer bowl, combine cream cheese, sugar, egg and lemon rind. Beat until smooth and creamy. Stir in raisins. Use about 2 teaspoons Filling for each Kolache.

Apricot Almond Filling

1 cup dried apricot halves
⅓ cup packed brown sugar
⅓ cup chopped almonds
½ teaspoon cinnamon

Filling for 18 Kolaches
Makes 1¼ cups

In small saucepan, cover apricot halves with water. Cook over medium heat until water is absorbed and apricots are tender. Purée apricots in blender. In small bowl, combine apricots, brown sugar, almonds and cinnamon. Use about 2½ teaspoons Filling for each Kolache.

Cranberry Orange Filling

⅔ cup canned (ready-to-serve) cranberry orange relish
⅓ cup vanilla wafer crumbs
¼ cup chopped nuts
Dash cinnamon

Filling for 18 Kolaches
Makes 1 cup

In small bowl, combine ingredients. Use about 2 teaspoons Filling for each Kolache.

My Notes: _____

_____

_____

_____

_____

_____

Panettone
(pah-neh-toh-nee)

An Italian bread—anise, candied fruit and raisins are a delicious flavor blend in this sweet bread. Flavor improves when stored tightly wrapped.

4¼ to 4¾ cups all-purpose flour
2 packages Red Star Instant Blend Dry Yeast
½ cup sugar
1½ teaspoons anise seeds
1 teaspoon salt
½ cup milk
½ cup water
¼ cup butter or margarine
¾ teaspoon vanilla
2 eggs
½ cup raisins
½ cup chopped nuts
⅓ cup chopped candied fruit
1 egg, slightly beaten
1 tablespoon water

Oven 375°   2 Round Loaves

In large mixer bowl, combine 1¾ cups flour, yeast, sugar, anise seed and salt; mix well. In saucepan, heat milk, water and butter until warm (120-130°; butter does not need to melt). Add to flour mixture. Add vanilla and eggs. Blend at low speed until moistened; beat 3 minutes at medium speed. By hand, gradually stir in raisins, nuts, candied fruit and enough remaining flour to make a soft dough. Knead on floured surface, 5 to 8 minutes. Place in greased bowl, turning to grease top. Cover; let rise in warm place until double, about 1 hour.

Punch down dough. Divide into 2 parts. On lightly floured surface, shape each half into a round loaf. Place on greased large cookie sheet. Cover; let rise in warm place until double, 30 to 45 minutes. Combine egg and water; brush loaves. Bake at 375° for 30 to 35 minutes until golden brown. Remove from cookie sheet; cool.

Pineapple Bars – Mazurek

The Polish use many different fruit fillings with this rich yeast crust. This mellow pineapple filling is a favorite.

1 package Red Star Instant Blend Dry Yeast
¼ cup warm water
2½ cups all-purpose flour
1 tablespoon sugar
¼ teaspoon salt
¾ cup butter or margarine, cut in pieces
2 tablespoons milk
4 egg yolks

Filling:

½ cup sugar
3 tablespoons cornstarch
½ cup water
1 egg
1 can (20 oz.) crushed pineapple in heavy syrup
2 tablespoons lemon juice

Powdered sugar

Oven 375°   **Thirty 2½x2-inch Bars**

In small bowl, dissolve yeast in warm water (110-115°); let stand 5 minutes. In large bowl, combine flour, sugar and salt; mix well. With pastry blender, cut in butter until the consistency of cornmeal. Add dissolved yeast, milk and egg yolks to flour mixture. Mix lightly with fork. Shape dough into a ball. Cover bowl with plastic wrap and foil. Refrigerate 4 to 24 hours. (This is a rich dough; it rises very little.)

Prepare Filling: In saucepan, combine sugar, cornstarch, water, egg and crushed pineapple. Cook and stir over low heat until thickened. Add lemon juice; cool. Set aside.

Divide dough into 2 parts. On lightly floured surface, roll each half to a 16x12-inch rectangle. Roll rectangle onto rolling pin to transfer to greased 15x10-inch jelly roll pan. Press gently into pan. Spread cooled Filling over dough. Place remaining 16x12-inch rectangle over Filling. Fold top edges over bottom; seal. Cover; let rise in warm place for 45 minutes. Bake at 375° for 20 to 25 minutes until golden brown. Remove from pan; cool. Sift powdered sugar over top; cut into bars.

Pineapple Brazilian Easter Bread

This coffee bread is rich with Brazil nuts, pineapple, lemon rind and candied orange peel. A mark of the season—a dough cross— is baked atop each loaf.

1 can (20 oz.) crushed pineapple, in its own juice
6½ to 7 cups all-purpose flour
2 packages Red Star Instant Blend Dry Yeast
½ cup sugar
1 tablespoon grated lemon rind
1 teaspoon salt
1 teaspoon cinnamon
½ cup milk
½ cup water
½ cup butter or margarine
4 eggs
½ cup chopped Brazil nuts
2 tablespoons chopped candied orange peel

Trinity Easter Bread

A traditional Greek bread which according to tradition represents the Trinity. At Eastertime, each person is served a slice from each of the breads.

4 to 4½ cups all-purpose flour
2 packages Red Star Instant Blend Dry Yeast
⅓ cup sugar
½ teaspoon salt
½ cup water
⅓ cup milk
⅓ cup butter or margarine
2 eggs
2 tablespoons grated lemon rind
1 jar (10 oz.) maraschino cherries, well drained and halved, (about 1 cup)

Oven 375°   **One Large Coffee Bread**

In large mixer bowl, combine 1½ cups flour, yeast, sugar and salt; mix well. In saucepan, heat water, milk and butter until warm (120-130°; butter does not need to melt). Add to flour mixture. Add eggs. Blend at low speed until moistened; beat 3 minutes at medium speed. By hand, gradually stir in lemon rind, cherries and enough remaining flour to make a firm dough. Knead on floured surface until smooth and elastic, 5 to 8 minutes. Place in greased bowl, turning to grease top. Cover; let rise in warm place until light and doubled, about 1 hour.

Punch down dough. Divide into 3 parts. Shape each third into a smooth ball. On greased large cookie sheet, place 3 balls together in shape of a cloverleaf. Cover; let rise until double, about 45 minutes. Bake at 375° for 30 to 35 minutes. If too dark, cover loosely with foil last 5 to 10 minutes of baking. Remove from cookie sheet; cool. Drizzle with powdered sugar Glaze and Garnish with chopped nuts and cherries, if desired.

Oven 350°   **2 Round Loaves**

Drain pineapple very well, pressing out all liquid. In large mixer bowl, combine 2 cups flour, yeast, sugar, lemon rind, salt and cinnamon; mix well. In saucepan, heat milk, water and butter until warm (120-130°; butter does not need to melt). Add to flour mixture. Add eggs. Blend at low speed until moistened; beat 3 minutes at medium speed. By hand, gradually stir in well drained pineapple, nuts, candied orange peel and enough remaining flour to make a soft dough. Knead on floured surface 5 to 8 minutes. Place in greased bowl, turning to grease top. Cover; let rise in warm place until double, about 1 hour.

Punch down dough. Divide into 2 parts. Cut off a piece of dough about the size of an egg from each half. Shape each half into a round loaf. Place on greased cookie sheet. Divide each small piece in half. Roll each half into a rope the length of the diameter of the loaves. Place 2 ropes on each loaf in the shape of a cross. Cover; let rise in warm place until almost doubled, 30 to 45 minutes. Bake at 350° for 35 to 40 minutes until golden brown. Remove from cookie sheets; cool.

143

Potica (poh-tee-kah)

A rich, very special recipe popular in many southern European countries. This version captures the wonderful flavors and tender dough in an easy-to-form snail shape.

2½ to 2¾ cups all-purpose flour
1 package Red Star Instant
  Blend Dry Yeast
2 tablespoons sugar
½ teaspoon salt
½ cup sour cream
¼ cup water
¼ cup butter or margarine
1 egg

Filling:

2 cups ground walnuts
¼ cup sugar
¼ cup packed brown sugar
2 tablespoons Half and Half
¼ cup butter or margarine,
  softened
1 egg
½ teaspoon vanilla

Oven 350°   **2 Coffeecakes**

In large mixer bowl, combine 1 cup flour, yeast, sugar and salt; mix well. In saucepan, heat sour cream, water and butter until warm (120-130°; butter does not need to melt). Add to flour mixture. Add egg. Blend at low speed until moistened; beat 3 minutes at medium speed. By hand, gradually stir in enough remaining flour to make a soft dough. Knead on floured surface until smooth and elastic, 5 to 8 minutes. Place in greased bowl, turning to grease top. Cover; let rise in warm place until double, about 1 hour.

Prepare Filling: In small bowl, combine walnuts, sugar, brown sugar, Half and Half, butter, egg and vanilla; mix well.

Punch down dough. Divide into 2 parts. On lightly floured surface, roll each half to a 15x12-inch rectangle. Spread with half of Filling. Starting with longer side, roll up dough tightly. Pinch edge and ends to seal. Place roll seam-side down on greased cookie sheet. Loosely coil dough to form a snail shape. Cover; let rise in warm place until double, about 30 minutes. Bake at 350° for 20 to 25 minutes until golden brown. Remove from cookie sheet; cool. Sift powdered sugar over top, if desired.

Raisin Filled Holiday Ring

A festive holiday bread. A "crown" of dough tops a raisin-filled ring.

3 to 3½ cups all-purpose flour
2 packages Red Star Instant
  Blend Dry Yeast
1 teaspoon salt
⅓ cup sugar
¼ cup milk
½ cup water
¼ cup butter or margarine
1 egg
2 tablespoons butter, softened
⅓ cup sugar
1 tablespoon orange rind
1 teaspoon cinnamon
½ cup chopped almonds
1 cup raisins

Glaze:

1 cup powdered sugar
2 tablespoons butter or
  margarine, softened
½ teaspoon vanilla
1 to 2 tablespoons milk

Swiss Christmas Bread

Oven 375°   **1 Coffeecake**

In large mixer bowl, combine 1½ cups flour, yeast, salt and ⅓ cup sugar; mix well. In saucepan, heat milk, water and ¼ cup butter until warm (120-130°; butter does not need to melt). Add to flour mixture. Add egg. Blend at low speed until moistened; beat 3 minutes at medium speed. By hand, gradually stir in enough remaining flour to make a firm dough. Knead on floured surface until smooth and elastic, 5 to 8 minutes. Place in greased bowl, turning to grease top. Cover; let rise in warm place until light and doubled, about 1 hour.

Prepare Filling: Combine 2 tablespoons butter, ⅓ cup sugar, orange rind, cinnamon and almonds. Mix well.

Punch down dough. Divide dough into 3 parts. Set aside one third of dough. On lightly floured surface, roll remaining two thirds of dough to a 14x10-inch rectangle. Spread Filling over dough; sprinkle with raisins. Starting with longer side, roll up tightly. Pinch edge to seal. Form ring; pinch ends to seal. Place ring seam side down on greased cookie sheet. Brush top of dough with water. Roll reserved dough to an 18-inch rope. Place on top of filled ring, sealing ends together. With scissors, make 12 cuts in the rope; alternate the cut petals, bringing one to center and next to outside of ring. Cover; let rise in warm place until double, about 30 minutes. Bake at 375° for 25 to 30 minutes until golden brown. Remove from cookie sheet; cool.

Prepare Glaze: Combine Glaze ingredients; blend until smooth. Glaze cooled coffeecake. Garnish with colored sugar and chopped almonds, if desired.

Spices blend with candied fruit and nuts in an easy round holiday loaf.

4½ to 5 cups all-purpose flour
2 packages Red Star Instant Blend Dry Yeast
¼ cup sugar
1 teaspoon salt
½ teaspoon nutmeg
½ teaspoon mace
¼ teaspoon ground cloves
1 cup milk
½ cup water
¼ cup butter or margarine
1 egg
½ cup raisins
½ cup halved candied cherries
¼ cup chopped citron
¼ cup chopped nuts
1 tablespoon butter or margarine, melted
1 teaspoon sugar

Oven 375°   **1 Loaf**

In large mixer bowl, combine 2 cups flour, yeast, sugar, salt, nutmeg, mace and cloves; mix well. In saucepan, heat milk, water and butter until warm (120-130°; butter does not need to melt). Add to flour mixture. Add egg. Blend at low speed until moistened; beat 3 minutes at medium speed. By hand, gradually stir in raisins, cherries, citron, nuts and enough remaining flour to make a firm dough. Knead on floured surface until smooth and elastic, 5 to 8 minutes. Place in greased bowl, turning to grease top. Cover; let rise in warm place until double, about 1 hour.

Punch down dough. Shape into round loaf. Place in greased 2-quart casserole. Cover; let rise in warm place until double, about 1 hour. Brush top of loaf with melted butter; sprinkle lightly with sugar. Bake at 375° for 40 to 45 minutes until deep golden brown. If too dark, cover loosely with foil last 5 to 10 minutes of baking. Remove from casserole; cool.

Queen Ann Holiday Brunch Cake

★ This beautiful coffeecake has a "jeweled" look. Because of all the fruit, it takes a long time to rise, but it's well worth the wait!

4 to 4½ cups all-purpose flour
2 packages Red Star Instant Blend Dry Yeast
¾ cup sugar
1 teaspoon salt
¼ teaspoon ground ginger
1 tablespoon grated orange rind
½ cup milk
½ cup water
1 cup butter or margarine
4 eggs
1 package (3 oz.) cream cheese, softened
½ cup currants
½ cup chopped candied mixed fruit
¼ cup chopped candied cherries
½ cup flaked coconut
½ cup sliced almonds

Orange Glaze:

1 cup powdered sugar
1 teaspoon grated orange rind
¼ teaspoon vanilla
5 to 6 teaspoons orange juice

Oven 375°   One 10-inch
                   Bundt® Coffeecake

In large mixer bowl, combine 1½ cups flour, yeast, sugar, salt, ginger and orange rind; mix well. In saucepan, heat milk, water and butter until warm (120-130°; butter does not need to melt). Add to flour mixture. Add eggs and cream cheese. Blend at low speed until moistened; beat 3 minutes at medium speed. By hand, gradually stir in fruit, coconut and enough remaining flour to make a stiff batter.

Arrange almond slices on bottom of well-greased and floured 12-cup Bundt® pan. Spoon batter into pan. Cover; let rise in warm place until double, about 1½ hours. Bake at 375° for 35 to 40 minutes until golden brown. Cool 15 minutes in pan; remove from pan. Drizzle Glaze over cooled cake.

Prepare Glaze: Combine Glaze ingredients; blend until smooth.

Spicy Fruit-Filled Christmas Buns

☽ ★ A special Christmas treat! Spicy fruit-filled diamonds glazed with Vanilla Sugar.

4 cups all-purpose flour
2 packages Red Star Instant Blend Dry Yeast
½ cup sugar
2 teaspoons salt
¾ cup milk
½ cup water
½ cup butter or margarine
1 egg
1 cup chopped walnuts
½ cup currants
½ cup chopped dried apricots
¼ cup honey
¼ teaspoon cinnamon
¼ teaspoon ground allspice
¼ teaspoon ground ginger
Vanilla Sugar*

Oven 400°   32 Buns

In large mixer bowl, combine 2 cups flour, yeast, sugar and salt; mix well. In saucepan, heat milk, water and butter until warm (120-130°; butter does not need to melt). Add to flour mixture. Add egg. Blend at low speed until moistened; beat 3 minutes at medium speed. By hand, gradually stir in remaining flour to make a soft dough. Cover bowl with plastic wrap and foil; refrigerate several hours.

Prepare Filling: Combine nuts, currants and apricots. Blend honey and spices together; combine with fruit mixture. Cover; refrigerate until dough is ready.

Punch down dough. Divide into 2 parts. On lightly floured surface, roll each half to a 16-inch square. Cut each square into 16 squares. Spoon 1 tablespoon Filling in center of each square. Fold corners to center and pinch edges together. Place on greased cookie sheets. Cover; let rise in warm place until double, about 45 minutes. Bake at 400° for 10 to 12 minutes until light brown. Sprinkle with Vanilla Sugar; bake 5 minutes longer until golden brown.

*VANILLA SUGAR: Fill pint jar with sugar. Split vanilla bean in half lengthwise; push down into center of sugar. Cover tightly; let stand several days. Use as needed.

Snow Ring Holiday Bread

For winter holidays, sprinkle extra coconut on top to resemble "snow." Garnish with halved candied cherries for color. With only one short rise, this coffeecake is so quick to make, you'll want to enjoy it year round!

4½ to 5 cups all-purpose flour
2 packages Red Star Instant Blend Dry Yeast
⅓ cup sugar
1 tablespoon grated orange rind
1 teaspoon salt
1 cup milk
½ cup water
⅓ cup butter or margarine
1 egg

Topping:
1½ cups sugar
⅓ cup butter
¼ cup orange juice
2 tablespoons honey
1 cup flaked coconut

Oven 400°   **Two 10-inch Bundt® Coffeecakes**

In large mixer bowl, combine 2 cups flour, yeast, sugar, orange rind and salt; mix well. In saucepan, heat milk, water and butter until warm (120-130°; butter does not need to melt). Add to flour mixture. Add egg. Blend at low speed until moistened; beat 3 minutes at medium speed. By hand, gradually stir in enough remaining flour to make a firm dough. Knead on floured surface until smooth and elastic, 3 to 5 minutes.

Prepare Topping: In saucepan, combine sugar, butter, orange juice and honey; heat until sugar is dissolved. Divide half of Topping between two well-greased Bundt® pans or 11-cup ring molds. Sprinkle ¼ cup coconut into each pan.

Divide dough into 4 parts. Divide each fourth into 5 pieces. Place 10 pieces in each pan. Pour remaining Topping over dough in pans. Sprinkle with remaining coconut. Cover; let rise in warm oven (Turn oven to lowest setting for 1 minute, turn off.) for 25 minutes. Bake at 400° for 15 to 20 minutes. Cover pans with foil; invert onto rack. Cool 1 minute; remove pans. Cool. Sprinkle with additional coconut, if desired.

Guglehupf
(goo-gl-hoopf)

Guglehupf, an Austrian specialty, is a rich, sweet, cake-like yeast bread flavored with lemon rind, golden raisins and almonds. Baked in the classic, fancy-shaped Guglehupf mold, it's an excellent accompaniment to coffee or to serve as dessert.

> 1 to 2 tablespoons sliced almonds
> 3 cups all-purpose flour
> 1 package Red Star Instant Blend Dry Yeast
> ½ cup sugar
> 1 teaspoon grated lemon rind
> ½ teaspoon salt
> 1¼ cups milk
> ¼ cup water
> ½ cup butter or margarine, softened
> 3 eggs
> ¾ cup golden raisins
> ¼ cup finely chopped almonds

Oven 375°   **One Guglehupf or One 9-inch Coffeecake**

Arrange sliced almonds on bottom of well-greased 9-cup Guglehupf or fluted tube pan. In large mixer bowl, combine 2¾ cups flour, yeast, sugar, lemon rind and salt; mix well. In saucepan, heat milk and water until warm (120-130°); add to flour mixture. Add butter and eggs. Blend at low speed until moistened; beat 2 minutes at medium speed. Mix raisins and almonds with remaining ¼ cup flour; stir into batter. Pour batter carefully into pan. Cover; let rise in warm place for 30 minutes. Bake at 375° for 40 to 45 minutes until golden brown. Cool 10 minutes in pan; invert onto serving plate. Cool.

TIP: If using a shiny copper tone Guglehupf mold, reduce the baking temperature to 350°.

Saint Lucia Crown

In Sweden, this double tiered braided coffeecake, which looks like a crown, is served with hot coffee at dawn on St. Lucia's Day, December 13, to signal the opening of the Christmas season. Even if you're not Scandinavian, this "crown" makes a beautiful centerpiece for holiday brunches or buffets. To be more authentic, use a pinch of saffron instead of the food color.

> 6 to 6½ cups all-purpose flour
> 2 packages Red Star Instant Blend Dry Yeast
> ½ cup sugar
> 2 teaspoons salt
> 1¼ cups buttermilk
> ½ cup water
> ½ cup butter or margarine
> 2 to 3 drops yellow food color
> 2 eggs
> ½ cup chopped candied citron
> ¼ cup chopped almonds
> 1 tablespoon chopped candied lemon peel
> Red and green candied cherries
> Pecan halves

Glaze:
> 2 cups powdered sugar
> 2 to 3 tablespoons water

Oven 350°   **One Large Coffeecake**

In large mixer bowl, combine 2½ cups flour, yeast, sugar and salt; mix well. In saucepan, heat buttermilk, water, butter and yellow food color until warm (120-130°; butter does not need to melt). Add to flour mixture. Add eggs. Blend at low speed until moistened; beat 3 minutes at medium speed. By hand, gradually stir in citron, almonds, lemon peel and enough remaining flour to make a soft dough. Knead on floured surface, 5 to 8 minutes. Cover; let rest 10 minutes.

Cut off one third of dough; set aside. Divide remaining dough into 3 parts. On lightly floured surface, roll each third to a 25-inch rope. On greased cookie sheet, loosely braid from center to ends. Shape into a circle; pinch ends to seal. Cover; let rise in warm place until double, about 30 minutes. Divide remaining dough into 3 parts. Roll each third to a 16-inch rope. On greased cookie sheet, loosely braid from center to ends. Shape into a circle; pinch ends to seal. Cover; let rise in warm place until almost doubled, 20 to 30 minutes. Bake at 350° for 25 to 30 minutes for large wreath and 20 to 25 minutes for small wreath until golden brown. Remove from cookie sheets; cool. Make holes for 16 candles in small braid. Place small braid on large braid. Drizzle Glaze on braids. Garnish with cherries and nuts. Insert candles.

Prepare Glaze: Combine powdered sugar and water; blend until smooth.

Sugar Plum Trees

This special Christmas coffeecake in the shape of a tree is made with a sour cream dough and fruits of the season.

> 3 to 3¼ cups all-purpose flour
> 2 packages Red Star Instant Blend Dry Yeast
> 3 tablespoons sugar
> 1 teaspoon salt
> ¾ cup sour cream
> ½ cup water
> 2 tablespoons shortening
> 1 egg
> ½ cup chopped candied fruit
> ¼ cup chopped nuts
> 2 tablespoons sugar
> 2 tablespoons butter, softened

Oven 375°　　　　　　　**2 Trees**

In large mixer bowl, combine 1½ cups flour, yeast, 3 tablespoons sugar and salt; mix well. In saucepan, heat sour cream, water and shortening until warm (120-130°; shortening does not need to melt). Add to flour mixture. Add egg. Blend at low speed until moistened; beat 3 minutes at medium speed. By hand, gradually stir in enough remaining flour to make a soft dough. Knead on floured surface until smooth and elastic, 5 to 8 minutes. Cover; let rest 5 minutes.

Prepare Filling: Combine candied fruit, nuts and 2 tablespoons sugar; set aside.

Divide dough into 2 parts. On lightly floured surface, roll each half to a 12x6-inch rectangle. Spread with half of butter. Spread half of Filling over half of the long side of dough. Fold dough over Filling. Press top gently to seal in Filling. Cut dough into twelve 1-inch strips.

To shape tree, place three strips vertically on a greased cookie sheet to form trunk. Place one strip horizontally at bottom of trunk to form the stand. To form branches, place remaining strips on both sides of the trunk in a diagonal pattern. Place folded ends of each strip toward the outside and press ends to cookie sheet. Cover; let rise in warm place until almost doubled, 15 to 20 minutes. Bake at 375° for 15 to 20 minutes until golden brown. Drizzle with powdered sugar glaze, if desired.

Raisin Orange Holiday Trees

An easy-to-make festive Christmas coffeecake. Arrange raisin orange rolls in the shape of a tree. Give as hostess gifts or enjoy with family and friends.

5 to 5½ cups all-purpose flour
2 packages Red Star Instant Blend Dry Yeast
½ cup sugar
2 tablespoons grated orange rind
1 teaspoon salt
1 cup milk
½ cup water
¼ cup butter or margarine
2 eggs
1½ cups raisins
½ cup packed brown sugar
½ cup chopped toasted almonds
1 teaspoon cinnamon
3 tablespoons butter or margarine, melted

Oven 350°   3 Holiday Trees

In mixer bowl, combine 2½ cups flour, yeast, sugar, orange rind and salt; mix well. Heat milk, water and butter until warm (120-130°; butter does not need to melt). Add to flour mixture. Add eggs. Blend at low speed until moistened; beat 3 minutes at medium speed. By hand, gradually stir in raisins and enough remaining flour to make a soft dough. Knead on floured surface 5 to 8 minutes. Place in greased bowl, turning to grease top. Cover; let rise in warm place until double, about 1 hour.

Prepare Filling: Combine brown sugar, almonds, and cinnamon.

Punch down dough. Divide into 3 parts. On lightly floured surface, roll each third to an 11-inch square. Brush with 1 tablespoon melted butter; sprinkle with ⅓ of Filling. Roll up tightly. Pinch edge and ends to seal. Cut into 11 slices. Place slices, edges touching, on greased cookie sheet, making a tree shape. Cover; let rise in warm place until almost double, about 30 minutes. Bake at 350° for 20 to 25 minutes until golden brown. Remove from cookie sheets. Drizzle with Orange Powdered Sugar Glaze and Garnish with candied cherries, if desired. Serve warm or cold.

Sweetheart Coffeecake

Love is a universal word and what better way to say it than with this beautiful heart coffeecake. Celebrate Valentine's Day, an anniversary, Mother's Day, Father's Day or just surprise your loved one.

4 to 4½ cups all-purpose flour
2 packages Red Star Instant Blend Dry Yeast
⅓ cup sugar
2 teaspoons salt
½ cup milk
½ cup water
⅓ cup butter or margarine
2 eggs
1 cup coconut
1 cup snipped maraschino cherries
¾ cup chopped almonds
2 tablespoons sugar
2 tablespoons chopped almonds
1 tablespoon sugar
2 tablespoons butter, softened

Oven 350°   2 Coffeecakes

In large mixer bowl, combine 1½ cups flour, yeast, ⅓ cup sugar and salt; mix well. In saucepan, heat milk, water and ⅓ cup butter until warm (120-130°; butter does not need to melt). Add to flour mixture. Add eggs. Blend at low speed until moistened; beat 3 minutes at medium speed. By hand, gradually stir in enough remaining flour to make a soft dough. Knead on floured surface until smooth and elastic, 5 to 8 minutes. Place in greased bowl, turning to grease top. Cover; let rise in warm place until light and doubled, about 1 hour.

Prepare Filling: Combine coconut, cherries, ¾ cup almonds and 2 tablespoons sugar.

Prepare Topping: Combine 2 tablespoons almonds and 1 tablespoon sugar.

Punch down dough. Divide into 2 parts. On lightly floured surface, roll each half to a 15x10-inch rectangle. Spread with half of softened butter. Sprinkle half of Filling over dough. Starting with longer side, roll up tightly. Pinch edge to seal. Place seam side up on greased cookie sheet. Fold half of the roll over on top of other half, sealing ends. Starting at folded end, cut with scissors down center of roll to within 1 inch of other end. Turn cut halves out, cut side up, to form a heart. Sprinkle half of Topping over dough. Cover; let rise in warm place until double, about 30 minutes. Bake at 350° for 18 to 20 minutes until golden brown. Remove from cookie sheets; cool. Drizzle with powdered sugar Glaze, if desired.

My Notes: _____

_____

_____

_____

_____

_____

_____

_____

_____

_____

_____

Contemporary

**Wheat Germ
Herb Bread**

**Granola Crunch
Coffeecake**

breads

Many Grains Bread

Sunflower Nut Crescents

CONTEMPORARY BREADS

Throughout the 100 years of our company's history, many different trends in food have been popular. During the 70's, there was a renewed interest in nutrition and a swing back to ingredients that could be called old-fashioned because they are natural and wholesome. Since this trend in foods is still popular, we've taken some of these "naturally good" ingredients and incorporated them into breads along with Red Star Yeast—the all natural one.

In this chapter, you'll find breads using natural cereals and granola. Because of the interest in whole grain products, we've included two breads using a combination of several grains—*Many Grains Bread* and *Four Grain English Muffins.* You'll find a potato bread using yogurt. There are some breads using sunflower nuts—*Seed And Wheat Bread, Sunflower Nut Crescents* and *Granola Crunch Coffeecake.*

We hope you'll enjoy these breads, not just because they represent a trend, but because they are delicious breads that can add variety to your menus. They have distinctive flavors and textures, as well as added nutrients.

Burlap Bread

🎖 The delightful "natural whole-some" flavor of this bread comes from the combination of several grain products. The texture looks like burlap.

5 to 5½ cups all-purpose flour
2 packages Red Star Instant Blend Dry Yeast
1 cup rolled oats
⅓ cup wheat germ
½ cup whole bran cereal
1 tablespoon salt
2 cups water
½ cup molasses
2 tablespoons butter or margarine

Oven 375°   2 Loaves

In large mixer bowl, combine 2 cups flour, yeast, oats, wheat germ, cereal and salt; mix well. In saucepan, heat water, molasses and butter until warm (120-130°; butter does not need to melt). Add to flour mixture. Blend at low speed until moistened; beat 3 minutes at medium speed. By hand, gradually stir in enough remaining flour to make a firm dough. Knead on floured surface, 5 to 8 minutes. Place in greased bowl, turning to grease top. Cover; let rise in warm place until double, about 1 hour.

Punch down dough. Divide into 2 parts. On lightly floured surface, roll or pat each half to a 14x7-inch rectangle. Starting with shorter side, roll up tightly, pressing dough into roll with each turn. Pinch edges and ends to seal. Place in greased 9x5-inch bread pans. Cover; let rise in warm place until double, about 1 hour. Bake at 375° for 35 to 40 minutes until loaves sound hollow when tapped. Remove from pans; cool.

Dilled Brown Bread

🎖 Dill seed, bran cereal and whole wheat flour add flavor and texture to these round loaves baked in casserole or soufflé dishes.

3½ to 4 cups all-purpose flour
1 cup whole wheat flour
2 packages Red Star Instant Blend Dry Yeast
2 tablespoons dill seed
2 teaspoons salt
1 cup buttermilk
½ cup shortening
½ cup honey
½ cup water
2 eggs
½ cup whole bran cereal

Oven 375°   2 Round Loaves

In large mixer bowl, combine 1 cup all-purpose flour, 1 cup whole wheat flour, yeast, dill seed and salt; mix well. In saucepan, heat buttermilk, shortening, honey and water until warm (120-130°; shortening does not need to melt). Add to flour mixture. Add eggs. Blend at low speed until moistened; beat 3 minutes at medium speed. By hand, gradually stir in cereal and enough remaining flour to make a firm dough. Knead on floured surface, 5 to 8 minutes. Place in greased bowl, turning to grease top. Cover; let rise in warm place until double, about 1 hour.

Punch down dough. Divide into 2 parts. Shape each half into a round loaf. Place in greased 1-quart soufflé dishes or casseroles. Cover; let rise in warm place until double, about 45 minutes. Bake at 375° for 25 to 30 minutes until golden brown. Remove from baking dishes; cool.

Seed and Wheat Bread

These large, hearty loaves, fragrant with cumin and molasses, have added flavor from sunflower nuts and sesame seed.

5½ to 6 cups all-purpose flour
2 packages Red Star Instant Blend Dry Yeast
¼ cup sesame seeds
2 tablespoons sugar
1 tablespoon salt
½ teaspoon cumin seeds
2 cups water
¼ cup oil
¼ cup light molasses
2 eggs
¼ cup salted sunflower nuts
1½ cups whole wheat flour
1 egg white, slightly beaten
1 tablespoon water
2 tablespoons chopped salted sunflower nuts or sesame seeds

Oven 375°   **2 Loaves**

In large mixer bowl, combine 3 cups all-purpose flour, yeast, sesame seed, sugar salt and cumin seed; mix well. In saucepan, heat water, oil and molasses until warm (120-130°). Add to flour mixture. Add eggs. Blend at low speed until moistened; beat 3 minutes at medium speed. By hand, gradually stir in ¼ cup sunflower nuts, whole wheat flour and enough remaining all-purpose flour to make a firm dough. Knead on floured surface until smooth and elastic, 5 to 8 minutes. Place in greased bowl, turning to grease top. Cover; let rise in warm place until double, about 1 hour.

Punch down dough. Divide into 2 parts. On lightly floured surface, roll or pat each half to a 14x7-inch rectangle. Starting with shorter side, roll up tightly, pressing dough into roll with each turn. Pinch edges and ends to seal. Place in greased 9x5-inch bread pans. Cover; let rise in warm place until double, about 30 minutes. Combine egg white and water; gently brush loaves. Sprinkle with 2 tablespoons sunflower nuts or sesame seed. Bake at 375° for 35 to 40 minutes until golden brown. If too dark, cover loosely with foil last 5 to 10 minutes of baking. Remove from pans; cool.

Wheat Germ Herb Bread

Slightly nutty tasting, with just the right touch of herbs. Wheat germ also adds extra nutrients. A delicious bread to team with all your favorite foods.

5½ to 6 cups all-purpose flour
2 packages Red Star Instant Blend Dry Yeast
⅓ cup sugar
1 teaspoon salt
1 teaspoon thyme leaves, crushed
1 teaspoon marjoram leaves, crushed
1½ cups milk
½ cup water
½ cup butter or margarine
2 eggs
1 egg yolk
1⅓ cups wheat germ
1 egg white, slightly beaten
1 tablespoon wheat germ

Wheat Germ Bread

Oven 350°	**2 Loaves**

In large mixer bowl, combine 3 cups flour, yeast, sugar, salt and herbs; mix well. In saucepan, heat milk, water and butter until warm (120-130°; butter does not need to melt). Add to flour mixture. Add eggs and egg yolk. Blend at low speed until moistened; beat 3 minutes at medium speed. By hand, gradually stir in 1⅓ cups wheat germ and enough remaining flour to make a soft dough. Knead on floured surface until smooth and elastic, 5 to 8 minutes. Place in greased bowl, turning to grease top. Cover; let rise in warm place until light and doubled, about 1 hour.

Punch down dough. Divide into 2 parts. On lightly floured surface, roll or pat each half to a 12x8-inch rectangle. Cut each rectangle into two 12-inch strips. Pinch edges of each strip together to make a rope. Twist 2 ropes together; seal ends and tuck under loaf. Place in greased 8x4 or 9x5-inch bread pans. Cover; let rise in warm place until almost doubled, 30 to 40 minutes. Brush with egg white; sprinkle with 1 tablespoon wheat germ. Bake at 350° for 35 to 40 minutes. If too dark, cover loosely with foil last 5 to 10 minutes of baking. Remove from pans; cool.

Whole wheat flavor in a nutritious wheat germ batter bread.

2¾ cups all-purpose flour
2 packages Red Star Instant Blend Dry Yeast
½ cup wheat germ
1½ teaspoons salt
1 cup water
¼ cup molasses
2 tablespoons shortening
1 egg

Oven 375°	**1 Round Loaf**

In large mixer bowl, combine 1½ cups flour, yeast, wheat germ and salt; mix well. In saucepan, heat water, molasses and shortening until warm (120-130°; shortening does not need to melt). Add to flour mixture. Add egg. Blend at low speed until moistened; beat 3 minutes at medium speed. By hand, gradually stir in remaining flour to make a stiff batter. Cover; let rise in warm place until double, about 1 hour.

Stir down batter. Spoon into greased 2-quart casserole. Cover; let rise in warm place until double, about 45 minutes. Bake at 375° for 40 to 45 minutes until golden brown. Remove from casserole; cool.

My Notes: _____

_____

_____

_____

_____

_____

"Vita-B" Bread

🎖 The name for this bread comes from the bran cereal, which is a good source of Vitamin B.

1 cup whole bran cereal
1 cup hot water
6 to 6½ cups all-purpose flour
2 packages Red Star Instant Blend Dry Yeast
1½ tablespoons salt
1 cup water
⅔ cup honey
½ cup shortening
2 eggs

Oven 375°　　　**2 Loaves**

In small bowl, pour 1 cup hot water over bran cereal; let stand. In large mixer bowl, combine 2 cups flour, yeast and salt; mix well. In saucepan, heat 1 cup water, honey and shortening until warm (120-130°; shortening does not need to melt). Add to flour mixture. Add eggs. Blend at low speed until moistened; beat 3 minutes at medium speed. By hand, gradually stir in bran mixture and enough remaining flour to make a firm dough. Knead on floured surface, 5 to 8 minutes. Place in greased bowl, turning to grease top. Cover; let rise in warm place until double, about 1½ hours.

Punch down dough. Divide into 2 parts. On lightly floured surface, roll or pat each half to a 14x7-inch rectangle. Starting with shorter side, roll up tightly, pressing dough into roll with each turn. Pinch edges and ends to seal. Place in greased 9x5-inch bread pans. Cover; let rise in warm place until double, about 1 hour. Bake at 375° for 40 to 45 minutes until loaves sound hollow when tapped. Remove from pans; cool.

Four Grain English Muffins

🎖 These hearty muffins are extra nutritious—and so good! In addition to serving for breakfast or brunch, serve these with soup for lunch or a light supper.

4 to 4½ cups all-purpose flour
1 package Red Star Instant Blend Dry Yeast
½ cup whole wheat flour
½ cup wheat germ
½ cup quick rolled oats
1 cup nonfat dry milk solids
3 tablespoons sugar
2 teaspoons salt
2 cups water
¼ cup oil
¼ cup cornmeal

Electric griddle 325°　**18 to 20 Muffins**

In large mixer bowl, combine 2 cups all-purpose flour, yeast, whole wheat flour, wheat germ, oats, dry milk, sugar and salt; mix well. In saucepan, heat water and oil until warm (120-130°). Add to flour mixture. Blend at low speed until moistened; beat 3 minutes at medium speed. By hand, gradually stir in enough remaining all-purpose flour to make a firm dough. Knead on floured surface, 5 to 8 minutes. Place in greased bowl, turning to grease top. Cover; let rise in warm place until double, about 1 hour.

Punch down dough. On surface sprinkled with cornmeal, roll dough to ½-inch thickness. With biscuit or cookie cutter, cut into 3-inch circles. Place muffins on ungreased cookie sheets. Cover; let rise in warm place until double, about 30 minutes. Bake on lightly oiled electric griddle or fry pan at 325° for about 8 minutes on each side until deep golden brown. Cool. To serve, split and toast.

Many Grains Bread

A dense, dark bread made with an interesting blend of grains. Cornmeal and oatmeal add a crunchy texture. Excellent served freshly baked and well buttered.

2¾ to 3¼ cups all-purpose flour
3 cups graham flour
2 packages Red Star Instant Blend Dry Yeast
4 teaspoons salt
3 cups water
½ cup dark molasses
¼ cup oil
½ cup buckwheat flour
½ cup rye flour
½ cup soy flour
½ cup yellow cornmeal
½ cup quick rolled oats
Butter

Oven 375°   2 Round Loaves

In large mixer bowl, combine 1½ cups all-purpose flour and 2 cups graham flour, yeast and salt; mix well. In saucepan, heat water, molasses and oil until warm (120-130°). Add to flour mixture. Blend at low speed until moistened; beat 3 minutes at medium speed. By hand, gradually stir in buckwheat, rye and soy flours, cornmeal, rolled oats, remaining graham flour and enough remaining all-purpose flour to make a firm dough. Knead on floured surface, 5 to 8 minutes. Place in greased bowl, turning to grease top. Cover; let rise in warm place until double, about 1 hour.

Punch down dough. Divide into 2 parts. On lightly floured surface, shape each half into a round loaf. Place on greased cookie sheet. Cover; let rise in warm place until double, about 30 minutes. With very sharp knife, make cross slash across top of each loaf. Bake at 375° for 35 to 40 minutes until bread sounds hollow when tapped. If too dark, cover loosely with foil last 5 to 10 minutes of baking. Remove from cookie sheets. Brush with butter; cool.

My Notes: _____

_____

_____

_____

_____

_____

_____

_____

Maple Buck Wheat Loaf

Maple syrup adds a touch of sweetness; wheat cereal adds some crunch. Ideal toasted for breakfast.

3 to 3½ cups all-purpose flour
1 package Red Star Instant Blend Dry Yeast
2 teaspoons salt
½ cup milk
½ cup water
¼ cup maple syrup
2 tablespoons shortening
1 egg
1 cup maple flavored buck wheat ready-to-eat cereal

Oven 375°   **1 Loaf**

In large mixer bowl, combine 1½ cups flour, yeast and salt; mix well. In saucepan, heat milk, water, syrup and shortening until warm (120-130°; shortening does not need to melt). Add to flour mixture. Add egg. Blend at low speed until moistened; beat 3 minutes at medium speed. By hand, gradually stir in cereal and enough remaining flour to make a firm dough. Knead on floured surface, 5 to 8 minutes. Place in greased bowl, turning to grease top. Cover; let rise in warm place until double, about 1½ hours.

Punch down dough. On lightly floured surface, roll or pat to a 14x7-inch rectangle. Starting with shorter side, roll up tightly, pressing dough into roll with each turn. Pinch edges and ends to seal. Place in greased 9x5-inch bread pan. Cover; let rise in warm place until double, about 1 hour. Bake at 375° for 35 to 40 minutes until golden brown. Remove from pan; cool.

Honey of a Granola Loaf

Two favorites—honey and granola—team up to make these delicious loaves. They are braided for a pretty look.

6¼ to 6¾ cups all-purpose flour
2 packages Red Star Instant Blend Dry Yeast
1 tablespoon salt
1¼ cups water
1 cup milk
½ cup honey
¼ cup shortening
2 eggs
2 cups granola (any flavor), crushed

Oven 375°   **2 Loaves**

In large mixer bowl, combine 3 cups flour, yeast and salt; mix well. In saucepan, heat water, milk, honey and shortening until warm (120-130°; shortening does not need to melt). Add to flour mixture. Add eggs. Blend at low speed until moistened; beat 3 minutes at medium speed. By hand, gradually stir in granola and enough remaining flour to make a firm dough. Knead on floured surface 5 to 8 minutes. Place in greased bowl, turning to grease top. Cover; let rise in warm place until double, about 1½ hours.

Punch down dough. Divide into 2 parts. Divide each half into 3 pieces. On lightly floured surface, roll each piece to a 14-inch rope. Loosely braid from center to ends. Seal ends and tuck under loaf. Place in greased 9x5-inch bread pans. Cover; let rise in warm place until double, about 1 hour. Bake at 375° for 30 to 35 minutes until loaves sound hollow when tapped. If too dark, cover loosely with foil last 5 to 10 minutes of baking. Remove from pans; cool.

Granola Crunch Coffeecake

Start the day right with this easy coffeecake—granola and sunflower nuts add the crunchy nutrition.

3 cups all-purpose flour
2 packages Red Star Instant Blend Dry Yeast
½ cup granola
⅓ cup sugar
½ teaspoon salt
½ cup milk
½ cup water
¼ cup shortening
2 eggs
½ cup sugar
½ cup all-purpose flour
½ cup salted sunflower nuts
1 teaspoon cinnamon
¼ cup butter or margarine, melted

Oven 375°   **One 13x9-inch Coffeecake**

In large mixer bowl, combine 1½ cups flour, yeast, granola, sugar and salt; mix well. In saucepan, heat milk, water and shortening until warm (120-130°; shortening does not need to melt). Add to flour mixture. Add eggs. Blend at low speed until moistened; beat 3 minutes at medium speed. By hand, gradually stir in remaining 1½ cups flour to make a stiff batter. Cover; let rise in warm place until double, about 45 minutes.

Prepare Topping: Combine ½ cup sugar, ½ cup flour, sunflower nuts, cinnamon and butter; set aside.

Stir down batter; spread in greased 13x9-inch cake pan. Sprinkle Topping over batter. With back of a spoon, make random indentations in batter. Cover; let rise in warm place until double, about 30 minutes. Bake at 375° for 30 to 35 minutes until golden brown. Serve warm or cold.

Zucchini Rich Buns

 "Milk" made from puréed zucchini gives an excellent flavor and lowers the calories of these special rolls.

3½ cups all-purpose flour
1 package Red Star Instant Blend Dry Yeast
¼ cup sugar
1 teaspoon salt
1 cup zucchini milk*
¼ cup water
¼ cup oil
1 egg

Oven 375°   **24 Rolls**

In large mixer bowl, combine 1½ cups flour, yeast, sugar and salt; mix well. In saucepan, heat zucchini milk, water and oil until warm (120-130°). Add to flour mixture. Add egg. Blend at low speed until moistened; beat 3 minutes at medium speed. By hand, gradually stir in remaining flour to make a soft dough. Cover; let rise in warm place until light and doubled, about 1½ hours.

Punch down dough. Divide into 4 parts. Divide each fourth into 6 pieces. Shape each piece into a smooth ball. Place in greased 8-inch layer cake pans. Cover; let rise in warm place until double, about 45 minutes. Bake at 375° for 20 to 25 minutes until golden brown. Remove from pans; cool.

*Zucchini Milk: In blender or food processor, purée 2 to 3 peeled zucchini until smooth.

Yogurt Potato Bread

🎗 The flavor and moistness in this potato bread comes from potato soup and yogurt.

6 to 6½ cups all-purpose flour
2 packages Red Star Instant Blend Dry Yeast
2 tablespoons sugar
2 teaspoons salt
½ cup water
1 carton (8 oz.) plain yogurt
2 tablespoons butter or margarine
1 can (10½ oz.) condensed cream of potato soup, undiluted

Oven 400°   2 Loaves

In large mixer bowl, combine 2½ cups flour, yeast, sugar and salt; mix well. In saucepan, heat water, yogurt and butter until warm (120-130°; butter does not need to melt). Add to flour mixture. Add undiluted soup. Blend at low speed until moistened; beat 3 minutes at medium speed. By hand, gradually stir in enough remaining flour to make a firm dough. Knead on floured surface until smooth and elastic, 5 to 8 minutes. Place in greased bowl, turning to grease top. Cover; let rise in warm place until light and doubled, about 1 hour.

Punch down dough. Divide into 2 parts. On lightly floured surface, roll or pat each half to a 14x7-inch rectangle. Starting with the shorter side, roll up tightly, pressing dough into roll with each turn. Pinch edges and ends to seal. Place in greased 9x5-inch bread pans. Cover; let rise in warm place until double, about 40 minutes. Bake at 400° for 30 to 35 minutes until golden brown. Remove from pans; cool.

Porcupine Bread

🎗 An unusual blend of ingredients—rolled oats, buttermilk, raisins, sunflower nuts and sesame seeds—a combination that is a success!

5 to 5½ cups unbleached flour
1 cup rolled oats
2 packages Red Star Instant Blend Dry Yeast
¼ cup sugar
1 tablespoon salt
1½ cups buttermilk
½ cup water
¼ cup oil
1 cup raisins
½ cup salted sunflower nuts
¼ cup toasted sesame seeds

Oven 375°   2 Loaves

In large mixer bowl, combine 2 cups flour, rolled oats, yeast, sugar and salt; mix well. In saucepan, heat buttermilk, water and oil until warm (120-130°). Add to flour mixture. Blend at low speed until moistened; beat 3 minutes at medium speed. By hand, gradually stir in raisins, sunflower nuts, sesame seeds and enough remaining flour to make a firm dough. Knead on floured surface until smooth and elastic, 5 to 8 minutes. Place in greased bowl, turning to grease top. Cover; let rise in warm place until double, about 1 hour.

Punch down dough. Divide into 2 parts. On lightly floured surface, roll or pat each half to a 14x7-inch rectangle. Starting with shorter side, roll up tightly, pressing dough into roll with each turn. Pinch edges and ends to seal. Place in greased 9x5-inch bread pans. Cover; let rise in warm place until double, about 1 hour. Bake at 375° for 35 to 40 minutes until golden brown. Remove from pans; cool.

Natural Cereal Bread

Add your favorite natural cereal to this bread. For a special look, make the swirl loaves.

6 to 6½ cups all-purpose flour
2 packages Red Star Instant Blend Dry Yeast
1 cup all natural cereal, any flavor
¼ cup packed brown sugar
1 tablespoon salt
2 cups water
¼ cup oil
1 egg

Oven 375°   **2 Loaves**

In large mixer bowl, combine 2 cups flour, yeast, cereal, brown sugar and salt; mix well. In saucepan, heat water and oil until warm (120-130°). Add to flour mixture. Add egg. Blend at low speed until moistened; beat 3 minutes at medium speed. By hand, gradually stir in enough remaining flour to make a firm dough. Knead on floured surface 5 to 8 minutes. Place in greased bowl, turning to grease top. Cover; let rise in warm place until double, about 1½ hours.

Punch down dough. Divide into 2 parts. On lightly floured surface, roll or pat each half to a 14x7-inch rectangle. Starting with shorter side, roll up tightly, pressing dough into roll with each turn. Pinch edges and ends to seal. Place in greased 9x5-inch bread pans. Cover; let rise in warm place until double, about 45 minutes. Bake at 375° for 40 to 45 minutes until golden brown. Remove from pans; cool.

Natural Cereal Swirl Loaves

After rolling out dough to a 14x7-inch rectangle, brush each half with 1 tablespoon melted butter; sprinkle each half with ½ cup chopped natural cereal. Continue shaping and bake as directed above.

Sunflower Nut Crescents

Complement a salad luncheon with these pretty rolls. Salted sunflower nuts add the unique flavor and texture.

4 cups all-purpose flour
2 packages Red Star Instant Blend Dry Yeast
2 tablespoons sugar
2 teaspoons salt
1 cup milk
½ cup water
¼ cup shortening
1 egg
½ cup salted sunflower nuts, chopped
1 egg, slightly beaten
3 tablespoons salted sunflower nuts, chopped

Oven 400°   **30 Rolls**

In large mixer bowl, combine 2 cups flour, yeast, sugar and salt; mix well. In saucepan, heat milk, water and shortening until warm (120-130°; shortening does not need to melt). Add to flour mixture. Add egg. Blend at low speed until moistened; beat 3 minutes at medium speed. By hand, gradually stir in sunflower nuts and remaining flour to make a soft dough. Cover; let rise in warm place until double, 20 to 30 minutes.

Stir down dough. On well floured surface turn dough to coat with flour. Divide into 3 parts. Roll each third to a 10-inch circle. Cut into 10 wedges. Starting with wide end of wedge, roll toward point. Place point side down on greased cookie sheets. Curve to form crescent. Brush with egg; sprinkle sunflower nuts over top of rolls. Cover; let rise in warm place until almost doubled, about 15 minutes. Bake at 400° for 10 to 12 minutes until golden brown. Remove from cookie sheets; cool.

Savory breads

Whole Wheat Herb Bread

Spaghetti French Bread

**Corn Cheddar
Bubble Loaf**

Beef 'N Brew Braid

SAVORY BREADS

We have grouped together a collection of recipes we call Savory Breads. They include special flavoring ingredients such as a variety of cheeses, herbs, soups or soup mixes and seasoning mixes. These breads are great with hearty soups, stews, as sandwiches or they can accompany any meal.

This chapter includes breads in a variety of shapes in addition to special flavors. There are long French bread type loaves—*Spaghetti French Bread* and *Sourdough-Like Beer Bread. Beef 'N Brew Braid* and *Chicken Dressing Braid* are both long braided breads; *Corn-Fetti Bread* is a braided loaf. You'll find pull-apart bubble loaves made from balls of dough that are baked in a bread pan or a tubed cake pan. There are also several special recipes for rolls and buns.

When you want a bread that's a little different, we think you'll find a favorite here.

Herb Twist Bread

🕐 Add interest to your table with this different loaf shape and a different herb flavor.

**4½ to 5 cups all-purpose flour
2 packages Red Star Instant
  Blend Dry Yeast
2 tablespoons sugar
2 teaspoons salt
1½ teaspoons dill weed
1 teaspoon caraway seeds
½ teaspoon celery seeds
¾ cup milk
¾ cup water
2 tablespoons shortening
1 egg**

Oven 400°   **2 Loaves**

In large mixer bowl, combine 2 cups flour, yeast, sugar, salt and herbs; mix well. In saucepan, heat milk, water and shortening until warm (120-130°; shortening does not need to melt). Add to flour mixture. Add egg. Beat at low speed until moistened; beat 3 minutes at medium speed. By hand, gradually stir in enough remaining flour to make a firm dough. Knead on floured surface until smooth and elastic, 5 to 8 minutes. Place in greased bowl, turning to grease top. Cover; let rise in warm oven (Turn oven to lowest setting for 1 minute, turn off.) for 20 minutes.

Punch down dough. Divide into 2 parts. On lightly floured surface, roll or pat each half to a 12x8-inch rectangle. Cut each rectangle into two 12-inch strips. Pinch edges of each strip together to make a rope. Twist 2 ropes together; seal ends and tuck under loaf. Place in greased 9x5-inch bread pans. Cover; let rise in warm oven until double, about 30 minutes. Bake at 40° for 20 to 25 minutes until golden brown. Remove from pans; cool.

Herb Whole Wheat Bread

🎖 An excellent flavor blend of herbs and honey enhances this Greek wheat bread.

**3½ to 4 cups unbleached flour
3 cups whole wheat flour
2 packages Red Star Instant
  Blend Dry Yeast
2½ teaspoons salt
1 teaspoon dill seed
1 teaspoon basil leaves
1 teaspoon thyme leaves
2 cups water
⅓ cup honey
⅓ cup oil
1 egg**

Oven 400°   **2 Loaves**

In large mixer bowl, combine 1½ cups unbleached flour, 1 cup whole wheat flour, yeast, salt, dill seed, basil and thyme; mix well. In saucepan, heat water, honey and oil until warm (120-130°). Add to flour mixture. Add egg. Blend at low speed until moistened; beat 3 minutes at medium speed. By hand, gradually stir in remaining whole wheat flour and enough remaining unbleached flour to make a firm dough. Knead on floured surface until smooth and elastic, 5 to 8 minutes. Place in greased bowl, turning to grease top. Cover; let rise in warm place until double, about 1 hour.

Punch down dough. Divide into 2 parts. On lightly floured surface, roll or pat each half to a 14x7-inch rectangle. Starting with the shorter side, roll up tightly, pressing dough into roll with each turn. Pinch edges and ends to seal. Place in greased 8x4-inch bread pans. Cover; let rise in warm place until double, about 45 minutes. Bake at 400° for 15 minutes; reduce heat to 375° and bake 20 to 25 minutes longer until loaves sound hollow when tapped. Remove from pans; cool.

Garlic Bubble Loaf

An easy one-rise garlic bread in a buttery pull-apart bubble loaf.

2½ to 3 cups all-purpose flour
1 package Red Star Instant Blend Dry Yeast
1 tablespoon sugar
1 teaspoon salt
½ cup milk
½ cup water
2 tablespoons shortening
1 egg
¼ cup butter or margarine, melted
1 teaspoon paprika
½ teaspoon garlic powder
1 tablespoon sesame seeds

Oven 375°   **1 Loaf**

In large mixer bowl, combine 1½ cups flour, yeast, sugar and salt; mix well. In saucepan, heat milk, water and shortening until warm (120-130°; shortening does not need to melt). Add to flour mixture. Add egg. Blend at low speed until moistened; beat 3 minutes at medium speed. By hand, gradually stir in enough remaining flour to make a soft dough. Knead on floured surface, about 2 minutes.

Divide dough into 2 parts. Divide each half into 6 pieces. Shape each piece into a smooth ball. Combine melted butter, paprika and garlic powder; mix well. Dip balls into butter mixture; place in greased 9x5-inch bread pan, using 6 balls on each layer. Sprinkle with sesame seed. Cover; let rise in warm place until double, about 45 minutes. Bake at 375° for 40 to 45 minutes until golden brown. Remove from pan; serve warm.

Spaghetti French Bread

The tantalizing flavors of garlic bread are baked right in this tempting loaf.

3½ to 4 cups all-purpose flour
2 packages Red Star Instant Blend Dry Yeast
1 tablespoon sugar
1 teaspoon garlic salt
1 teaspoon salt
½ cup Stella grated Parmesan cheese
½ teaspoon basil leaves, crumbled
1 teaspoon dried parsley
1½ cups water
1 tablespoon oil
Cornmeal

Oven 375°   **2 Loaves**

In large mixer bowl, combine 2 cups flour, yeast, sugar, garlic salt, salt, cheese, basil and parsley; mix well. Add warm water (120-130°) and oil. Blend at low speed until moistened; beat 3 minutes at medium speed. By hand, gradually stir in enough remaining flour to make a firm dough. Knead on floured surface until smooth and elastic, 5 to 8 minutes. Place in greased bowl, turning to grease top. Cover; let rise in warm place until light and doubled, about 45 minutes.

Punch down dough. Divide into 2 parts. On lightly floured surface, roll or pat dough to an 11x7-inch rectangle. Starting with longer side, roll up tightly, pressing dough into roll with each turn. Pinch edges and ends to seal. Place seam-side down on greased large cookie sheet sprinkled with cornmeal. With a very sharp knife, make 3 or 4 diagonal slashes across top. Cover; let rise in warm place until light and doubled, about 30 minutes. Bake at 375° for 30 to 35 minutes until golden brown. Remove from cookie sheets; cool.

Corn-Fetti Bread

🎗 If you like the taste of corn-bread but not the texture, you'll like this flavorful white bread with real corn.

5½ to 6 cups all-purpose flour
2 packages Red Star Instant Blend Dry Yeast
1 teaspoon salt
¼ cup sugar
¼ teaspoon dill weed
1 cup canned cream-style corn
½ cup water
¼ cup milk
¼ cup butter or margarine
3 tablespoons chopped pimento stuffed olives
2 eggs
1 tablespoon butter
1 tablespoon poppy seeds

Oven 375°   **2 Braids**

In large mixer bowl, combine 2½ cups flour, yeast, sugar and dill weed; mix well. In saucepan, heat corn, water, milk and butter until warm (120-130°; butter does not need to melt). Add to flour mixture. Add eggs. Blend at low speed until moistened; beat 3 minutes at medium speed. By hand, gradually stir in olives and enough remaining flour to make a firm dough. Knead on floured surface until smooth and elastic, 5 to 8 minutes. Place in greased bowl, turning to grease top. Cover; let rise in warm place until double, about 1 hour.

Punch down dough; divide into 2 parts. Divide each half into 3 pieces. On lightly floured surface, roll each piece to an 8-inch rope. Loose-ly braid from center to ends. Pinch ends and tuck under to seal. Place in greased 9x5-inch bread pans. Cover; let rise in warm place until double, about 1 hour. Bake at 375° for 35 to 40 minutes until golden brown. Remove from pans. Brush with butter and sprinkle with poppy seeds; cool.

Eureka Bread

🎗 A seasoned snack bread that is especially good with sausage and sharp Cheddar cheese. The color makes an attractive contrast on a plate of assorted light and dark breads.

5 to 5½ cups all-purpose flour
2 packages Red Star Instant Blend Dry Yeast
2 tablespoons sugar
2 tablespoons instant minced onion
1 tablespoon salt
1 teaspoon dried oregano
1 teaspoon dried basil
1 tablespoon caraway seeds
1 can (15 oz.) tomato sauce
½ cup water
2 tablespoons butter or margarine

Oven 375°   **2 Round Loaves**

In large mixer bowl, combine 2 cups flour, yeast, sugar, onion, salt, oregano, basil and caraway seed; mix well. In saucepan, heat toma-to sauce, water and butter until warm (120-130°; butter does not need to melt). Add to flour mixture. Blend at low speed until moist-ened; beat 3 minutes at medium speed. By hand, gradually stir in enough remaining flour to make a firm dough. Knead on floured sur-face 5 to 8 minutes. Place in greased bowl, turning to grease top. Cover; let rise in warm place until double, 1 to 1½ hours.

Punch down dough. Divide into 2 parts. On lightly floured surface, shape each half into a round loaf. Place on large greased cookie sheet. Cover; let rise in warm place until almost doubled, about 1 hour. Bake at 375° for 30 to 35 minutes until golden brown. Remove from cookie sheet; cool.

Yankee Bean Pot Bread

🎖 A subtle bean flavor makes this bread perfect for a hearty picnic menu.

5½ to 6 cups all-purpose flour
2 packages Red Star Instant Blend Dry Yeast
2 tablespoons packed brown sugar
1 tablespoon salt
1¼ cups water
1 can (11½ oz.) bean with bacon soup, undiluted
2 large shredded wheat biscuits, crumbled
¼ cup molasses
2 tablespoons butter or margarine
2 tablespoons imitation bacon-flavored pieces
2 eggs
1 teaspoon liquid smoke
Butter

Oven 375°   **2 Loaves**

In large mixer bowl, combine 1½ cups flour, yeast, brown sugar and salt; mix well. In saucepan, heat water, soup, shredded wheat biscuits, molasses, butter and bacon pieces until warm (120-130°; butter does not need to melt). Add to flour mixture. Add eggs and liquid smoke. Blend at low speed until moistened; beat 3 minutes at medium speed. By hand, gradually stir in enough remaining flour to make a firm dough. Knead on floured surface until smooth and elastic, 5 to 8 minutes. Place in greased bowl, turning to grease top. Cover; let rise in warm place until double, about 1 hour.

Punch down dough. Divide into 2 parts. On lightly floured surface, roll or pat each half to a 14x7-inch rectangle. Starting with shorter side, roll up tightly, pressing dough into roll with each turn. Pinch edges and ends to seal. Place in greased 9x5-inch bread pans. Cover; let rise in warm place until double, about 45 minutes. Bake at 375° for 35 to 40 minutes until loaves sound hollow when tapped. Remove from pans; brush with butter. Cool.

Chicken Dressing Braid

🎖 It has all the favorite flavors of poultry stuffing blended to make a prize winning bread.

5½ to 6 cups all-purpose flour
2 packages Red Star Instant Blend Dry Yeast
⅔ cup nonfat dry milk solids
3 tablespoons sugar
3 tablespoons chopped fresh parsley
1 tablespoon dry onion soup mix
1½ teaspoons poultry seasoning
1 teaspoon salt
½ teaspoon thyme leaves
2 cups water
2 teaspoons instant chicken bouillon
3 tablespoons shortening
1 egg white, slightly beaten
1 tablespoon water
2 tablespoons sesame seeds

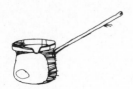

Bread "Stew-Pendous"

Oven 350°   2 Braids or Loaves

In large mixer bowl, combine 3 cups flour, yeast, milk, sugar, parsley, soup mix, poultry seasoning, salt and thyme; mix well. In saucepan, heat water, bouillon and shortening until warm (120-130°; shortening does not need to melt). Add to flour mixture. Blend at low speed until moistened; beat 3 minutes at medium speed. By hand, gradually stir in enough remaining flour to make a firm dough. Knead on floured surface until smooth and elastic, 5 to 8 minutes. Place in greased bowl, turning to grease top. Cover; let rise in warm place until light and doubled, about 45 minutes.

Punch down dough. Divide into 2 parts. Divide each half into 3 pieces. On lightly floured surface, roll each piece to a 14-inch rope. Loosely braid from center to ends. Pinch ends and tuck under to seal. Place on greased cookie sheets or in greased 8x4-inch bread pans. Cover; let rise in warm place until double, about 35 minutes. Combine egg white and water; gently brush tops of braids. Sprinkle with sesame seed. Bake at 350° for 45 to 50 minutes until golden brown. Remove from pans; cool.

Beef stew seasoning mix adds a unique flavor to these loaves. Good to serve with soups or beef stew!

4 to 4½ cups all-purpose flour
2 packages Red Star Instant
**   Blend Dry Yeast**
¼ cup sugar
1 envelope (about 1⅝ oz.) beef
**   stew seasoning mix**
¾ cup milk
½ cup water
¼ cup butter or margarine
2 eggs
Butter

Oven 375°   2 Loaves

In large mixer bowl, combine 2 cups flour, yeast, sugar and seasoning mix; mix well. In saucepan, heat milk, water and butter until warm (120-130°; butter does not need to melt). Add to flour mixture. Add eggs. Blend at low speed until moistened; beat 3 minutes at medium speed. By hand, gradually stir in enough remaining flour to make a firm dough. Knead on floured surface 5 to 8 minutes. Place in greased bowl, turning to grease top. Cover; let rise in warm place until double, about 1½ hours.

Punch down dough. Divide into 2 parts. On lightly floured surface, roll or pat each half to a 14x7-inch rectangle. Starting with shorter side, roll up tightly, pressing dough into roll with each turn. Pinch edges and ends to seal. Place in greased 8x4-inch bread pans. Cover; let rise in warm place until double, about 1½ hours. Bake at 375° for 35 to 40 minutes. Remove from pans; brush with butter. Cool.

Beer Limpa

 A hearty, robust bread that's a favorite of men.

3 to 3½ cups all-purpose flour
3 cups rye flour
2 packages Red Star Instant
  Blend Dry Yeast
¼ cup packed brown sugar
2 tablespoons fennel seeds
1 tablespoon salt
1½ cups beer
½ cup water
¼ cup dark molasses
2 tablespoons shortening
1 tablespoon vinegar

Oven 375°   2 Round Loaves

In large mixer bowl, combine 1 cup all-purpose flour, 2 cups rye flour, yeast, sugar, fennel seed and salt; mix well. In saucepan, heat beer, water, molasses, shortening and vinegar until warm (120-130°; shortening does not need to melt). Add to flour mixture. Blend at low speed until moistened; beat 3 minutes at medium speed. By hand, gradually stir in remaining rye flour and enough remaining all-purpose flour to make a firm dough. Knead on floured surface 5 to 8 minutes. Place in greased bowl, turning to grease top. Cover; let rise in warm place until double, about 1½ hours.

Punch down dough. Divide into 2 parts. On lightly floured surface, shape each half into a round loaf. Place on large greased cookie sheet. Cover; let rise in warm place until almost doubled, about 1 hour. Bake at 375° for 30 to 35 minutes until loaves sound hollow when tapped. Remove from cookie sheet; cool.

Beef 'N Brew Braid

 This handsome braid is made delicious with beer, dried beef and mustard.

4 to 4½ cups all-purpose flour
2 packages Red Star Instant
  Blend Dry Yeast
2 tablespoons sugar
1 teaspoon salt
1 cup beer
½ cup water
2 tablespoons shortening
1 egg, slightly beaten
1 jar (2½ oz.) dried beef, snipped
2 teaspoons prepared mustard
1 egg
2 teaspoons water

Oven 375°   1 Large Braid

In large mixer bowl, combine 2 cups flour, yeast, sugar and salt; mix well. In saucepan, heat beer, ½ cup water and shortening until warm (120-130°; shortening does not need to melt). Add to flour mixture. Add egg, dried beef and mustard. Blend at low speed until moistened; beat 3 minutes at medium speed. By hand, gradually stir in enough remaining flour to make a firm dough. Knead on floured surface 5 to 8 minutes. Place in greased bowl, turning to grease top. Cover; let rise in warm place until double, about 1 hour.

Punch down dough. Divide into 3 parts. On lightly floured surface, roll each third to make a 15-inch rope. On greased cookie sheet, braid loosely from center to ends. Pinch ends and tuck under to seal. Cover; let rise in warm place until double, about 30 minutes. Combine egg and water; brush braid. Bake at 375° for 30 to 35 minutes until golden brown. Remove from cookie sheet; cool.

Double Onion Cheese Bread

Onion in the bread and an onion-cheese filling makes this bread a favorite for onion lovers.

6 to 6½ cups all-purpose flour
2 packages Red Star Instant Blend Dry Yeast
1 teaspoon salt
1 tablespoon instant minced onion
1 can (10½ oz.) condensed onion soup, plus enough water to make 2¼ cups
2 tablespoons butter or margarine

Filling:
1 medium onion, finely chopped
2 tablespoons butter or margarine
⅔ cup Stella shredded Cheddar cheese

Oven 375°　　　　　　　　**2 Loaves**

In large mixer bowl, combine 3 cups flour, yeast, salt and minced onion; mix well. In saucepan, heat soup, water and butter until warm (120-130°; butter does not need to melt). Add to flour mixture. Blend at low speed until moistened; beat 3 minutes at medium speed. By hand, gradually stir in enough remaining flour to make a firm dough. Knead on floured surface until smooth and elastic, 5 to 8 minutes. Place in greased bowl, turning to grease top. Cover; let rise in warm place until light and doubled, about 1 hour.

Prepare Filling: In small skillet, sauté onion in butter until lightly browned. Drain well. Add cheese; set aside.

Punch down dough. Divide into 2 parts. On lightly floured surface, roll each half to a 15x7-inch rectangle. Spread each rectangle with half of onion-cheese mixture. Starting with shorter side, roll up tightly, pressing dough into roll with each turn. Pinch edges and ends to seal. Place in greased 8x4-inch bread pans. Cover; let rise in warm place until double, about 30 minutes. Bake at 375° for 35 to 40 minutes until golden brown. Remove from pans; cool.

My Notes: _____

_____

_____

_____

_____

_____

_____

_____

_____

_____

_____

_____

Pepper Cheese Bread

⏱ A new medium for the pepper cheese flavor combination.

4½ to 5 cups all-purpose flour
2 packages Red Star Instant Blend Dry Yeast
2 tablespoons sugar
2 teaspoons salt
2 teaspoons coarse pepper
¾ cup milk
¾ cup water
¼ cup shortening
1 egg
1 cup Stella shredded Cheddar cheese

Oven 375°　　　**2 Round Loaves**

In large mixer bowl, combine 2 cups flour, yeast, sugar, salt and pepper; mix well. In saucepan, heat milk, water and shortening until warm (120-130°; shortening does not need to melt). Add to flour mixture. Add egg. Beat at low speed until moistened; beat 3 minutes at medium speed. By hand, gradually stir in cheese and enough remaining flour to make a firm dough. Knead on floured surface until smooth and elastic, 5 to 8 minutes. Cover; let rise in warm oven (Turn oven to lowest setting for 1 minute; turn off.) for 20 minutes.

Punch down dough. Divide into 2 parts. Shape each half into a round loaf. Place on greased baking sheet. Cover; let rise in warm oven until double, about 30 minutes. Bake at 375° for 20 to 25 minutes until golden brown. Remove from cookie sheet; cool.

Sourdough-Like Beer Bread

🎖 This easy-to-make bread tastes like sourdough but doesn't require a starter.

5 to 5½ cups all-purpose flour
2 packages Red Star Instant Blend Dry Yeast
¼ cup sugar
1½ teaspoons salt
1½ cups beer
½ cup water
3 tablespoons oil
Cornmeal

Oven 375°　　　**2 Loaves**

In large mixer bowl, combine 2 cups flour, yeast, sugar and salt; mix well. In saucepan, heat beer, water and oil until warm (120-130°). Add to flour mixture. Blend at low speed until moistened; beat 3 minutes at medium speed. By hand, gradually stir in enough remaining flour to make a firm dough. Knead on floured surface until smooth and elastic, 5 to 8 minutes. Place in greased bowl, turning to grease top. Cover; let rise in warm place until light and doubled, about 1 hour.

Punch down dough. Divide into 2 parts. On lightly floured surface, roll or pat each half to an 11x7-inch rectangle. Starting with longer side, roll up tightly, pressing dough into roll with each turn. Pinch edges and ends to seal. Place seam-side down on large greased cookie sheet sprinkled with cornmeal. With very sharp knife, make 3 or 4 diagonal slashes across top of each loaf. Cover; let rise in warm place until light and doubled, about 30 minutes. Bake at 375° for 30 to 35 minutes until golden brown. Remove from cookie sheet; cool.

Corn Cheddar Bubble Loaf

🎗 A marvelous pull-apart bubble loaf that can be made the day before, refrigerated overnight and baked before serving. Great for summer barbecues or to serve with hearty winter soups.

4¾ to 5¼ cups all-purpose flour
2 packages Red Star Instant
   Blend Dry Yeast
1 cup cornmeal
2 tablespoons sugar
2 teaspoons salt
1¾ cups milk
½ cup water
2 tablespoons butter or
   margarine
½ cup Stella shredded sharp
   Cheddar cheese
⅓ cup butter or margarine,
   melted

Oven 375°   One 10-inch
                   Bubble Loaf

In large mixer bowl, combine 1½ cups flour, yeast, cornmeal, sugar and salt; mix well. In saucepan, heat milk, water and 2 tablespoons butter until warm (120-130°; butter does not need to melt). Add to flour mixture. Blend at low speed until moistened; beat 3 minutes at medium speed. By hand, gradually stir in cheese and enough remaining flour to make a firm dough. Knead on floured surface 5 to 8 minutes. Place in greased bowl, turning to grease top. Cover; let rise in warm place until double, about 1 hour.

Punch down dough; divide into 4 parts. Divide each fourth into 10 pieces. Shape each piece into a smooth ball; dip in melted butter. Place in greased 10-inch solid bottom tubed cake pan or 12-cup Bundt® pan. Cover; refrigerate 2 to 24 hours. Bake at 375° for 55 to 60 minutes until golden brown. Remove from pan; brush with butter. Serve warm.

Choosey Cheesy Bread

🎗 Tender, cheesy bread breaks into buttery flakes for easy serving.

5 to 5½ cups all-purpose flour
2 packages Red Star Instant
   Blend Dry Yeast
2 tablespoons sugar
2 teaspoons salt
1½ cups buttermilk
½ cup water
2 tablespoons oil
1 cup grated Stella Parmesan
   cheese
2 tablespoons butter, melted

Oven 375°   2 Loaves

In large mixer bowl, combine 2½ cups flour, yeast, sugar and salt; mix well. In saucepan, heat buttermilk, water and oil until warm (120-130°). Add to flour mixture. Blend at low speed until moistened; beat 3 minutes at medium speed. By hand, gradually stir in cheese and enough remaining flour to make a firm dough. Knead on floured surface until smooth and elastic, 5 to 8 minutes. Place in greased bowl, turning to grease top. Cover; let rise in warm place until light and doubled, about 1 hour.

Punch down dough. Divide into 2 parts. On lightly floured surface, roll each half to a 16x10-inch rectangle. Brush with half of melted butter. Cut into four 10x4-inch rectangles. Stack together, butter-side up. Cut into five stacks, 4x2 inches. Arrange stacks in a row, placing cut-side down in a 9x5-inch greased bread pan. Cover; let rise in warm place until doubled, about 30 minutes. Bake at 375° for 30 to 35 minutes until golden brown. Remove from pans; cool.

175

Caraway Cheese Sandwich Bread

This delicious bread would be a welcome addition to any buffet table, or it would make an excellent holiday gift.

7 to 7½ cups all-purpose flour
2 packages Red Star Instant Blend Dry Yeast
2 tablespoons sugar
1 tablespoon salt
1 tablespoon caraway seeds
¼ cup grated Stella Parmesan cheese
1½ cups water
1 can (11 oz.) Cheddar cheese soup, undiluted
2 tablespoons butter or margarine
2 eggs

Oven 375°   **2 Loaves**

In large mixer bowl, combine 3 cups flour, yeast, sugar, salt, caraway seed and Parmesan cheese. In saucepan, heat water, soup and butter until warm (120-130°; butter does not need to melt). Add to flour mixture. Add eggs. Blend at low speed until moistened; beat 3 minutes at medium speed. By hand, gradually stir in enough remaining flour to make a firm dough. Knead on floured surface until smooth and elastic, 5 to 8 minutes. Place in greased bowl, turning to grease top. Cover; let rise in warm place until double, about 1 hour.

Punch down dough. Divide into 2 parts. On lightly floured surface, roll or pat each half to a 14x7-inch rectangle. Starting with shorter side, roll up tightly, pressing dough into roll with each turn. Pinch edges and ends to seal. Place in two greased 9x5-inch bread pans. Cover; let rise in warm place until double, about 30 minutes. Bake at 375° for 35 to 40 minutes until golden brown. Remove from pans; cool.

Blushing Sandwich Buns

These flavorful sandwich buns are especially good for hamburgers or "sloppy joes."

5 to 5½ cups all-purpose flour
2 packages Red Star Instant Blend Dry Yeast
¼ cup wheat germ
¼ cup sugar
2 teaspoons salt
½ teaspoon celery salt
½ teaspoon oregano leaves, crushed
¼ teaspoon basil leaves, crushed
¼ teaspoon ground ginger
1½ cups tomato juice
½ cup water
¼ cup shortening

Oven 375°   **18 Buns**

In large mixer bowl, combine 3 cups flour, yeast, wheat germ, sugar, salt, celery salt, oregano, basil and ginger; mix well. In saucepan, heat tomato juice, water and shortening until warm (120-130°; shortening does not need to melt). Add to flour mixture. Blend at low speed until moistened; beat 3 minutes at medium speed. By hand, gradually stir in enough remaining flour to make a firm dough. Knead on floured surface until smooth and elastic, 5 to 8 minutes. Place in greased bowl, turning to grease top. Cover; let rise in warm place until double, about 1 hour.

Punch down dough. Divide into 3 parts. Divide each third into 6 pieces. Shape each piece into a smooth ball; place on greased cookie sheets. Flatten to a 4-inch diameter. Cover; let rise in warm place until double, about 30 minutes. Bake at 375° for 15 to 20 minutes. Remove from cookie sheets; cool.

Speedy Seedy Muffins

Three seeds—poppy, celery and dill—add interest and flavor to these cheese and mushroom flavored dinner rolls. Bake them in small cans for a special occasion.

3½ cups all-purpose flour
1 package Red Star Instant Blend Dry Yeast
2 tablespoons sugar
2 tablespoons instant minced onion
1 teaspoon onion salt
1 tablespoon poppy seeds
1½ teaspoons celery seeds
1½ teaspoons dill seed
1 can (10¾ oz.) cream of mushroom soup, undiluted
¼ cup water
2 tablespoons butter or margarine
1 egg
1 cup shredded American process cheese
1 tablespoon butter or margarine, melted

Oven 375°   **18 Muffins**

In large mixer bowl, combine 1 cup flour, yeast, sugar, onion and onion salt; mix well. Combine poppy seed, celery seed and dill seed. Reserve 1 tablespoon for Topping; add remaining seeds to flour mixture. In saucepan, heat soup, water and 2 tablespoons butter until warm (120-130°; butter does not need to melt). Add to flour mixture. Add egg. Blend at low speed until moistened; beat 3 minutes at medium speed. By hand, gradually stir in cheese and enough remaining flour to make a stiff batter. Cover; let rise in warm place until light and doubled, about 1 hour.

Punch down dough. Using spoon dipped in melted butter, fill well greased muffin pan cups almost full. Sprinkle tops with reserved seeds. Cover; let rise in warm place until doubled, 50 to 60 minutes. Bake at 375° for 12 to 15 minutes. Remove from pans; serve warm.

My Notes: _____

_____

_____

_____

_____

_____

_____

_____

_____

_____

_____

_____

One Hour Pan Rolls Italiano

⏱ Plan to serve these rolls hot with your next spaghetti dinner. Excellent flavor!

3½ to 4 cups all-purpose flour
2 packages Red Star Instant Blend Dry Yeast
2 tablespoons sugar
2 teaspoons garlic salt
1 teaspoon Italian seasoning
1 cup milk
½ cup water
2 tablespoons butter or margarine
1 egg
½ cup grated Stella Parmesan cheese
2 tablespoons butter, melted
¼ cup grated Stella Parmesan cheese

Oven 375°   **16 Rolls**

In large mixer bowl, combine 1½ cups flour, yeast, sugar, garlic salt and seasoning; mix well. In saucepan, heat milk, water and butter until warm (120-130°; butter does not need to melt). Add to flour mixture. Add egg. Blend at low speed until moistened; beat 3 minutes at medium speed. By hand, gradually stir in ½ cup cheese and enough remaining flour to make a firm dough. Knead on floured surface until smooth and elastic, 3 to 5 minutes. Place in greased bowl, turning to grease top. Cover; let rise in warm oven (Turn oven to lowest setting for 1 minute; turn off.) for 15 minutes.

Punch down dough. Divide dough into 4 parts. Divide each fourth into 4 pieces. Shape each piece into a smooth ball. Dip tops into melted butter and ¼ cup cheese. Place in well greased 13x9-inch cake pan or two 9-inch layer cake pans. Cover; let rise in warm oven about 10 minutes. Bake at 375° for 20 minutes until golden brown. Remove from pans; cool.

Savory Jonni Buns

🏵 These delicious and unusual cornmeal buns with onion soup mix inside and on top will draw raves.

3½ to 4 cups all-purpose flour
2 packages Red Star Instant Blend Dry Yeast
2 tablespoons sugar
1 teaspoon salt
⅓ cup nonfat dry milk solids
¾ cup yellow cornmeal
2 tablespoons dry onion soup mix
1¼ cups water
¼ cup butter or margarine
1 egg
2 tablespoons butter, melted

Onion Wine Crescent Twists

Oven 375°	15 Rolls

In large mixer bowl, combine 1½ cups flour, yeast, sugar, salt and milk solids; mix well. Combine cornmeal and onion soup mix; reserve ¼ cup for Topping. Add remaining cornmeal and soup mix to flour mixture. In saucepan, heat water and butter until warm (120-130°; butter does not need to melt). Add to flour mixture. Add egg. Blend at low speed until moistened; beat 3 minutes at medium speed. By hand, gradually stir in enough remaining flour to make a firm dough. Knead on floured surface until smooth and elastic, 5 to 8 minutes. Place in greased bowl, turning to grease top. Cover; let rise in warm place until light and doubled, about 45 minutes.

Punch down dough. Divide into 3 parts. Divide each third into 5 pieces. Shape each piece into a smooth ball. Dip each piece into melted butter; roll in reserved cornmeal mixture, turn to coat. Place in greased 13x9-inch cake pan. Cover; let rise in warm place until double, about 30 minutes. Bake at 375° for 20 to 25 minutes until golden brown. Remove from pan; cool.

These rolls are reminiscent of soft pretzels. They are great picnic "take alongs" — better than chips for snacking.

3 to 3½ cups all-purpose flour
1 package Red Star Instant Blend Dry Yeast
½ cup cornmeal
2 tablespoons sugar
2 teaspoons salt
½ teaspoon garlic powder
1 cup chopped onions
2 tablespoons butter or margarine
1 cup water
½ cup dry sherry

Oven 375°	20 Rolls

In large mixer bowl, combine 1½ cups flour, yeast, cornmeal, sugar, salt and garlic powder; mix well. In saucepan, sauté onions in butter until soft. Add water and heat until warm (120-130°). Add to flour mixture. Add sherry. Blend at low speed until moistened; beat 3 minutes at medium speed. By hand, gradually stir in enough remaining flour to make a soft dough. Knead on floured surface 5 to 8 minutes. Place in greased bowl, turning to grease top. Cover; let rise in warm place until double, about 1½ hours.

Punch down dough. Divide into 2 parts. Roll or pat each half to a 10x6-inch rectangle. Cut into ten 6x1-inch strips. Twist each strip into a crescent shape; place on greased cookie sheet. Cover; let rise in warm place until double, about 30 minutes. Bake at 375° for 15 to 20 minutes until golden brown. Remove from cookie sheets; cool.

Main dish & snacks

Vienna Snack Loaves

Baked Rueben

**Sauerkraut Rye
Party Snack Loaves**

Corned Beef Party Rounds

Pita Bread with Taco Filling   Whole Wheat Pita Bread
with Falafel Filling

Chicago-Style Deep Dish Pizza   181

MAIN DISH AND SNACK BREADS

Who would think a yeast breads cookbook would have a chapter filled with great recipes for main dishes and snacks! A yeast bread can be an excellent base for the addition of meat, fish, eggs or cheese.

The main dish recipes in this chapter include the classic thin-crust *Pizza* and the popular *Chicago-Style Deep Dish Pizza*, along with a *Mexican Pizza*. There are three flavor variations of a spectacular *High Hat Soufflé*—a Salmon, Tuna or Italian Beef filling carries a yeast-raised bread topping that puffs up like an egg soufflé. We are proud of our *Pita* breads that are bound to be a baking success with pockets every time. Choose from five delicious fillings. The popular Reuben sandwich takes on a new twist with an all-in-one *Baked Reuben* that's perfect for lunch or supper.

You'll find several breads which could double as snacks or as soup and salad accompaniments. The *Little Filled Pies* are delightful for snacking or to serve for lunch. For hors d'oeuvres or just snacks, make either the *Sauerkraut Rye Party Snack Loaves* or the *Vienna Snack Loaves*, then slice and spread with a topping.

We hope you'll make these main dish and snack breads some of your favorite menu ideas to be served again and again.

Yeast-Crust-Quiche

🕑 A press-in-the-pan yeast crust with a delightful quiche filling.

1 cup all-purpose flour
1 package Red Star Instant Blend Dry Yeast
½ teaspoon salt
½ cup warm water
1 tablespoon shortening
8 slices bacon, cooked and crumbled
1 cup (4 oz.) Stella shredded Fontinella cheese
3 eggs
2 cups Half and Half
1 teaspoon salt
Dash pepper

Oven 400°   4 to 6 Servings

In medium mixer bowl, combine ½ cup flour, yeast and salt; mix well. Add water (120-130°) and shortening to flour mixture. Mix by hand until almost smooth. Gradually stir in remaining flour to make a firm dough. With lightly floured fingers, press into greased 10-inch pie pan to make a crust. If desired, flute edges. Sprinkle bacon and cheese in pie shell. In large mixing bowl, beat eggs until foamy. Add remaining ingredients; mix well. Pour over bacon and cheese. Bake at 400° for 30 to 35 minutes until knife inserted in center comes out clean. Serve warm.

Pizza Burger Pie

🕑 Favorite pizza filling in a moist spread-in-the-pan crust.

Filling:
1 lb. lean ground beef
1 teaspoon salt
¼ teaspoon pepper
1 tablespoon instant minced onion
½ teaspoon Italian herb seasoning
1 can (6 oz.) tomato paste
1 can (4 oz.) sliced mushrooms, drained

Crust:
1½ cups all-purpose flour
1 package Red Star Instant Blend Dry Yeast
1 teaspoon sugar
½ teaspoon salt
½ cup sour cream
½ cup water
¼ cup shortening
1 egg
1 cup (4 oz.) Stella shredded Mozzarella cheese

Oven 375°   4 to 6 Servings

Prepare Filling: In skillet, lightly brown beef with salt and pepper; drain. Add onion, Italian seasoning, tomato paste and mushrooms; mix well. Cool.

In medium bowl, combine flour, yeast, sugar and salt; mix well. In saucepan, heat sour cream, water and shortening until warm (120-130°; shortening does not need to melt). Add to flour mixture. Add egg. Mix by hand until smooth. Spread in greased 9 or 10-inch pie pan to make a crust. Spoon Filling into crust; sprinkle with cheese. Bake at 375° for 30 to 35 minutes until light golden brown. Serve immediately.

TIP: Filling can be prepared ahead and refrigerated; assemble and bake as directed.

Pizza

Traditional pizza dough adds an easy-homemade touch to a thin crust pizza. Using a prepared pizza sauce, you can make and bake this pizza in an hour. The combination of Mozzarella and Cheddar cheeses on top gives extra flavor.

**2½ cups all-purpose flour
1 package Red Star Instant
　Blend Dry Yeast
1½ teaspoons salt
1 cup warm water
2 tablespoons shortening**

Oven 400°　　Two 12-inch Pizzas

In medium mixing bowl, combine 1 cup flour, yeast and salt; mix well. Add warm water (120-130°) and shortening. Mix by hand until almost smooth. Gradually stir in remaining flour to make a firm dough. Let rest 15 minutes.

Prepare Toppings.

Divide dough into 2 parts. With well-floured or greased fingers, press each half into greased 12 or 14-inch pizza pan. Spread half of pizza sauce over dough. Sprinkle half of ground beef, mushrooms, green pepper and cheeses over sauce. Bake at 400° for 25 to 30 minutes until edge is crisp and light golden brown and cheeses are melted. Serve immediately.

NOTE: Pizza dough can be frozen, thawed and assembled as directed or assembled pizza can be frozen, thawed and baked as directed.

**Pizza Sauce
and Toppings**

**1½ lbs. lean ground beef
1 teaspoon salt
1½ cups prepared pizza sauce
1 to 1½ teaspoons Italian
　seasoning
1 cup sliced mushrooms
½ cup diced green pepper
1 package (8 oz.) Stella shredded
　Mozzarella cheese
1 package (8 oz.) Stella shredded
　Cheddar cheese**

In large skillet, lightly brown beef with salt; drain. Combine with pizza sauce and Italian seasoning. Prepare other ingredients and set aside.

Chicago-Style Deep Dish Pizza

A spectacular one-dish meal! Serve this Italian inspired specialty with a tossed salad and beverage. Add your favorite toppings, if desired.

**3¼ to 3¾ cups all-purpose flour
1 package Red Star Instant
　Blend Dry Yeast
1½ teaspoons salt
1¼ cups warm water
3 tablespoons oil**

**Oven 425°　　　　One 14-inch
　　　　　　　　Deep Dish Pizza**

In large mixer bowl, combine 1½ cups flour, yeast and salt; mix well. Add warm water (120-130°) and oil to flour mixture. Blend at low speed until moistened; beat 3 minutes at medium speed. By hand, gradually stir in enough remaining flour to make a firm dough. Knead on floured surface, 3 to 5 minutes. Cover dough with plastic wrap and a towel. Let rest 20 minutes.

Mexican Pizza

Prepare Pizza Sauce and Toppings. On lightly floured surface, roll dough to a 16-inch circle. Place in oiled 14-inch round deep dish pizza pan, pushing dough halfway up sides of pan. Cover; let rise in warm place until puffy, about 30 minutes.

Spread pizza sauce over dough. Sprinkle sausage over sauce; then arrange mushrooms, green pepper and onion over sausage. Sprinkle cheese on top. Bake at 425° for 20 to 25 minutes until edge is crisp and golden brown and cheese is melted.

TIP: This recipe has been developed for a 14-inch round deep dish pizza pan. The pizza could also be baked in a 13x9x2-inch cake pan. Roll dough to a 15x11-inch rectangle. Baking time may be slightly less.

Pizza Sauce and Toppings

1 lb. pork sausage
1 can (8 oz.) tomato sauce
1 can (6 oz.) tomato paste
2 teaspoons sugar
1 to 1½ teaspoons oregano
1 teaspoon parsley flakes
½ to ¾ teaspoon basil
½ teaspoon salt
⅛ teaspoon garlic powder
⅛ teaspoon crushed red pepper
1 cup sliced mushrooms
⅓ cup diced green pepper (use part red pepper, if desired)
¼ cup chopped onion
1 package (8 oz.) Stella shredded Mozzarella cheese

In large skillet, lightly brown sausage; drain. Combine tomato sauce and paste with seasonings; simmer 10 to 15 minutes. Prepare other ingredients and set aside.

🏅 A pizza crust made different with cornmeal is topped with favorite taco ingredients. This recipe is for all who love pizza and Mexican food.

2½ cups all-purpose flour
1 package Red Star Instant Blend Dry Yeast
½ cup cornmeal
1 teaspoon sugar
1 teaspoon salt
1 cup warm water
2 tablespoons oil
1½ lbs. lean ground beef
2 cans (7½ oz. each) taco sauce
2 cans (4 oz. each) green chilies, drained and chopped
8 ounces natural Monterey Jack cheese, sliced ⅛-inch thick
Sliced green onions
Shredded lettuce

Oven 425°   Two 12-inch Pizzas

In large mixer bowl, combine 1 cup flour, yeast, cornmeal, sugar and salt; mix well. Add water (120-130°), and oil to flour mixture. Blend at low speed until moistened; beat 3 minutes at medium speed. By hand, gradually stir in enough remaining flour to make a soft dough. Knead on floured surface, 5 to 8 minutes. Place in greased bowl, turning to grease top. Cover; let rise in warm place until double, about 45 minutes.

Prepare Topping: In large skillet, lightly brown beef; drain. Stir in taco sauce. Cook, uncovered, 5 to 10 minutes until almost dry. Remove from heat; cool.

Punch down dough. Divide into 2 parts. Shape each half into a ball; place on greased cookie sheets. Using palms of hands, pat dough into a 12-inch circle, making edges slightly thick. Spread meat mixture over dough. Arrange chilies and cheese over meat. Bake at 425° for 15 to 20 minutes until crust is golden brown. Sprinkle with onions and lettuce. Serve immediately.

High Hat Salmon Soufflé

🎖 An ideal luncheon main dish. The light, yeast-raised topping puffs up like a traditional egg soufflé—serve immediately before it falls! There's a choice of three flavors: salmon, tuna or Italian Beef.

Bread Soufflé Topping:
1 cup all-purpose flour
1 package Red Star Instant Blend Dry Yeast
2 tablespoons sugar
1 teaspoon salt
¾ cup milk
¼ cup butter or margarine
2 eggs, separated

Salmon Base:
1 can (15¼ oz.) salmon, drained and flaked
1 can (10¾ oz.) cream of celery soup, undiluted
¼ cup milk
2 tablespoons diced pimento
2 teaspoons grated onion

Oven 375°   4 to 6 Servings

Prepare Topping: In large mixer bowl, combine ½ cup flour, yeast, sugar and salt; mix well. In saucepan, heat milk and butter until warm (120-130°; butter does not need to melt). Add to flour mixture. Blend at low speed until moistened; beat 2 minutes at medium speed. Add egg yolks and remaining flour. Beat at high speed 2 minutes, scraping bowl occasionally. Cover; let rise in warm place until light and double, about 40 minutes.

Prepare Salmon Base: Combine salmon, soup, milk, pimento and onion; place mixture in greased 1½-quart casserole.

Stir down batter. Beat egg whites until stiff, but not dry; fold into batter. Pour over salmon mixture. Bake at 375° for 40 to 45 minutes until brown. Serve immediately.

High Hat Tuna Soufflé

Prepare Bread Soufflé Topping as for High Hat Salmon Soufflé *except* mix in ½ teaspoon dill weed with the dry ingredients in mixer bowl.

Tuna Base:
1 can (6½ oz.) chunk tuna, drained and flaked
1 can (10¾ oz.) cream of mushroom soup, undiluted
½ cup chopped celery
2 hard cooked eggs, diced
2 tablespoons diced pimento
2 teaspoons grated onion
⅛ teaspoon pepper

Combine all ingredients for Tuna Base. Place in greased 1½-quart casserole. Bake as directed above.

High Hat Italian Beef Soufflé

Prepare Bread Soufflé Toppping as for High Hat Salmon Soufflé.

Italian Beef Base:
1 lb. lean ground beef
½ cup chopped onion
¼ cup chopped green pepper
½ teaspoon salt
1 can (10¾ oz.) condensed tomato soup, undiluted
1 can (4 oz.) mushroom stems and pieces, drained
¾ teaspoon Italian herb seasoning

In large skillet, lightly brown ground beef, onion, green pepper and salt, about 10 minutes, until onion and green pepper are soft; drain. Cool.

Combine meat mixture with soup, mushrooms and herb seasoning. Place meat mixture in greased 1½-quart casserole. Bake as directed above.

Yaroslav's Snack Bread

A Russian recipe translated for the American kitchen. It's great with soup or salad.

3 cups all-purpose flour
1 package Red Star Instant Blend Dry Yeast
1 tablespoon sugar
1 teaspoon salt
1 cup warm water
1 tablespoon butter or margarine, softened
1 egg
½ cup chopped onion
2 tablespoons butter
4 hard-cooked eggs, chopped
4 slices bacon, cooked and crumbled
1 cup sour cream
1 tablespoon milk
1 teaspoon salt
1 teaspoon all-purpose flour
Dill weed

Oven 425°   **2 Large Snack Breads**

In large mixer bowl, combine 1½ cups flour, yeast, sugar and 1 teaspoon salt; mix well. Add water (120-130°) and 1 tablespoon butter to flour mixture. Add egg. Blend at low speed until moistened; beat 3 minutes at medium speed. By hand, gradually stir in remaining 1½ cups flour to make a soft dough. Knead on floured surface until smooth and elastic, 5 to 8 minutes. Place in greased bowl, turning to grease top. Cover; let rise in warm place until light and doubled, about 1 hour.

Prepare Topping: In small saucepan, sauté onion in 2 tablespoons butter. Add chopped eggs and bacon; set aside.

Punch down dough. Divide into 2 parts. Roll each half to a 12x9-inch rectangle. Place on greased cookie sheets. Cover; let rise until almost doubled, about 30 minutes. In small bowl combine sour cream, milk, 1 teaspoon salt and 1 teaspoon flour. Spoon half of egg mixture on dough. Spread with half of sour cream mixture, spreading to within ¾ inch of edges. Sprinkle dill on top. Place in cold oven and turn heat to 425°. Bake 15 minutes; reduce heat to 375° and bake about 15 minutes longer until crust is golden brown. Let stand a few minutes; cut into serving size pieces. Serve warm.

My Notes: _____

_____

_____

_____

_____

_____

_____

_____

_____

_____

Pita Bread

⭐ Pita bread is becoming a favorite in the United States. It originated in the Middle East and was eaten at every meal. As it bakes, it opens up like a "pocket" and delicious sandwich fillings can be placed in this pocket.

4½ to 4¾ cups all-purpose flour
1 package Red Star Instant Blend Dry Yeast
1½ teaspoons sugar
1½ teaspoons salt
1¾ cups warm water
2 tablespoons oil

Oven 500°   12 Pocket Breads

In large mixer bowl, combine 2 cups flour, yeast, sugar and salt; mix well. Add warm water (120-130°) and oil. Blend at low speed until moistened; beat 3 minutes at medium speed. By hand, gradually stir in enough remaining flour to make a firm dough. Knead on floured surface until smooth and elastic, about 10 minutes. Cover with plastic wrap, then a towel. Let rest 20 minutes.

Punch down dough. Divide into 2 parts. Divide each half into 6 pieces. Shape each piece into a smooth ball. Cover; let rise 30 minutes. On lightly floured surface, roll each ball to a 5-inch circle. Place 6 circles on a large cooling rack. Place cooling rack on oven rack. Bake at 500° for 5 minutes until puffed and tops just begin to brown. Remove from rack; cool. Cut circles in half; fill.

VARIATION: Stir in 1 cup wheat germ with second addition of flour.

TIP: The rolling and baking instructions should be carefully followed to be sure the bread bakes with the "pocket."

100% Whole Wheat Pita Bread

This is an excellent quality all whole wheat recipe. The breads provide a tasty flavor for the fillings suggested.

6 cups whole wheat flour
1 package Red Star Instant Blend Dry Yeast
1 tablespoon salt
1½ teaspoons sugar
2½ cups warm water
2 tablespoons oil

Oven 500°   24 Pocket Breads

In large mixer bowl, combine 3 cups flour, yeast, salt and sugar; mix well. Add warm water (120-130°) and oil. Blend at low speed until moistened; beat 3 minutes at medium speed. By hand, gradually stir in remaining flour to make a firm dough. Knead on floured surface until smooth and elastic, about 10 minutes. Cover with plastic wrap, then a towel. Let rest 20 minutes.

Punch down dough. Divide into 4 parts. Divide each fourth into 6 pieces. Shape each piece into a smooth ball. On lightly floured surface, roll each ball to a 5-inch circle. Cover; let rise 30 minutes. Place 6 circles on a large cooling rack. Place cooling rack on oven rack. Bake at 500° for 5 minutes until puffed and tops just begin to brown. Remove from rack; cool. Cut circles in half; fill.

TIP: The rolling and baking instructions should be carefully followed to be sure the bread bakes with the "pocket."

Pita Bread Fillings

Falafel Filling

1 cup wheat germ
½ cup plain yogurt
½ cup shredded Monterey Jack
  cheese
¼ cup chopped almonds
2 tablespoons chopped fresh
  parsley
2 tablespoons finely chopped
  green onion
½ teaspoon oregano
¼ to ½ teaspoon ground cumin
½ teaspoon salt
¼ teaspoon garlic powder
2 tablespoons oil
1 cup alfalfa sprouts

16 Small Patties
Filling for 5 to 8 Pita Halves

Dressing:

1 cup plain yogurt
2 teaspoons horseradish
  mustard
½ teaspoon tarragon leaves
¼ teaspoon basil leaves
⅛ teaspoon salt

1 Cup Dressing

In medium bowl, combine ¾ cup wheat germ, yogurt, cheese, almonds, parsley, onion and seasonings. Shape into 16 small flat patties. Coat with ¼ cup wheat germ. In small skillet, heat oil. Brown patties 2 minutes on each side.

Prepare Dressing: Combine yogurt, mustard and seasonings.

Place 2 or 3 patties in each Pita half; top with sprouts. Spoon Dressing over sprouts.

Vegetable Sloppy Joe Filling

1 lb. lean ground beef
½ cup chopped onion
½ teaspoon salt
1 cup catsup
1 teaspoon prepared mustard
½ teaspoon chili powder
¼ cup chopped celery
¼ cup chopped green pepper
¼ cup chopped zucchini

2½ Cups
Filling for 6 to 8 Pita Halves

In large skillet, lightly brown beef, onion and salt, about 10 minutes until onion is soft; drain. Add catsup, mustard and chili powder; simmer 15 minutes over low heat. Add vegetables; heat 5 minutes. Spoon into Pita halves.

Taco Filling

1 lb. lean ground beef
½ cup chopped onion
½ teaspoon salt
1 can (8 oz.) tomato sauce
¼ teaspoon ground cumin
¼ teaspoon garlic powder
⅛ to ¼ teaspoon cayenne
1 cup shredded Stella Cheddar
  cheese
1 cup shredded lettuce
1 cup chopped tomato, drained

2 Cups
Filling for 6 to 8 Pita Halves

In large skillet, lightly brown beef, onion and salt, about 10 minutes until onion is soft; drain. Add tomato sauce, cumin, garlic powder and cayenne. Simmer 15 minutes over low heat. Spoon into Pita halves. Top with Cheddar cheese, lettuce and tomato.

(More fillings on next page)

Pita Bread Fillings

Chicken Salad Filling

¼ cup mayonnaise
¼ cup sour cream
2 teaspoons orange juice
   concentrate, thawed and
   undiluted
¼ teaspoon salt
¼ teaspoon ground ginger
2 cups cubed cooked chicken
1 cup green grapes, halved
½ cup thinly sliced celery
1 cup alfalfa sprouts

3½ Cups
Filling for 6 to 8 Pitas

In medium bowl, combine mayonnaise, sour cream, orange juice concentrate, salt and ginger; mix well. Add chicken, grapes and celery; toss lightly. Spoon into Pita halves; top with sprouts.

Italian Beef and Vegetables

½ cup sliced cherry tomatoes
½ cup chopped green pepper
½ cup thinly sliced cucumber
½ cup sliced mushrooms
¼ cup thinly sliced green onions
2 tablespoons Italian dressing
   Lettuce leaves
4 thin slices of cooked roast beef
   or steak, cut into strips

2 Cups Vegetables
Filling for 4 Pita Halves

In medium bowl, combine vegetables, except lettuce. Add dressing; toss lightly. Line each Pita half with a lettuce leaf; add sliced beef. Top with vegetables.

Speedy Supper Bread

⏱ A quick pizza flavored main dish! For a "round" bread, use a 10-inch ovenproof skillet for cooking the meat, then spoon bread topping on meat and bake right in the skillet.

1½ lbs. lean ground beef
½ cup chopped onion
½ teaspoon salt
1 cup catsup
1½ teaspoons parsley flakes
1½ cups all-purpose flour
1 package Red Star Instant
   Blend Dry Yeast
2 tablespoons sugar
1 teaspoon salt
⅛ teaspoon oregano leaves
⅛ teaspoon thyme leaves
⅛ teaspoon marjoram leaves
½ cup milk
¼ cup butter or margarine
2 eggs
2 cups (8 oz.) Stella shredded
   Mozzarella cheese
1 tablespoon butter or
   margarine, melted
2 tablespoons Stella grated
   Parmesan cheese

Oven 350°   6 Servings

In large skillet, lightly brown beef, onion and ½ teaspoon salt; drain. Stir in catsup and parsley flakes. Simmer while preparing bread topping.

In large mixer bowl, combine 1 cup flour, yeast, sugar, 1 teaspoon salt and herbs; mix well. In saucepan, heat milk and butter until warm (120-130°; butter does not need to melt). Add to flour mixture. Add eggs. Blend at low speed until moistened; beat 3 minutes at medium speed. By hand, stir in remaining flour.

Stir Mozzarella cheese into meat mixture. Spoon into greased 9-inch square cake pan or 1½-quart shallow casserole. Spoon bread topping over meat mixture. Drizzle with melted butter. Sprinkle Parmesan cheese on top. Let rise in warm place for 30 minutes. Bake at 350° for 20 to 25 minutes until light brown. Let stand for 5 minutes before cutting. Serve hot.

Soup or Salad Snack Bread

An unusual snack bread with a cheese, bacon and onion filling. It can be baked ahead and reheated in foil before serving. Perfect for all those football game parties.

3 to 3½ cups all-purpose flour
1 package Red Star Instant Blend Dry Yeast
1 tablespoon sugar
1½ teaspoons salt
1½ teaspoons dry mustard
½ cup water
½ cup milk
1 tablespoon oil
1 egg
1 egg, slightly beaten
3 cups Stella shredded Cheddar cheese
8 slices bacon, cooked and crumbled
½ teaspoon garlic salt
2 tablespoons instant minced onion

Oven 400°   **One 12-inch Snack Bread**

In small mixer bowl, combine 1½ cups flour, yeast, sugar, salt and dry mustard; mix well. In saucepan, heat water, milk and oil until warm (120-130°). Add to flour mixture. Add one egg. Blend at low speed until moistened; beat 3 minutes at medium speed. By hand, gradually stir in enough remaining flour to make a firm dough. Knead on floured surface until smooth and elastic, 5 to 8 minutes. Place in greased bowl, turning to grease top. Cover; let rise in warm place until light and doubled, about 1 hour.

Prepare Filling: Combine slightly beaten egg, cheese, bacon, garlic salt and onion; mix well. Set aside.

Punch down dough. Divide into 2 parts. On lightly floured surface, roll each half to a 13-inch circle. Place one half in greased 12-inch round pizza pan. Spread Filling over dough. Place remaining 13-inch circle over Filling. Pinch and press edges to seal; flute. Bake at 400° for 20 to 25 minutes until golden brown. Serve warm.

My Notes: _____

_____

_____

_____

_____

_____

_____

_____

Cheese 'N Beef Snack Bread

An easy no-rise snack bread for hors d'oeuvres or lunch.

3 cups all-purpose flour
1 package Red Star Instant Blend Dry Yeast
2 tablespoons sugar
1 tablespoon instant minced onion
1 teaspoon salt
1 teaspoon caraway seeds
1 cup milk
¼ cup water
3 tablespoons shortening
1 egg, separated
1 package (2.5 oz.) smoked sliced beef or corned beef, snipped
1½ cups Stella shredded Cheddar cheese

Oven 375°   One 15x10-inch Snack Bread

In large mixer bowl, combine 2 cups flour, yeast, sugar, onion, salt and caraway seed; mix well. In saucepan, heat milk, water and shortening until warm (120-130°; shortening does not need to melt). Add to flour mixture. Add egg yolk. Blend at low speed until moistened; beat 3 minutes at medium speed. By hand, gradually stir in remaining flour to make a stiff batter. Spread evenly in greased 15x10-inch jelly roll pan. Brush with slightly beaten egg white. Sprinkle beef and cheese on dough. Bake at 375° for 25 to 30 minutes until golden brown. Serve warm.

Sauerkraut Rye Party Snack Loaves

Bake these long narrow rye snack loaves and freeze to have on hand when you need an appetizer or want a nutritious snack. For a hot appetizer or snack, spread the bread slices with the corned beef mixture. To serve cold, spread with the cheese and shrimp mixture. They are delicious— and so easy!

2½ to 3 cups all-purpose flour
2 packages Red Star Instant Blend Dry Yeast
½ cup non-fat dry milk solids
2 tablespoons sugar
1 tablespoon whole caraway seeds
1½ teaspoons salt
¼ teaspoon ground ginger
1¼ cups warm water
2 tablespoons oil
1 can (8 oz.) undrained sauerkraut, room temperature
2 cups medium rye flour

Oven 375°   4 Snack Loaves

In large mixer bowl, combine 1¼ cups all-purpose flour, yeast, dry milk, sugar, caraway seed, salt and ginger; mix well. Add warm water (120-130°) and oil to flour mixture. Blend at low speed until moistened; beat 3 minutes at medium speed. By hand, gradually stir in sauerkraut, rye flour and enough remaining all-purpose flour to make a firm dough. (The amount of flour will depend upon how much juice the sauerkraut has.) Knead on floured surface until smooth and elastic, about 5 minutes.

Divide dough into 4 parts. On lightly floured surface, roll or pat each fourth to a 12x4-inch rectangle. Starting with longer side, roll up tightly, pressing dough into roll with each turn. Pinch edges and ends to seal. Place on greased cookie sheets. Cover; let rise in warm place until almost doubled, 20 to 30 minutes. Bake at 375° for 20 to 25 minutes until loaves sound hollow when tapped. Remove from cookie sheets; cool.

Corned Beef Party Rounds

Sauerkraut Rye Party Snack Loaves
2½ ounces sliced cooked corned beef, finely snipped
½ cup butter or margarine, softened
3 tablespoons horseradish mustard
4 teaspoons snipped fresh parsley or 2 teaspoons parsley flakes, crushed

Oven 375°   **1 cup**
Spread for about 45 Rounds

Cut loaves into slices about ¼-inch thick. Combine remaining ingredients. Spread about 1 teaspoon topping on each slice of bread. Place on ungreased cookie sheet. Bake at 375° for 5 to 7 minutes until crisp. Remove from cookie sheets. Serve hot.

Shrimp 'N Cheese Party Rounds

Sauerkraut Rye Party Snack Loaves
1 container (5 oz.) Boursin cheese with garlic and herb
1 cup drained tiny shrimp
1 tablespoon finely chopped chives or green onion
2 teaspoons lemon juice
4 drops tabasco

1 cup
Spread for about 45 Rounds

Cut loaves into slices about ¼-inch thick. Combine remaining ingredients. Spread about 1 teaspoon cheese mixture on each slice of bread. Place on serving plate. Refrigerate until serving time.

My Notes: _____

_____

_____

_____

_____

_____

_____

_____

_____

_____

_____

Vienna Snack Loaves

Delicious snacks to make from long, narrow loaves of Vienna bread. Spread with a cheesy, garlic butter or herbed mustard butter. Bake until crisp and serve hot.

5½ to 6 cups all-purpose flour
2 packages Red Star Instant Blend Dry Yeast
1 tablespoon sugar
1 tablespoon salt
1¼ cups water
1 cup milk
1 tablespoon shortening

Oven 425°   4 Snack Loaves

In large mixer bowl, combine 2½ cups flour, yeast, sugar and salt; mix well. In saucepan, heat 1¼ cups water, milk and shortening until warm (120-130°; shortening does not need to melt). Add to flour mixture. Blend at low speed until moistened; beat 3 minutes at medium speed. By hand, gradually stir in enough remaining flour to make a firm dough. Knead on floured surface until smooth and elastic, 5 to 8 minutes. Place in greased bowl, turning to grease top. Cover; let rise in warm place until light and doubled, about 1 hour.

Punch down dough. Divide into 4 parts. On lightly floured surface, roll each fourth to a 15x4-inch rectangle. Starting with longer side, roll up tightly, pressing dough into roll with each turn. Pinch edges and ends to seal. Place on greased cookie sheet. Cover; let rise at room temperature until double, about 30 minutes. Bake at 425° for 15 to 20 minutes until golden brown. Remove from cookie sheets; cool.

Cheesy Garlic Snack Rounds

Vienna Snack Loaves
½ cup butter or margarine, softened
¼ cup grated Stella Parmesan cheese
½ teaspoon garlic powder

Oven 375°   ¾ cup
Spread for about 70 Rounds

Cut loaves into slices about ¼-inch thick. Combine remaining ingredients. Spread about ½ teaspoon butter mixture on each slice of bread. Place on ungreased cookie sheet. Bake at 375° for 8 to 10 minutes until crisp. Remove from cookie sheets. Serve hot.

Herbed Mustard Snack Rounds

Vienna Snack Loaves
½ cup butter or margarine, softened
1 tablespoon Dijon mustard
4 teaspoons snipped fresh parsley or 2 teaspoons parsley flakes, crushed
½ teaspoon tarragon leaves, crushed

Oven 375°   ½ cup
Spread for about 45 Rounds

Cut loaves into slices about ¼-inch thick. Combine remaining ingredients. Spread about ½ teaspoon butter mixture on each slice of bread. Place on ungreased cookie sheet. Bake at 375° for 8 to 10 minutes until crisp. Remove from cookie sheets. Serve hot.

Baked Reuben

⏱ 📝 The traditional Reuben sandwich makings—corned beef, sauerkraut and Swiss cheese—top an onion-caraway flavored rye dough. An easy to make luncheon or supper entrée. Serve with a vegetable or salad.

1 cup all-purpose flour
1 package Red Star Instant Blend Dry Yeast
2 teaspoons instant minced onion
1½ teaspoons caraway seeds
¾ teaspoon salt
1 cup warm water
2 tablespoons dark molasses
2 tablespoons oil
1 cup medium rye flour
¼ cup mayonnaise or salad dressing
2 tablespoons horseradish mustard
½ lb. sliced corned beef, torn into bite-size pieces
1 can (8 oz.) sauerkraut, well drained
4 ounces sliced Swiss cheese, cut in half

Oven 375°   4 to 6 Servings

In large mixer bowl, combine 1 cup all-purpose flour, yeast, onion, caraway seed and salt; mix well. Add warm water (120-130°), molasses and oil to flour mixture. Blend at low speed until moistened; beat 3 minutes at medium speed. By hand, gradually stir in rye flour to make a stiff batter. Spread in greased 9-inch square cake pan. Combine mayonnaise and mustard; spread over dough. Cover; let rise in warm place until almost doubled, about 20 minutes.

Sprinkle corned beef over dough, then sprinkle sauerkraut over beef. Place cheese slices on top, overlapping edges. Bake at 375° for 30 to 35 minutes until cheese is melted. Serve hot.

TIP: Remove any remaining servings from pan, wrap in foil and refrigerate. Reheat at 300° for about 15 minutes.

My Notes: _____

_____

_____

_____

_____

_____

_____

_____

_____

_____

_____

_____

Little Filled Pies

You'll describe these little turnover pies as versatile and delicious! They are equally sensational served warm with a cheese or sausage filling or date filled with a crisp sugar topped crust.

3¼ to 3¾ cups all-purpose flour
2 packages Red Star Instant Blend Dry Yeast
2 tablespoons sugar
1 teaspoon salt
1 cup water
½ cup butter or margarine
1 egg, beaten

Oven 400°   30 Little Pies

In large mixer bowl, combine 1¼ cups flour, yeast, sugar and salt; mix well. In saucepan, heat water and butter until warm (120-130°; butter does not need to melt). Add to flour mixture. Blend at low speed until moistened; beat 3 minutes at medium speed. By hand, gradually stir in enough remaining flour to make a soft dough. Knead on floured surface until smooth and elastic, 3 to 5 minutes. Place in greased bowl, turning to grease top. Cover; let rise in warm place until light and doubled, about 30 minutes.

Prepare desired Filling.

Punch down dough. Divide into 6 parts. Divide each sixth into 5 pieces. On lightly floured surface, roll or pat each piece to a 4-inch circle. Spoon Filling on each circle. Brush edge lightly with egg. Fold half of circle over Filling. Seal edge by pressing with fingers, then press edge with a fork. Place on greased cookie sheet. Brush tops with egg. Bake at 400° for 12 to 15 minutes until golden brown. Remove from cookie sheets. Serve warm.

Romano-Muenster Cheese Filling

1½ cups (5 oz.) finely grated Stella Romano cheese
¾ cup (3½ oz.) shredded Muenster cheese
2 eggs, beaten

Filling for 30 Little Pies

Combine all ingredients. Spoon about 1 tablespoon Filling on each circle.

Spinach Cheese Filling

1½ cups (5 oz.) finely grated Stella Romano cheese
¾ cup (3½ oz.) shredded Muenster cheese
½ cup well-drained chopped cooked spinach
2 eggs, beaten

Filling for 30 Little Pies

Combine all ingredients. Spoon about 1 tablespoon Filling on each circle.

Sausage Cheese Filling

1 lb. pork sausage
1 cup (4 oz.) shredded processed Swiss cheese
2 teaspoons Dijon mustard

Filling for 30 Little Pies

In large skillet, lightly brown sausage; drain well. In small bowl, combine sausage, cheese and mustard. Spoon about 1 tablespoon Filling on each circle.

Coconut Date-Nut Filling

2 cups chopped dates
½ cup water
⅓ cup orange juice
¾ cup coconut
½ cup chopped nuts
   Sugar or pearl sugar

Filling for 30 Little Pies

In small saucepan, combine dates, water and orange juice. Bring to a boil. Simmer about 3 minutes, until thickened; cool. Stir in coconut and nuts. Spoon about 1 tablespoon Filling on each circle. After brushing with egg, sprinkle sugar over tops of pies. Serve cold.

My Notes: _____

_____

_____

_____

_____

_____

_____

_____

_____

_____

Wiener Bread

Bake a wiener and bun all in one easy dish. It will delight "kids" of any age!

1½ cups warm water
1 tablespoon shortening
1 package Red Star Instant
   Blend Dry Yeast
3¼ cups all-purpose flour
2 tablespoons sugar
1½ teaspoons salt
1 egg
¾ lb. wieners or Polish sausage
   Butter, softened

Oven 375°   **8 Servings**

In large mixer bowl, combine warm water (110-115°), shortening and yeast. Let stand 3 to 5 minutes. In separate bowl, combine flour, sugar, and salt. Add egg and 2 cups of the flour mixture to the yeast mixture. Blend at low speed until moistened; beat 2 minutes at medium speed. By hand, gradually stir in remaining flour and beat 1 minute. Cover; let rise in warm place until double, about 30 minutes. Stir down batter and beat about 2 minutes. Spread evenly in greased 13x9-inch cake pan.

Cut wieners in half, crosswise; press down into batter. Cover; let rise in warm place until double, about 25 minutes. Push wieners down into batter. Bake at 375° for 25 to 30 minutes until golden brown. Brush with butter. Serve warm with mustard.

Vintage fruit sauce™

Vintage Fruit Crown

Vintage Fruit Sauce

Tart 'N Creamy
Vintage Pie

198

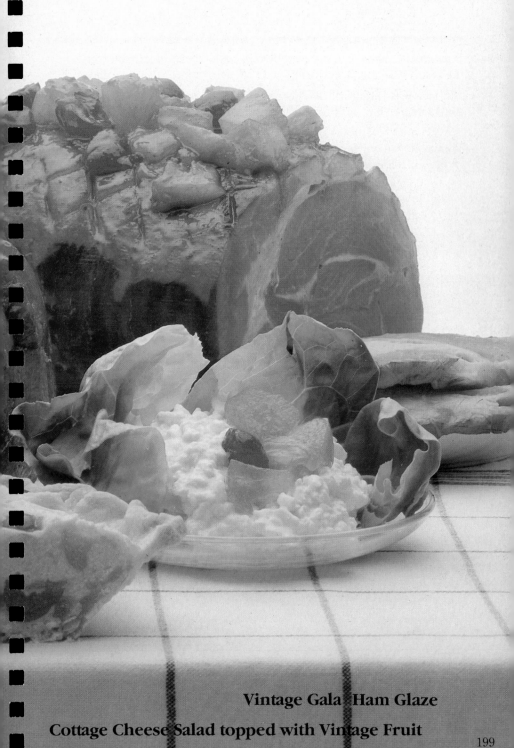

Vintage Gala Ham Glaze
Cottage Cheese Salad topped with Vintage Fruit

199

"VINTAGE FRUIT SAUCE" RECIPES

Back in 1972 we created a secret recipe using yeast to ferment fruit— the result was a fruit sauce with a deliciously different, *vintage* flavor.

Our idea was enthusiastically received from coast to coast, and homemakers wrote to tell us how they were inspired to create their own favorite ways to use "Vintage Fruit Sauce."

We developed our favorite recipes using "Vintage Fruit Sauce," and this chapter includes the best of our collection.

Many people prepare "Vintage Fruit Sauce" in decorative jars as gifts for friends. The fermented fruit recipe makes enough for two batches of "Vintage Fruit Sauce," so one can be given to a friend along with the recipe or it can be used to start a second batch of sauce.

Vintage Fruit Sauce

An innovative use of yeast in fermenting favorite fruits for a sauce used on desserts, meats and many other foods.

To Ferment Fruit:

¾ cup canned peaches in heavy syrup, drained and cut into pieces
¾ cup canned pineapple tidbits in heavy syrup, drained
6 maraschino cherries, cut in half
1½ cups sugar
1 package Red Star Instant Blend Dry Yeast

2 Cups

Combine ingredients and place in a glass jar with a loose cover—an apothecary jar is perfect. Stir several times the first day, then stir once a day. At the end of two weeks the starter has fermented enough to make sauce.

Prepare Sauce:

1 cup fermented fruit
½ cup canned peaches in heavy syrup, drained and cut into pieces
½ cup canned pineapple tidbits in heavy syrup, drained
6 maraschino cherries, cut in half
1 cup sugar

Combine all ingredients in a glass jar with a loose cover; stir well. Set in a fairly warm place. Continue to stir once a day. Sauce can be served after one week. Fruit and sugar must be repeated every two weeks.

Every Day Uses...

For Desserts:

spoon over:

• angel food or pound cake
• ice cream or sherbet
• pudding

layer with ice cream for:

• parfaits
• your favorite dessert crepes
• your favorite cheesecake

For Toppings:

combine Vintage Fruit with:

• sour cream and brown sugar
• whipped cream
• sweetened whipped cream cheese
• macaroon cookie crumbs
• granola cereal
• chopped nuts

For Main Dishes:

• spoon over ham slice
• spoon over Canadian bacon
• add to rice stuffing for poultry or game
• spoon over pancakes or French toast for breakfast/brunch

For Salads:

• spoon over cottage cheese
• fold into your favorite gelatin
• spoon onto lettuce cups, top with sunflower nuts or cashews

For Vegetables:

• add to cooked carrots
• add to cooked squash

For Fruit Compotes:

• heat Vintage Fruit, spiced grapes and sliced bananas
• combine Vintage Fruit, sliced pears and green grapes
• combine Vintage Fruit, orange slices and toasted almonds for breakfast

201

Vintage Fruit Crown

Vintage Fruit crowns this moist, rich coffeecake—the star at your next brunch.

3½ to 4 cups all-purpose flour
2 packages Red Star Instant Blend Dry Yeast
⅓ cup sugar
½ teaspoon salt
½ cup milk
½ cup water
⅓ cup shortening
1 egg
¼ cup Vintage Fruit syrup
⅓ cup packed brown sugar
⅓ cup sugar
3 tablespoons butter or margarine
1 cup drained Vintage Fruit
¼ cup chopped walnuts

Oven 350°   One 10-inch
              Bundt® Coffeecake

In large mixer bowl, combine 1½ cups flour, yeast, ⅓ cup sugar and salt; mix well. In saucepan, heat milk, water and shortening until warm (120-130°; shortening does not need to melt). Add to flour mixture. Add egg. Blend at low speed until moistened; beat 3 minutes at medium speed. By hand, gradually stir in enough remaining flour to make a firm dough. Knead on floured surface until smooth and elastic, 3 to 5 minutes. Place in greased bowl, turning to grease top. Cover; let rise in warm place until light and doubled, about 1 hour.

Prepare Filling: In medium saucepan, combine Vintage Fruit syrup, brown sugar, ⅓ cup sugar and butter. Cook over low heat, stirring occasionally, until sugar has dissolved and butter melts; keep warm. Spoon Vintage Fruit into bottom of greased 12-cup Bundt® pan. Sprinkle nuts over fruit.

Punch down dough. Divide into pieces the size of walnuts; shape each piece into a smooth ball. Place balls in layers in pan; pouring warm sauce over layers and top. Cover; let rise in warm place until double, about 30 minutes. Bake at 350° for 40 to 45 minutes until dark golden brown. Cool 10 minutes in pan; invert onto serving plate. Serve warm.

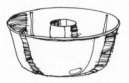

Vintage Coffee Ring

Granola and Vintage Fruit make the delicious chewy filling for this moist coffee ring.

2¼ to 2¾ cups all-purpose flour
1 package Red Star Instant Blend Dry Yeast
¼ cup sugar
½ teaspoon salt
½ cup milk
¼ cup water
2 tablespoons shortening
1 egg
1 cup drained Vintage Fruit
1½ cups granola
1 teaspoon cinnamon
1 egg
2 tablespoons Vintage Fruit syrup

Vintage Fruit Sauce Upside Down Cake

Oven 375°	1 Coffee Ring

In large mixer bowl, combine 1 cup flour, yeast, sugar and salt; mix well. In saucepan, heat milk, water and shortening until warm (120-130°; shortening does not need to melt). Add to flour mixture. Add 1 egg. Blend at low speed until moistened; beat 3 minutes at medium speed. By hand, gradually stir in enough remaining flour to make a soft dough. Knead on floured surface until smooth and elastic, 5 to 8 minutes. Place in greased bowl, turning to grease top. Cover; let rise in warm place until light and doubled, about 1 hour.

Prepare Filling: Combine Vintage Fruit, granola, cinnamon and 1 egg; set aside.

Punch down dough. On lightly floured surface, roll dough to an 18x12-inch rectangle. Brush with syrup; spread with Filling. Starting with longer side, roll up tightly. Pinch edge to seal. Form ring; pinch ends to seal. Place seam-side down on greased cookie sheet. With scissors, make cuts 1 inch apart through top of ring to 1 inch from center. Turn each slice on its side. Cover; let rise in warm place until almost doubled, about 30 minutes. Bake at 375° for 20 to 25 minutes until golden brown. Remove from cookie sheet. Serve warm or cold. Drizzle with powdered sugar Glaze, if desired.

A one bowl upside down cake mixed by hand. The Fruit Sauce nestles on top of a rich, moist cake and caramel topping.

¼ cup butter or margarine
⅓ cup packed brown sugar
1 cup drained Vintage Fruit
⅓ cup chopped nuts
1¼ cups all-purpose flour
¾ cup sugar
1 teaspoon baking powder
1 teaspoon cinnamon
½ teaspoon salt
½ teaspoon ground nutmeg
½ cup Vintage Fruit syrup
¼ cup oil
2 eggs
Whipped cream or ice cream

Oven 350°	One 8-inch Square Cake

Melt butter in 8-inch square cake pan. Add brown sugar, Vintage Fruit and nuts; mix well. Set aside. In medium mixing bowl, combine remaining ingredients; mix well. Pour batter over topping in pan. Bake at 350° for 40 to 45 minutes until golden brown. Cool 5 minutes; loosen edges with knife and invert onto serving plate. Serve warm with whipped cream or ice cream.

Vintage Stuffed Turkey Roast

Vintage Fruit perks up the rice stuffing and glazes this tasty stuffed turkey roast entrée.

1 frozen turkey roast (about 2 lbs.), thawed
¾ cup uncooked brown rice
1½ cups water
½ teaspoon salt
¼ teaspoon ground nutmeg
Dash ground allspice
2 tablespoons butter or margarine
½ cup drained Vintage Fruit
¼ cup chopped slivered almonds
½ cup Vintage Fruit syrup
1 tablespoon lemon juice
1 tablespoon butter or margarine

Oven 375°   4 to 6 Servings

In medium saucepan, combine brown rice, water and salt; bring to a boil. Reduce heat and cook covered until water is absorbed and rice tender. Add nutmeg, allspice and 2 tablespoons butter; mix until butter has melted. Add Vintage Fruit and almonds; mix lightly. Slice turkey roast into ½-inch slices to within ½ inch of bottom. Spoon rice mixture in between slices. Skewer and place in shallow baking pan. Cover with foil. Bake at 375° for 2 hours and 15 minutes. Remove foil. In small saucepan, combine Vintage Fruit syrup, lemon juice and 1 tablespoon butter; heat until butter has melted. Spoon over turkey roast. Continue to bake uncovered until browned, about 15 minutes. Remove skewer and serve with pan juices, if desired.

Vintage Sauced Chicken

A rich wine and onion sauce glistens on the Vintage Fruit and chicken—delicious!

2½ to 3 lb. frying chicken, cut up
1 cup dry red wine
¾ cup Vintage Fruit syrup
1 envelope dry onion soup
2 tablespoons cornstarch
2 tablespoons water
1 cup drained Vintage Fruit
Cooked Rice

4 to 6 Servings

In large fry pan, brown chicken in small amount of shortening. Add wine, syrup and soup. Cover and simmer about 1 hour until tender. Remove chicken to platter. Combine cornstarch and water; add to pan juices. Cook over medium heat, stirring constantly, until thickened. Add fruit and chicken pieces. Heat through. Serve over rice.

Vintage Gala Ham Glaze

Top your ham with this delicious and colorful fruit glaze. Makes a most attractive entrée.

4 lbs. ready-to-eat fully cooked ham
¼ cup packed brown sugar
2 teaspoons cornstarch
¼ teaspoon cinnamon
⅛ teaspoon ground cloves
⅓ cup Vintage Fruit syrup
2 tablespoons lemon juice
½ cup drained Vintage Fruit

Vintage Sauced Ribs

Oven 325°   **6 to 8 Servings**

Bake ham according to label directions; score with sharp knife. In medium saucepan, combine remaining ingredients. Heat until thickened, stirring constantly. Spoon sauce over ham. Return to oven and bake until golden brown, 10 to 15 minutes.

TIP: Recipe can be doubled and half the Glaze served warm as a sauce. Makes 2 cups.

Vintage Stuffed Chops

A delicious variation for pork chops—a fruit and bread stuffing bakes atop.

4 pork chops, ¾ to 1-inch thick
3 cups (3 slices) soft bread crumbs
2 tablespoons chopped onion
¼ teaspoon salt
¼ teaspoon poultry seasoning
½ cup drained Vintage Fruit
¼ cup butter or margarine, melted
2 tablespoons Vintage Fruit syrup

Oven 325°   **4 Servings**

In fry pan, brown pork chops in small amount of shortening; place in shallow baking dish. In medium bowl combine bread crumbs, onion, salt and poultry seasoning; mix lightly. Add drained fruit, butter and syrup; mix lightly until thoroughly combined. Spoon onto each pork chop. Cover; bake at 325° until tender, about 1 hour and 15 minutes.

A sweet-sour sauce with the Vintage Fruit bakes atop ribs for a tasty, attractive main dish.

4 to 6 lbs. country-style ribs or spareribs
2 teaspoons salt
½ teaspoon pepper
¼ cup packed brown sugar
3 tablespoons cornstarch
½ teaspoon ground ginger
¼ teaspoon garlic powder
1 cup water
½ cup Vintage Fruit syrup
½ cup apple cider vinegar
2 tablespoons soy sauce
1 cup drained Vintage Fruit
1 small onion, sliced
Cooked Rice

Oven 350°   **4 to 6 Servings**

Sprinkle ribs with salt and pepper; wrap tightly in heavy foil packets, sealing well. Place on cookie sheets. Bake at 350° for 1 hour. In medium saucepan, combine brown sugar, cornstarch, ginger and garlic powder; gradually add water, stirring until smooth. Add syrup, vinegar and soy sauce. Cook over medium heat until thickened, stirring constantly. Add drained fruit; remove from heat. Place ribs in shallow baking dish; top with onion slices. Spoon sauce over ribs. Bake uncovered until tender, about 1½ hours. Serve over rice.

205

Vintage Sweet Potato Bake

📖 Dress up sweet potatoes with colorful Vintage Fruit, tasty sauce and coconut over all.

1 can (1 lb. 7 oz.) sweet potatoes, drained and thickly sliced
¾ cup drained Vintage Fruit
½ cup Vintage Fruit syrup
2 tablespoons packed brown sugar
¼ teaspoon salt
2 tablespoons butter or margarine
¼ cup flaked coconut

Oven 350°   **4 Servings**

Place sweet potatoes in 1-quart casserole; spoon fruit over. In small saucepan, combine syrup, brown sugar, salt and butter; cook over medium heat until butter has melted. Pour over sweet potatoes. Bake at 350° for 15 minutes; sprinkle with coconut and continue to bake until coconut is browned, about 15 minutes.

Vintage Stuffed Squash

📖 Attractive fruit-filled acorn squash will add the right touch to your next pork meal.

2 medium acorn squash
¼ teaspoon salt
¼ cup butter or margarine
1 cup Vintage Fruit Sauce
½ cup chopped walnuts
¼ teaspoon ground ginger

Oven 350°   **4 Servings**

Cut squash in half crosswise; remove seeds. Place cut-side down on shallow baking pan. Bake at 350° for 35 minutes. Turn over, cut side up; sprinkle with salt. Place a tablespoon of butter in each half. In small mixing bowl, combine remaining ingredients; spoon into squash halves. Continue to bake until tender, about 25 minutes.

Vintage Fruit Dressing

🌙 A delicious celery seed fruit salad dressing features the Vintage Fruit syrup. Use it on the Vintage Fruit with cottage cheese or your other favorite fruit combinations.

½ cup sugar
1 teaspoon dry mustard
1 teaspoon celery seeds
¼ teaspoon salt
⅓ cup vinegar
⅓ cup Vintage Fruit syrup
½ cup oil

1¼ Cups Dressing

In blender or jar, combine dry ingredients; add vinegar and syrup. Blend at medium speed or shake in jar until thoroughly combined. Add oil and continue to blend or shake until thoroughly combined. Store covered in refrigerator.

Vintage Salad Ring

❂ A creamy, cool salad features Vintage Fruit Sauce and sour cream with lemon gelatin in a pretty ribbon mold.

2 packages (3 oz.) lemon flavored gelatin
2 cups boiling water
½ cup cold water
1½ cups Vintage Fruit Sauce
1 cup sour cream

6 to 8 Servings

In large mixing bowl, add boiling water to gelatin; stir to dissolve. Add cold water. Remove 1 cup of gelatin mixture; add ½ cup Vintage Fruit Sauce, and pour into oiled 6-cup ring mold. To remaining gelatin, add sour cream; mix thoroughly. Chill both mixtures: clear gelatin in mold until firm, and creamy mixture until thickened. Add 1 cup Vintage Fruit Sauce to creamy mixture. Pour over layer in mold and chill until firm.

Heavenly Vintage Dessert

❂ An easy company dessert from convenience foods—prepared cake, canned pudding, and Vintage Fruit Sauce are layered for this tasty dessert.

1 loaf prepared angel food cake
1 can (18 oz.) prepared vanilla pudding
1 cup drained Vintage Fruit
1 cup whipped cream or whipped topping

6 to 8 Servings

Slice angel food cake into ½-inch slices; fit half of slices into 9-inch square cake pan to cover bottom of pan. In medium mixing bowl, combine pudding and Vintage Fruit; fold in whipped cream. Spoon half of pudding mixture evenly over cake slices in pan; cover with remaining cake slices and pudding mixture. Cover and refrigerate at least 4 hours. Garnish with toasted slivered almonds, if desired.

Tossed Vintage Fruit Salad

A colorful tossed fruit and onion salad made extra tasty with the Vintage Fruit Dressing.

4 cups torn head lettuce
1 cup drained Vintage Fruit
2 bananas, sliced
¼ cup sliced green onions
⅓ cup Vintage Fruit Dressing

6 Servings

In salad bowl, combine all ingredients except Dressing; toss lightly. Add Dressing and toss lightly. Serve immediately.

My Notes: _____

_____

_____

_____

_____

_____

_____

_____

_____

_____

_____

_____

Vintage Berry Cream

◖ A unique creamy dessert as simple as combining dry gelatin, Vintage Fruit, cottage cheese, and whipped cream. Good as a salad too!

1 cup drained Vintage Fruit
1 cup cream-style cottage cheese
1 package (3 oz.) strawberry or raspberry flavored gelatin
1 carton (4½ oz.) whipped topping or 2 cups whipped cream

4 to 6 Servings

In blender container, combine Vintage Fruit and cottage cheese; blend at medium speed until fruit is partially crushed. In medium mixing bowl, combine blended fruit mixture and dry gelatin; mix thoroughly. Fold in whipped topping. Spoon into serving bowl or individual serving dishes. Cover and refrigerate until served. Serve as salad or dessert.

Vintage Fruit Ice

◖ A quick and easy freezer dessert. Handy to do ahead. Completes a meal any time of the year.

1 cup drained Vintage Fruit
1 tablespoon lemon juice
2 egg whites
Dash salt
1 cup whipped topping

4 to 6 Servings

Spoon fruit into blender container; blend at medium speed until somewhat smooth. Add lemon juice. In small mixer bowl, beat egg whites and salt until stiff peaks form. In medium mixing bowl, gently fold egg whites and whipped topping into blended fruit. Spoon lightly into metal bowl or baking pan. Freeze until firm, about 4 hours. Spoon into dessert glasses to serve.

Tart 'N Creamy Vintage Pie

◖ Add Fruit Sauce and ice cream to lemon gelatin for the creamy filling of this refreshing pie.

½ cup water
½ cup Vintage Fruit syrup
1 package (3 oz.) lemon flavored gelatin
2 cups (1 pint) vanilla ice cream
½ cup drained Vintage Fruit
9- inch pastry or crumb crust

One 9-inch Pie

In small saucepan, combine water and Vintage Fruit syrup; bring to boil. In medium mixing bowl, add syrup to lemon gelatin; stir until dissolved. Gradually beat in ice cream with a wire whisk until smooth. Chill until thickened, about 30 minutes. Fold in Vintage Fruit. Spoon into prepared crust. Cover; refrigerate until set, about 4 hours.

Frosty Vintage Cups

◖ Macaroon crumbs and Fruit Sauce blend with ice cream for an easy family dessert in paper cups—add wooden sticks for the kids!

2 cups (1 pint) vanilla ice cream, slightly softened
½ cup drained Vintage Fruit
¾ cup coarsely crumbled macaroon cookies (about 6 cookies)

4 to 6 Servings

In medium mixing bowl, combine all ingredients, stirring gently. Spoon into 3 or 5-ounce paper cups or cupcake cups. Freeze until firm, about 4 hours.

TIP: For childrens' treats, insert wooden sticks into center of filled cups before freezing; remove paper cups just before serving "lollipops."

INDEX

INDEX

Contemporary Breads

Savory Breads

INDEX

INDEX

INDEX

NOTES

69
72
75
76
77
79
80
86
87
88
89
90
91
94
96
97
98
99
102
103